Marcos E. Kinevan

PERSONAL ESTATE PLANNING

**FINANCIAL AND LEGAL ASPECTS
OF ACCUMULATING, PROTECTING,
AND DISPOSING OF YOUR PERSONAL ESTATE**

Prentice-Hall, Inc. • Englewood Cliffs, N.J.

A SPECTRUM BOOK

Library of Congress Cataloging in Publication Data

Kinevan, Marcos E
    Personal estate planning.

    (Spectrum Book)
    1. Finance, Personal.   2. Estate planning—United States.   I. Title.
HG179.K555   332'.024   79-20997
ISBN 0-13-657528-5
ISBN 0-13-657510-2 pbk.

© 1980 by Prentice-Hall, Inc., Englewood Cliffs, New Jersey 07632

A SPECTRUM BOOK

All rights reserved.
No part of this book may be reproduced
in any form or by any means
without permission in writing from the publisher.

10 9 8 7 6 5 4 3 2 1

Printed in the United States of America

PRENTICE-HALL INTERNATIONAL, INC., *London*
PRENTICE-HALL OF AUSTRALIA PTY. LIMITED, *Sydney*
PRENTICE-HALL OF CANADA, LTD., *Toronto*
PRENTICE-HALL OF INDIA PRIVATE LIMITED, *New Delhi*
PRENTICE-HALL OF JAPAN, INC., *Tokyo*
PRENTICE-HALL OF SOUTHEAST ASIA PTE. LTD., *Singapore*
WHITEHALL BOOKS LIMITED, WELLINGTON, *New Zealand*

To Bobby

Contents

Preface

part 1
Estate Accumulation

chapter 1
Going From Broke
WHY SAVE? 3
WAYS TO SAVE 4
WHAT BUDGETING SHOULD BE 5
DETERMINING NET WORTH 8
CARTA PECUNIA 9

chapter 2
Buy Now, Pay Later?
WHEN DEBT IS JUSTIFIABLE 11
TYPES OF CONSUMER CREDIT 12
CREDIT LIFE INSURANCE 15

BORROWING MONEY 16
THE COST OF CREDIT 19

chapter 3

Sharing Risks

HOW INSURANCE DEVELOPED 23
LEGAL CONSIDERATIONS 24
AMOUNTS OF INSURANCE NEEDED 27
AUTOMOBILE INSURANCE 27
PERSONAL PROPERTY INSURANCE 38
PERSONAL LIABILITY INSURANCE 40
HOMEOWNERS' POLICIES 40
"UMBRELLA" COVERAGE 41
MEDICAL AND HOSPITALIZATION PROTECTION 42
MAXIM ONE 43

chapter 4

Big Brother Cares

THE IMPACT OF SOCIAL SECURITY 44
THE FICA—BANE OR BLESSING? 45
SOCIAL SECURITY TAXES 47
WHO QUALIFIES FOR BENEFITS? 48
HOW MUCH WILL BENEFICIARIES RECEIVE? 50
OTHER SURVIVOR BENEFITS 55
THE NEED TO KNOW 56

chapter 5

How Much is Enough?

EXPENSES INCIDENT TO DEATH 59
CONSTRUCTING AN ESTATE PROGRAMMING CHART 59
SOCIAL SECURITY AND OTHER SURVIVORS' BENEFITS 60
FILLING THE GAPS 62
OTHER REQUIREMENTS 67
GULP! 69
ARE YOU THERE? 71

chapter 6

The Fundamentals Of Life Insurance

MORTALITY RISK 74
LOADING CHARGES 76
FORCED SAVINGS 77
TYPES OF LIFE INSURANCE POLICIES 78
PARTICIPATING AND NONPARTICIPATING POLICIES 89
PRINCIPAL CONTRACTUAL PROVISIONS 95
NONFORFEITURE PROVISIONS 92
POLICY LOANS 97
DEATH BENEFIT PAYMENT PROVISIONS 98
SELECTING A LIFE INSURANCE COMPANY 102
THE "COST" OF LIFE INSURANCE 103
OTHER COST ANALYSES METHODS 107

chapter 7

The Fundamentals Of Investments

WHAT IS AN INVESTMENT? 112
FIXED-DOLLAR ASSETS 112
NON-FIXED-DOLLAR ASSETS 128

chapter 8

How to Allocate Your Resources

LIFE INSURANCE 156
TERM INSURANCE PLUS FIXED-DOLLAR INVESTMENT 164
INFLATION AND FIXED-DOLLAR ASSETS 170
PROTECTING PURCHASING POWER 174
IS TWISTING SINFUL? 178
WHAT SHOULD YOU DO? 179

Contents

part II
Estate Distribution

chapter 9
Trusts and Sundry Non-Probate Transfers

TRUSTS 185
SUNDRY NON-PROBATE TRANSFERS 199

chapter 10
What's Mine Is Thine

OWNERSHIP OF PROPERTY 203
COMMUNITY PROPERTY 208
FACTORS TO CONSIDER 210

chapter 11
Wills

PROBATE AND NON-PROBATE ASSETS 214
INTESTACY 215
WILLS 217
STATUTORY AND OTHER LIMITATIONS UPON TESTAMENTARY FREEDOM 227
THE EXECUTOR'S RESPONSIBILITIES 230

Appendices

A. ***WHAT'S YOUR INTEREST?*** 234
B. ***FEDERAL INCOME TAX WITHHOLDING RATES (1979)*** 237
C. ***FEDERAL INDIVIDUAL INCOME TAXES (1979)*** 238
D. ***FEDERAL ESTATE AND GIFT TAX RATES*** 239
E. ***COMPOUND INTEREST TABLE*** 241
F. ***PERIODIC INVESTMENT TABLE*** 242
G. ***CONSUMER PRICES, 1820–1978*** 243
H. ***INFORMATION FOR MY EXECUTOR*** 245

List of Figures and Tables

TABLES

1.1 Personal Balance Sheet 8
4.1 FICA Taxes on Employees 51
4.2 Primary Insurance Payable to Beneficiaries 53
4.3 Percentage of Average Indexed Earnings Replaced by Worker's Primary Insurance 54
5.1 Present Value of Annuity 63
5.2 Present Value 64
6.1 Extracts from Commissioners Standard Ordinary 1958 Mortality Table 74
6.2 Non-Forfeiture and Loan Values 98
6.3 Interest-Adjusted Surrender Cost Indices 107
6.4 Cost of Insurance if Death Were to Occur at End of the Policy Year 109
6.5 Death-Cost Index of Different Policies 109
7.1 Equivalent Taxable Yields from Tax-Exempt Income 121
7.2 Approximate Yields on Representative Fixed-Dollar Uses of Savings 127
7.3 Compound Growth Rates 136
7.4 Representative "Growth" Stocks 137

8.1 *What $240 a Year in Premiums Might Buy* 160
9.1 *Estate Tax Savings by Using Trusts* 191

FIGURES

4.1 *What Social Security Costs* 47
5.1 *Plotting the Adequacy of Social Security Benefits* 61
5.2 *How Much Is Enough?* 70
6.1 *Basic Policies* 90
7.1 *Possible Uses of Savings* 113
7.2 *Options Trading Table* 131
7.3 *New York Stock Exchange Table* 133
7.4 *Dollar Cost Averaging* 144
7.5 *Mutual Fund Table* 147
8.1 *Estate Requirements* 162
8.2 *Insurance Needs as the Difference between Estate Requirements and Other Assets* 162
8.3 *Endowment-at-65 vs. Term-to-65 plus Series E's* 166
8.4 *Whole Life vs. 5-year R&C Term plus Savings Bonds* 168
8.5 *Relative Value of the Dollar (1820–1978)* 171
8.6 *Consumer Prices Since World War II* 172
8.7 *Dow Jones Industrial Average (1945–1978)* 176
11.1 *Will of Thomas T. Testator* 221

Preface

The great problem in our culture is not faith versus complete knowledge. It is that of finding disinterested sources of information.
Hayakawa, *Symbol, Status and Personality* (1963)

Whenever you deposit money in a savings account, invest in securities, buy a house, insure your possessions against loss, purchase life insurance, take title to property jointly with your spouse instead of separately, execute a will, establish a trust, or engage in any of countless other acts that have a financial and legal effect upon you and your family, you will be doing what is called—for lack of a more palatable term—"estate planning."

Although many people associate estate planning only with legal documents, such as trusts or wills, or with various arrangements designed to avoid or reduce taxation, it actually involves a large number of interrelated activities. These range from first acquiring an estate (an obvious prerequisite), through productively managing and enjoying it, to finally taking measures to assure that it is preserved and used in whatever manner best suits your needs and desires.

Numerous books have been written about one facet or another of estate planning. Among the hundreds available, though, few attempt to integrate the various components in a way that will provide their readers—whether in the early or later stages of their careers—with the broad perspective and rudimentary understanding they need. It was this dearth of basic, comprehensive guides that led me to prepare the first version of this book in 1961. Since then, twelve editions have been published and used by thousands of college students and others. To the extent that it might have helped some of them to make better informed decisions about their estates, present and prospective, the effort will have been rewarded.

I assume you realize that merely reading, or for that matter studying, this book will not qualify you to recognize, appraise, and solve the many legal and other problems inherent in creating and planning an estate. Only a lawyer or other trained person specializing in this field or in some particular aspect of it is equipped to provide this kind of guidance. Instead, this book is a primer that merely surveys some—not all, but some—of the main topics with which you should be familiar. Beginning with a brief discussion of savings and credit, it progresses through such subjects as casualty insurance, survivors' benefits, estate programming, life insurance, and various types of investments; then it concludes by considering the nature and uses of trusts, other property arrangements between family members, and the ultimate dispositive device—a will.

Throughout, the aim has been to educate, not advocate; to inform, not indoctrinate. And, of course, nothing in this book should be construed as a specific suggestion as to how YOU, personally, should build, manage, or dispose of your estate. You should be aware that a great deal—sometimes, all—of the "estate planning" information and advice that most people acquire comes not from impartial sources, but instead from those who stand to profit from what is done. To avoid potentially costly errors, you must develop the ability to critically analyze what a salesman proposes, discriminatingly compare the alternatives, and intelligently decide whether it suits your particular needs. This book alone will not equip you for these tasks, but it might start you on a quest for further information and ideas to help you build and plan your estate effectively.

My purpose is to stimulate thought, not faith, and to provide basic information, not complete knowledge. I have tried to be objective, and what is presented comes from a source that is wholly disinterested, in a financial sense, in any estate planning decision you might make.

I am indebted to more people than could possibly be named for their assistance over the years, but I would be remiss not to single out Richard R. Lee, my Deputy Department Head; Robert F. McDermott, President of USAA; J. C. Douglas, Editor of AIDE magazine; and Julie Volosin, my indefatigable secretary. Also, a special thanks to all my colleagues, past and present, in the Academy's Department of Law, and to any teacher's severest and best critics—his students. Most of all, I am grateful to my understanding wife, Bobby, and our now-grown children, Mark and Joan, who missed many vacation trips and other activities so that I might pursue this effort.

This book was written off-duty in my private capacity, and none of the views I have expressed necessarily reflect those of the Air Force Academy or the United States Air Force.

MARCOS E. KINEVAN

Colorado Springs, Colorado
September 1979

part 1

Estate Accumulation

chapter 1

Going From Broke

WHY SAVE?

Grover Cleveland thought that "people should support the government; the government should not support the people." So did most other Americans—then. Today, though, more and more people seem to look upon the government as the Great Provider for their future financial needs. There are many reasons, of course, that they do so. These include the widespread instant-satisfaction and "rights" syndromes that have mushroomed over the last couple of decades, as well as the legislative largess that has markedly reduced the financial perils of unemployment, prolonged illness, serious injury, and old age. The point is not whether such changes have been good or bad; certainly few who lived through the Good Old Days would advocate a full return to their harsh conditions. Yet, paternalistic societies do not do much to encourage financial self-reliance.

Although rugged individualism and, with it, economic freedom have given ground in recent years, financial responsibility is still an essential ingredient of a mature individual. Government programs help, as we'll consider later, but they have not relieved you of your obligation to support your family and to provide for yourself and your family in old age. Also, of course, many needs and wants will arise over the course of any lifetime that can be met only with personal financial resources. Those who anticipate and plan for these needs will be able to handle them with some degree of equanimity. Those who don't, won't.

What, then, are these needs and wants? Basically, they might be characterized as *foreseeable* and *unforeseeable*. In the foreseeable category, most people have both short-term and long-term goals. The short-term goals normally are to acquire things or services that contribute to a better life: perhaps a new car, major appliances or furniture, a vacation trip, recreation equipment, or any of countless other things that might be important to you and your family. The major foreseeable long-term goals, which usually are far more costly, might be college and graduate school education for children, a mortgage-free home, a mountain cabin or seashore cottage, or additional retirement income. Unforeseeable future financial risks, which are unforeseeable only in the sense that their occurrence, nature, and scope cannot be predicted, include serious illness or disabling injuries to a family member, untimely deaths, and substantial losses or damages to your property.

WAYS TO SAVE

To meet these future needs and wants, you have only yourself (and perhaps your spouse) to rely upon. How, then, might you acquire the necessary financial resources? Obviously, the initial step is to save systematically from your income. Next, the sums saved should be appropriately invested until you reach your goals. In the meantime, financial protection against premature death in the form of life insurance, and against catastrophic losses or liabilities in the form of casualty insurance, should be maintained. We'll look at insurance and investments later; at the moment, our attention will center upon the preliminary problem of accumulating reserves through savings.

Saving, which is no more than deferred spending, isn't easy for most people. It requires planning, family cooperation, and considerable self-discipline. Nevertheless, family harmony and security are so dependent upon adequate financial reserves (money problems are a factor in over four-fifths of all divorces) that the small amount of work involved is worth the effort.

The first step is to devise a system for saving and adhere to it.

This might be no more than routinely putting aside every dime, quarter or other coin you receive in change, depositing a certain amount of your pay in a savings account, or purchasing Series E bonds through payroll deductions. None of these methods is ideal for long-range purposes, but any is better than none.

WHAT BUDGETING SHOULD BE

A more fruitful system would be to first learn how much you reasonably can save, then methodically accumulate these sums. Necessarily, this involves knowing what your income is and what your living costs are. Assuming that you know your income, determining your living costs is merely a matter of record keeping. If you find that your living costs leave little, if anything, to save from income, your spending records should enable you to intelligently curtail your expenditures so as to leave a surplus.

The approach suggested is no more than budgeting. But "budget" is an unpleasant word, conjuring up visions of bookkeepers or accountants—and not many people like to think about them. But you shouldn't cringe at the thought of a budget, unless it is one of those "average" budgets that purport to tell you what percentage of your income you are supposed to spend for various things. These smack too much of exercises indulged in by statisticians for the amusement of other statisticians. Forget them. First of all, they are arbitrary and unrealistic: who's to say whether you would rather live in a mobile home so you could afford an expensive car and foreign travel, or drive a VW so you can have a real house from which you seldom venture? Besides, "standard" or "average" budgets ignore some important geographic variables: the costs of year-round clothing, fresh produce, and utilities in places such as Santa Barbara or Newport Beach are a lot less than in Cambridge or Passaic. Similarly, housing is not nearly so expensive in Waco or Biloxi as it is in New York or the District of Columbia. Additionally, if anyone were actually to follow an "average" budget, it would soon become a master rather than a servant. That's not the idea.

Sensibly used, budgeting does not involve onerous bookkeeping or pennypinching, nor is it designed to deprive you of those things you need or really want. Instead, a budget should be regarded as no more than a financial management tool to let you know how you spend your income, and then help you make whatever reallocations you decide would be in your best interests.

Maintaining a Budget

The mechanics of maintaining a budget can be as elaborate or as simple as you want to make them. Lincoln is reputed to have recorded some memorable things on the back of an envelope. You probably would find a notebook easier to use; in most stationery stores, a couple of dollars will buy an inexpensive, bound booklet with preprinted forms. The categories of expenses you choose to record can be as detailed as you wish, but simplicity is likely to make the chore easier.

To begin the process, merely label some columns across the top of a page with descriptive terms for your principal types of expenses, such as rent (or mortgage payments), utilities, groceries, restaurants, entertainment, sports, clothing, laundry/dry cleaning, automobile operation and maintenance, debts, medical/dental, contributions, incidentals, and—most important—savings. Vertically, number the lines 1 through 31 if space permits, to accommodate data for an entire month. Then try to faithfully jot down every day what you have spent under each category. Total these sums at the end of each month. It shouldn't take long to reveal some interesting and prospectively valuable information to you.

Using a Budget

Obviously, few people can have everything they want. So once necessities are taken care of, decisions about how you want to use the balance of the funds available to you (your "discretionary income") must be made. These decisions should be keyed to whatever your personal and family priorities might be. Whether an expensive car is more important than an extensive vacation, whether a new carpet should come before a new wardrobe, or whether your child should go to work after high school or go to college (and if so, whether a prestigious private school—if he or she can qualify—would be preferable to a local JC or obscure state institution) are the types of decisions that depend to a large extent upon subjective values.

Once you know where your income has gone in the past, your

records will help you plan where your future income should go. First, analyze where you might have been overspending, then place dollar limits on these categories for the next month. You might decide, for example, that you should cut down in some areas, such as entertainment or clothing, so that more funds will be available for something else that is more important to you.

Savings should receive a high priority. The amount will differ, of course, in every case, but at the outset your minimum aim should probably be at least 10% of your income. Try setting some monthly objective, whatever it might be, then transfer this sum to a separate savings account soon after you receive it. If you have overestimated what you can save or if an unforeseen need develops, the funds will be readily available, but you are less likely to dip into a separate account for frivolous purposes.

Stretching Your Dollars

There are many things you can do that will help you stay within your budget, and eventually emerge from the financial quagmire most people slog around in all their lives. Becoming a savvy consumer is one of the best. This is not a book on personal finance, so I won't get into this subject much beyond urging you to plunk down $14.95 (or $5.95, paperback) for Sylvia Porter's book, *Money* (1975). Read it, then keep it handy as a reference. Also, before buying any major appliance or other costly item, check one of the popular consumer periodicals, such as *Consumer Reports.* Another publication that could help you toward financial self-reliance is Kiplinger's *Changing Times,* a basic but nevertheless valuable guide.

There are a few general rules that might help you live better for less, such as: buy quality goods (which doesn't necessarily mean the costliest); deal with reputable merchants only; avoid succumbing to any telephone sales pitch; steer clear of door-to-door peddlers of pots and pans, magazine subscriptions, home repairs, vacuum cleaners, or for that matter almost anything else; learn to recognize garden-variety ripoffs, such as many of the land sale schemes in Florida and Arizona; and don't be an impulse buyer, whether the impulse is rooted in gastronomy (take a list of what you need to the super market and stick to it), vanity (stay out of boutiques), or other frailty. So much for that.

DETERMINING NET WORTH

As an aid to an effective savings program, it is a good idea to periodically determine just what your net worth is and to set down your objectives for the coming months. In most cases, an annual review and forecast of this sort is satisfactory. Considerable detail is

TABLE 1-1. Personal Balance Sheet for 19____.

ASSETS	Value Today	Goal in One Year	Value in One Year	LIABILITIES	Value Today	Goal in One Year	Value in One Year
Cash				Notes and Accounts Payable			
Checking Account(s)							
Savings Account(s)				Bank Loans			
Other				Charge Accounts			
				Sales Contracts			
Securities				Real Estate Loans			
Stocks				Other Liabilities			
Bonds							
Personal Property							
Automobile(s)							
Furnishings							
Other							
Real Estate							
Other							
TOTAL				TOTAL			

	Value Today	Goal in One Year	Value in One Year
ASSETS			
LIABILITIES			
NET WORTH			

neither essential nor desirable, for the principal value of a family balance sheet lies in the thought that goes into finding out where you are, establishing where you want to be, and later comparing your performance with your goals. For this purpose, try devoting a few minutes annually to completing a form similar to Table 1-1 and to reviewing the changes that have occurred over the past year.

CARTA PECUNIA

In summary, the key to freedom from money worries and to the start of financial success is, essentially, a combination of attitudes and habits. *Initially,* money should be viewed in proper perspective as a means to an end, not as an end itself. *Second,* a long-range program for the use of money should be developed. *Third,* goals must be realistic and spending must be geared to income. *Fourth,* how money is to be spent should be a family decision. *Fifth,* where money goes should be determined (the primary purpose of budgeting). *Finally,* a high degree of self-discipline is required.

These attitudes and habits are not found in many people at the outset of their working careers, but there is no reason anyone cannot develop them. The sooner you do so, the greater will be the benefits.

chapter 2

Buy Now, Pay Later?

There was a time, in the not too distant past, when cash-on-the-barrelhead was the accepted practice between customers and merchants. Just ask anyone who has lived long enough to remember Upton Sinclair's EPIC ("End Poverty in California") political platform during the depths of the Great Depression in the 1930s. Of course, one incidental problem was that not many people had cash to plunk down for more than the bare necessities.

Buying on credit was not unknown even then, but it was generally confined to the relatively wealthy who didn't need it anyway. For most people, the use of consumer credit, even if it had been available, would have been considered a stigma just short of going on the dole or being forced to wear the "scarlet letter." Well, times and values have changed. Not only do tens of millions of people now subsist on government handouts—euphemistically labelled food stamps, aid to dependent children, unemployment compensation, Social Security, or whatever—rather than from work, but most who do seem to regard them as basic rights. And since World War II, credit has proliferated to the point that anyone who pays cash for everything is suspected of being either mildly eccentric or some kind of subversive.

The evolution of on-the-cuff buying has not been all bad, because no one can seriously question that the ready availability of some buy-now, pay-later arrangement has been a substantial factor in enabling Americans at all social and economic levels to achieve an extraordinarily high standard of living. Nevertheless, while the use of credit can be beneficial, its abuse can be injurious to your financial health, and to your marriage and career as well.

Family insolvency is seldom caused by a single wild spending spree; rather, it usually results from innocently assuming more and more debt, which immature people who lack financial self-discipline are particularly susceptible to doing. Borrowing to have something before you pay for it is the converse of saving. There might not be anything immoral about the practice, but debt, which is a classic example of Allen's Law ("almost anything is easier to get into than out of"), is something every family must learn to handle.

Although the original purpose of consumer credit was to spur the sales of goods and services, credit sellers have learned that in some situations, there is more profit in debt than in sales, so sales of merchandise frequently have been subordinated to sales of credit. Moreover, consumer credit can be intricate and deceptive; hence, there are certain rudimentary things you should know before you can decide intelligently whether or not to use it. Primarily, you should strictly confine time purchases to those situations in which the advantages outweigh the disadvantages. Beyond this, you should be aware of the types of credit that are available and what each costs.

WHEN DEBT IS JUSTIFIABLE

An indiscreet debtor, like an inveterate gambler or an alcoholic, can always rationalize his weakness in some sophistic way. Informed and mature consumers, on the other hand, recognize that only under certain conditions should they consider using credit rather than deferring a purchase until they can pay cash. For example, indebtedness may be justifiable if it is for a necessity rather than a luxury. Essential medical or dental care or, in some instances, an automobile, fall in this category. Also, incurring debt for something that results in saving more than the credit costs or from which distinct advantages accrue might not be imprudent. Buying a house rather than renting, acquiring labor-saving appliances or paying for an education might be in this category. Occasionally, too, there may be situations in which credit either costs no more than using cash, such as a conventional charge account, or when despite the cost, the convenience is worth more than the extra amount paid.

Even in situations in which the benefits of credit outweigh its cost, certain principles should not be ignored. The cardinal one is: *never assume more debt than you can reasonably repay.* Elementary as this is, large numbers of families disregard it. How much is too much differs with each family, of course, but most credit advisors would look askance at any indebtedness that calls for payments in excess of 20% of take-home pay. Another basic rule is to shop around for credit when you need it, for the costs vary considerably. Additionally, you are less likely to make a serious mistake on big-ticket purchases if you heed the following suggestions:

1. Read the contract carefully and be sure you understand it; don't skip the fine print.
2. Make sure all figures are entered; never leave blank spaces to be filled in later.
3. Determine that all disclosures (finance charges, annual percentage rate, etc.) required by the Truth-in-Lending Act have been entered.
4. Make sure what you are buying is described accurately.
5. Obtain and retain a copy of the contract.

TYPES OF CONSUMER CREDIT

Assuming a situation arises that, in your mind, warrants incurring debt, you should know what types of credit are available and what each costs. You may obtain the credit you need to make a purchase from or through the vendor (e.g., department store or automobile dealer) or you may borrow the money you need from a lender (e.g., commercial bank or credit union). If you finance your purchase with the vendor, one of the following plans probably will be used:

Regular Charge Account

Most department stores and specialty shops permit purchases to be charged, which enables the buyer to defer payment until the end of the month or for a 30-day period. This is a convenience, but anyone who has either compulsive or impulsive spending tendencies would do better to confine one's purchases to cash. The unusual feature of most charge accounts is that if payment is made promptly, the cost is the same as the store's cash price for whatever you buy. If you delay payment, though, a 1% to 2% per month service charge may be added to your bill. Also, identical merchandise often is available at substantially lower prices from low overhead stores that sell for cash only.

Revolving Charge Accounts

Many stores offer "revolving" accounts. This fairly recent credit innovation permits customers to charge purchases up to a certain amount, say $500, and pay for them in equal monthly installments rather than all at the end of the month of purchase. The usual cost for this service is 1% to 2% a month on the unpaid balance, or a true annual interest of 12% to 24%. Thus, revolving accounts are not only expensive, but by encouraging and facilitating buying they can lead to wasteful spending.

Extended Payment Plans

Stores may permit certain purchases to be paid for over a longer period of time than is possible with a regular charge account. These extended payment plans are variously referred to as budget accounts, monthly installment plans or, ironically, continuous easy payment plans. Generally, a purchaser has three to six months in which to pay the bill in installments. Finance charges of 1% to 2% a month (12% to 24% annually) are imposed for this privilege.

Installment Purchases

Almost all retailers and dealers, except some discounters, allow and encourage installment purchases of costly items. A down payment usually is required and payment of the balance is made in monthly installments over a 12- to 36-month period. A chattel mortgage or conditional sale of the property secures payment. Almost two-thirds of all new cars are bought on time, and most purchases from furniture and appliance stores are financed the same way. The small retailer or dealer seldom ties up his or her own capital in this manner but instead assigns rights ("sells the paper") to a sales finance company. As you might expect, installment purchases are not cheap. On a new car paid for over a three-year period, for example, the added cost is likely to exceed $1,000. Often, the seller derives more profit from finance charges than from cash sales. Roughly, half of many dealers' profits on new cars, for instance, come from rebates received from sales finance companies. The least it usually costs for the privilege of making easy, endless payments is 1½% a month on the unpaid balance, or 18% a year. When other charges are tacked on, the true annual interest may be substantially more.

Credit Cards

Another way to make purchases without cash is with a credit card. There are two basic types: special purpose cards and the comprehensive card. The special purpose cards, such as those issued by the oil companies, which started the system in the 1920s, are issued free and no added charge is made when they are used. These can be quite convenient and usually there is little danger of making imprudent purchases. Some other cards for special purposes, such as air travel or car rental, also are available.

The comprehensive cards came into vogue in the 1950s. Their aim is to permit a wide variety of goods and services to be acquired through a single card. The originators knew not what they wrought: in addition to facilitating the purchase of mundane merchandise and prosaic services, cardholders have used their magic-money passports for such wide-ranging purposes as buying houses and ski-lift tickets, and paying for tuition, court fines, medical bills, lawyers' fees, and even (where are you, Oliver Cromwell?) the services of prostitutes in Nevada.

Initially, the comprehensive cards were the exclusive province of firms such as Diners' Club, American Express, and Hilton Credit; their customers pay $20 or so a year for use of the cards, which isn't much these days for any kind of status symbol. The issuers' main revenues come, however, from the service charges levied on the businesses that honor the cards.

Commencing in the late 1960s, banks invaded what had become a lucrative field. The two most widely held bank credit cards are issued by Visa (formerly BankAmericard) and Master Charge; each has between 30 and 40 million customers. These firms are not quite as particular about whom they will issue cards to (the other companies require applicants to meet certain standards, such as a specified minimum income), but there is no charge for the bank cards, and they are accepted up to their usual limit of a few hundred dollars for most of the merchandise or services for which an American Express, Diners', or Hilton card might be used.

The credit card companies charge participating merchants anywhere from 2% to 6% of the amounts billed. Also, if a holder does not pay within 25 days of billing for the goods or services purchased, he or she is charged interest at the rate of 1½% a month (18% a year) in most states, and only slightly less in others.

If a credit card is lost or stolen and used by the finder or thief before the issuer is notified of the loss, the holder might be liable up to a maximum of $50. But he would not be responsible in any amount unless the issuer had notified him of his prospective liability and had provided a stamped, self-addressed envelope to use to report the loss or theft.

Just as guns don't kill, but people do, credit cards don't cause bankruptcy, but economic illiterates do. An estimated 5% or so of all credit buyers end up south of solvency. If you (or your spouse) discover in time that you have difficulty resisting temptations to overspend, you should consider consigning all your credit weapons, properly mutilated, to the nearest trash bin. On the other hand, if your spending habits are disciplined, credit cards can be used to advantage. There is less risk of loss with a card than with carrying large sums of cash, and purchases, especially when travelling, can usually be made much more readily by card than by check.

CREDIT LIFE INSURANCE

Before leaving credit sales, credit life insurance should be mentioned. The use of this device has become commonplace in the last few years, and over three-fourths of all consumer installment credit is tied into this type of coverage, often without the debtor's awareness.

The primary purpose of credit life insurance is to pay the creditor the balance due if the debtor dies before completing his installments. Generally, it is optional—despite the impression many sellers create—but it might be required as part of an installment sale. In any event, sellers usually like to include credit life insurance, and occasionally do this unknown to the buyer, by "packing" the premium together with other costs.

The fast growth of this coverage is not surprising, because not only does it protect the seller's or his assignee's interest, but commissions, which in some cases are over 50% of the premium, can be an important added source of income. Conventional credit life insurance may cost, for an individual policy, as much as $1 per $100 per year. In those states which have enacted the model law proposed by the National Association of Insurance Commissioners, rates generally have decreased to 75 cents per $100 for group coverage for one debtor, or $1.25 per $100 for husband-wife protection. This insures only the unpaid balance of the note. The latest innovation is "level benefit" insurance in the full amount of the initial debt. Individual policies of this type may cost as much as $2 per $100 per year. The benefits paid by the insurers range from about 10 cents to 25 cents per $100 coverage per year; adding an overhead of 5 cents to 25 cents per $100 per year results in profits on gross premiums of 100% or more.

Although not all credit life insurance policies are as expensive as indicated (General Motors Acceptance Corporation and Household Finance charge significantly less), informed prospective credit purchasers will flatly reject credit life insurance, assuming they have the option to do so. If the debt is so large that the buyer cannot prudently assume the risk of death before payment, far less expensive protection can be obtained in the form of term life insurance (see Chapter 6).

BORROWING MONEY

If a prospective buyer is planning a credit purchase of an expensive item, such as an automobile, furniture, or appliances, he frequently will save money if he borrows and pays cash rather than finances the purchase through the retailer or dealer. He must realize, though, that lending money, like selling merchandise, is a competitive business. The competition enables him to search out the best available value, assuming he knows where to look and what to look for. The principal sources of cash loans are:

Commercial Banks

Two types of loans are made by commercial banks: a single payment loan secured by collateral such as securities, and a personal (unsecured) loan that usually is repayable in installments. If you have collateral acceptable to a bank, the single payment, secured loan is the more advantageous, for unlike many forms of consumer credit, the nominal interest is the true interest and the rate charged in most cases is the lowest obtainable.

The true interest on a personal installment loan might be almost twice the nominal interest, because generally the interest is computed on the original amount of the loan rather than on the declining balance. By repaying the obligation in equal monthly installments, the borrower has the average use over the loan period of only slightly more than one-half the amount borrowed. Thus, an installment loan with a nominal interest rate of 8% actually costs about 15%. Even this rate varies, depending upon whether the lender adds-on or discounts the interest. To illustrate, if $100 is borrowed at 8% for one year and the cost is added-on, $100 is received and $108 is repaid. If the cost is discounted, $92 is received and $100 is repaid. In the first situation, the monthly payments are $9 and the borrower has the average use for the year of about $50.50. In the second situation, the monthly payments are $8.34 and the average amount available is about $42.20. Most banks also require credit life insurance on personal loans. This increases the cost by about ½%. The maximum amount a bank may lend on a personal loan varies, depending upon the state in which it is located, but generally $3,000 to $5,000 is permissible. The period of such loans is usually one year.

Another "service" now provided by most banks is an overdraft plan that permits a depositor to make a loan merely by writing a check for more money than is actually in the checking account. If you find yourself resorting to this temporarily painless technique frequently or for other than an extraordinary and temporary emergency, it's a sure sign that your Puritan ethic has slipped to a dangerous level.

Credit Unions

Credit unions are cooperative ventures formed by people who have something in common, such as the same employer, to encourage thrift and to provide a source of low-cost loans for members. Typically, the cost of borrowing is from ¾% to 1% a month on the unpaid balance, or a true 9% to 12% a year.

Life Insurance Loans

Cash value life insurance (such as ordinary life, limited payment life or endowment), as we shall see in a later chapter, is a combination of pure insurance and a long-range savings program. Because premiums paid by an insured exceed by a wide margin the combined cost of the mortality risk and the insurer's overhead, after the first or second year the policy acquires a "cash surrender value." Depending upon the provisions of the policy, an insured may borrow 95% or 100% of this sum. The annual interest under most policies is 5% or 6%, although recently some companies have been permitted to charge 8%. The borrower is not required to repay the loan, but the face value of the policy would be reduced by any outstanding indebtedness if death occurs. Consequently, until it is repaid, an insurance loan reduces the beneficiary's protection.

While some policyholders might resent what they regard as paying interest for the use of their own money, borrowing against the cash value of a life insurance policy is analogous to borrowing from a credit union or bank in which the debtor has a savings account: she will pay higher interest on the loan than her savings earn, but her savings remain intact. In any event, borrowing is the only way an insured has of ever obtaining the savings portion of her policy, short of surrendering her coverage or converting it to some form of annuity. And in times of dire need, when an insured's ability to repay any loan is doubtful, the insurer might be her only source of money. Also, at times when interest rates on money market instruments (see Chapter 7) are high, borrowing the cash value provides an opportunity to earn more with it in highly secure, short-term securities such as Treasury bills than the loan costs. In other circumstances, borrowing the cash value is a questionable practice.

Industrial Banks

Some 30 states charter industrial banks, such as the Morris Plan, which accept savings accounts and make consumer loans. Their charges range from 12% to 24% a year.

Small Loan Companies

Consumer finance or small loan companies are licensed dealers that operate under state loan laws. These laws limit the amounts that may be lent and the interest that may be charged. Permissible rates usually depend upon the amount borrowed, and might range from 3½% a month on smaller loans down to 1% a month on larger amounts. A common cost for an average-sized loan is about 2½% or 3% a month (30% to 36% annually). On top of this, "add-on charges for services" and other fees, such as credit life insurance and sometimes even health and accident insurance, may increase the actual costs substantially.

While small loan companies serve a useful purpose in the consumer credit field, an informed borrower will investigate all loan sources when he needs money. The principal advantages small loan firms offer are the speed with which loans can be negotiated and the fact that, in some cases, loans will be made without collateral or cosigners. Nevertheless, the borrower who can obtain funds elsewhere may pay dearly for these conveniences. "Mail order" loans are even more costly because of the greater risk assumed by the lender.

THE COST OF CREDIT

In discussing various types of consumer credit, frequent reference has been made to true annual interest. The Truth-in-Lending Act requires disclosure of the pertinent details of installment sales and cash loan transactions. These include the "finance charge" (the total dollar cost of interest, service, or carrying charges, credit life insurance premiums, credit report fees and other charges), when payments are due, prepayment penalties, and the annual percentage rate (unless no more than $75 credit is extended and the charge does not exceed $5). The Act does not place any limit on the amount or percentage a seller might charge. Instead, it is designed simply to provide buyers with information that could be used for comparative purposes. Although a Federal Trade Commission study found that less than one in five consumers even know the law exists, and probably far fewer ever compare credit costs, the disclosure requirements should at least make buyers more aware of how expensive credit can be.

An informed prospective borrower should be able to compute the costs himself. Few can or do. As mentioned before, there are three basic methods of calculating finance charges: interest may be added on, discounted, or charged on the unpaid balance. Also, aside from stated interest, many lenders impose various other charges, fees, or commissions.

The easiest way of comparing the costs of credit, regardless of the method used or the extra charges made, is to convert all costs into a simple annual interest rate. On installment contracts, the constant ratio method enables a consumer to do this readily. The formula is:

$$R = \frac{2pC}{A(n+1)}$$

R = true annual interest.
p = number of payment periods in one year, exclusive of any down payment.
C = the total interest or finance charges in dollars.
A = the amount borrowed.
n = the number of equal installment payments.

Thus, if you purchase a color television set for $595, paying $100 down and agreeing to pay $35 a month for 18 months, the total charges, regardless of how they are labeled, are 18 ($35) minus the $495 borrowed, or $135. In terms of true annual interest, your costs would be:

$$\frac{2(12)(135)}{495(18+1)} = \frac{3240}{9405} = 0.344 = 34.4\%$$

Sometimes the first payment on an installment loan is not due for a few months. The formula then is:

$$R = \frac{2pC}{A(2s+n+1)}$$

The letters represent the same things indicated above, and "s" is the number of "skip periods." For example, if repayment is to be made in equal monthly installments commencing seven months after the loan is made, "s" would be 7.

If the cost of an installment purchase or loan repayable in equal installments is expressed in terms of annual interest on the original balance, a convenient rule of thumb is that the true annual interest is roughly twice the nominal interest. This is so because, as previously mentioned, a debtor who repays in equal installments actually has the average use over the loan period of only slightly more than one-half the amount borrowed.

A fairly accurate comparison of nominal interest and true annual interest on installment sales or loans is:

4% a year really means 7.3%
6% a year really means 11.1%
8% a year really means 14.5%
10% a year really means 18.4%
1% per month really means 22.2%

If interest is a certain percentage per month on the unpaid balance, the true annual interest, of course, is 12 times the monthly interest.

chapter 3
Sharing Risks

While successful saving and investing are the basic ingredients for achieving long-range financial goals, continuous protection is required to avoid losses that might impair or destroy an estate while it is being built.

There are, of course, countless ways in which personal assets can be lost: the reckless investment of significant sums in highly speculative securities or in questionable business ventures probably is among the fastest and surest. But for that matter, as we shall explore in Chapter 8, there is considerable risk even in cash itself or in the highest quality fixed-dollar uses of money, such as government bonds, for while the dollars as such might be inviolable, the continual erosion in their purchasing power over a period of years could result in just as real a loss to the owner. Obviously, then, anything you do with your savings involves some degree of risk. But for the moment, our concern is not with the perils inherent in particular uses of money. Instead, we shall examine briefly how to reduce or eliminate the types of losses that could result from wholly independent events.

Financially debilitating losses might be caused by any of several incidents, ranging from the outright theft or destruction of valuable property to a sizeable adverse judgment in a negligence suit. If a loss were of considerable magnitude, years of effort in accumulating an estate, as well as the things it was intended to provide, could be wiped out. Although such misfortune might never befall you, no one has any assurance of immunity. Yet there is a simple, relatively inexpensive and readily available way to protect against devastating losses: insurance.

HOW INSURANCE DEVELOPED

Essentially, the insurance concept, which originated centuries ago among ancient merchants, involves no more than pooling small contributions from many people exposed to similar risks, so that those who incur losses can be indemnified. In the Anglo-American world, the development of insurance can be traced from amorphous customs of the sixteenth and seventeenth centuries, such as those engaged in at an establishment called Lloyd's Coffee House. Lloyd's, which opened in 1688 on London's Tower Street, was a popular gathering place for seafarers and merchants, many of whom staked their fortunes on commerce with other nations. And considering the none-too-trustworthy sailing craft and various other hazards of the day, the risks were substantial. To avoid what otherwise would be an all-or-nothing outcome, an owner would post or circulate a piece of paper setting forth the details of a proposed venture. Those customers who chose to share some of the risk would sign their names, indicating how much of the whole they would guarantee. Out of this informal practice, the vast marine insurance industry gradually emerged. And Lloyd's, incidentally, went on to become the largest body of individual underwriters in the world.

Over the years, numerous other forms of insurance against particular perils developed to meet the needs of an increasingly crowded and complex society. For example, after the holocaust that devastated London in 1666, fire insurance became a significant business. Life insurance, which in most individual cases is the least-dispensable type of protection against financial loss, is a relative newcomer, for it was not sold extensively until the latter part of the nineteenth century. Several factors were responsible for this deferred development, including the practice during Elizabethan times of sometimes using life insurance as a gaming device, which led to its being banned in several countries.

In the early twentieth century, the advent of the horseless carriage created the need for still another type of protection against financial loss. At first, however, not all insurers were enthusiastic about automobile insurance. In fact, in 1904 the president of one of the largest insurance companies declared, "I will never insure a gasoline can on wheels, the noisy stinking things." Noise and stench notwithstanding, the financial protection required by car owners spawned an entirely new underwriting business.

Today, some type of insurance is available to protect against losses that might be caused by almost any imaginable event. A partial list of the particular coverages include:

Fire insurance for property losses caused by fire, lightning, wind and hail

Accident insurance for losses from personal injuries to the insured

Health and hospitalization insurance for the costs incident to a disabling illness or injury

Automobile insurance for liability arising from the ownership, maintenance or use of a car, and for loss or damage caused by collision, theft, fire or other causes

Transportation insurance for loss or damage to goods in transit

Personal liability insurance for liability for injuries or property damage to others on the insured's premises or caused by the insured or by household members.

Before examining a few of these policies more closely, a glimpse of some of the more important legal aspects of insurance might be helpful.

LEGAL CONSIDERATIONS

Fundamentally, any insurance policy is simply a unilateral contract in which the act of one party (payment of a premium) is exchanged for the promise of the other party (to indemnify or pay a stated sum to the insured if the contingency contemplated by the contract occurs). Consequently, insurance law is based on contract law, with which it shares some of the problems relating to offer and acceptance, consideration, legality of object, and capacity of the parties. Over the years, however, so many special rules governing the rights and liabilities of the insurer and the insured have developed that to a large extent insurance law has become a separate highly specialized field.

In life insurance, for example, an important variation from the customary rule as to contractual capacity is sometimes found. In most states, a minor has the right to disaffirm his simple contracts and, unless he had received necessaries from the other party, have returned to him any consideration he might have given. But a few states have abrogated this rule if the contract is for life insurance. Thus (depending upon local law), a child as young as 15, despite lack of experience and judgment and bargaining disabilities, might be prohibited from disaffirming a life insurance policy.

Legality of purpose is another area in which some important rules peculiar to insurance have developed. In general, the law looks upon gambling with such repugnance that it refuses to invoke judicial remedies in any wagering dispute. Hence, the courts will neither enforce payment of a gambling debt if a loser has refused to pay, nor will they require a winner to reimburse a disgruntled loser who has paid. A few centuries ago, some types of insurance were accorded similar treatment. But as the use of insurance became less reprehensible, the law's disdain slowly gave way, and today insurance contracts are recognized as valid and enforceable to the extent that they are not subterfuges for gambling. To prevent insurance from being used for illicit purposes, the law now requires an insured to have what is known as an *insurable interest* in the subject matter.

Essentially, an insurable interest simply means that the insured would incur a pecuniary loss from the occurrence of the event contemplated by the policy. For example, a person who insures her own house against fire would be entitled, within the dollar limits and other provisions of the policy, to recover her actual loss if her house is damaged or destroyed by this cause. On the other hand, if the same person insures someone else's house in which she has no financial interest, the contract would amount to an unenforceable wager. But if she held a mortgage on the other house, she would have an insurable interest to the extent of the unpaid balance of the debt that the mortgage secured. Note, however, that regardless of the amount of a policy, an insured cannot normally collect more than her actual loss, for the purpose of insurance is *indemnification,* which means to restore an insured to the same position she was in before the loss. Thus, an owner could not insure a $20,000 house for $50,000, then collect more than $20,000 if the house were totally destroyed, for receiving more than her insurable interest smacks of gambling.

As applied to life insurance, most courts regard the insurable interest concept as immaterial if the insured owned the policy, as usually is the case. Moreover, except for limitations which a few community property states impose when community funds are used to pay premiums, an insured has the right to designate anyone he pleases as beneficiary of the proceeds, regardless of whether the beneficiary has any financial interest in the insured's continued existence. An insurable interest is required, though, if the owner is someone other than the insured. Such an interest would exist if the owner had a reasonable expectation of some financial benefit from the insured's continued life, or conversely an expectation of financial loss from the insured's death. Expectations of this type usually arise from various relationships, such as husband-wife, parent-child, creditor-debtor, employer-key employee and even fiancée-fiancé.

Assuming that an insurable interest in the life of another exists, the dollar value of such interest is generally presumed to be the face value of the policy, irrespective of the monetary worth of the insured, insofar as this might be measured in terms of future earnings and other factors. The one exception to this rule is that the extent of a creditor's insurable interest in the life of a debtor must have a reasonable relationship to the amount the debtor owed him.

Insurance is sometimes treated differently than other property in the area of creditors' rights. Thus, while the proceeds from fire or casualty policies normally are subject to the claims of an insured's creditors, the opposite usually is true of all or at least a minimum part of the proceeds of a life insurance policy that a deceased debtor had owned. Moreover, prior to an insured debtor's death, most states accord the same preferential treatment to the cash surrender values of any life insurance policies he might own. On the other hand, though, life insurance proceeds to which a beneficiary is entitled seldom are exempt from claims of the beneficiary's creditors, unless the insured had elected to have the proceeds paid under a settlement option that contained a spendthrift clause. But even then, a few states regard such clauses as contrary to public policy.

These few illustrations of the law's role in insurance should suggest at least one thing: consult an attorney whenever a serious question arises as to the rights and liabilities under any insurance contract.

AMOUNTS OF INSURANCE NEEDED

Another question that warrants brief consideration is how much insurance generally is adequate. Deferring the consideration of life insurance until Chapter 6, and assuming that a prospective buyer can afford whatever types and amounts of other insurance his circumstances require, the answer depends primarily upon how much financial hardship a particular loss would create, for while not insuring (underinsuring) is foolhardy, buying unnecessary insurance (overinsuring) is equally senseless.

As a rule of thumb, a reasonable approach might be to *insure only in those amounts necessary to protect against financial losses that the buyer cannot afford to assume himself.* If a maximum potential loss could be absorbed without creating a financial hardship, insurance might be regarded as more of a needless luxury than a necessity. Just how extensive a risk can or should be assumed depends, obviously, upon the particular individual and his resources. But to illustrate the point, an owner of a car valued at $500 normally would not need coverage to compensate him in the event the car is stolen or irreparably damaged, for while a $500 loss might be inconvenient, rarely would it seriously impair estate assets. On the other hand, the negligent operation of the same car could cause bodily injuries to another just as serious as those which a new Mercedes might inflict. Consequently, ordinary prudence would dictate that the owner buy ample insurance as protection against personal injury claims. With these very general principles in mind, we shall now consider in more detail a few of the more common forms of insurance, other than life insurance, which most informed individuals own.

AUTOMOBILE INSURANCE

Types of Automobile Insurance

Basically, there are two principal forms of automobile insurance: *liability,* and *physical damage.* Liability coverage protects an insured if he becomes liable to another, while physical damage coverage (collision and comprehensive) indemnifies him for losses or damages to his own car. In addition, many car owners purchase medical payment, uninsured motorists, and other coverages.

Liability

Liability insurance comes in two distinct forms: that which pertains to personal injuries caused to others and that which relates to damages done to the property of others. Both provide for *indemnification* if the insured, due to the ownership, maintenance, or use of his car, becomes *legally obligated* to another. Thus, the insurer does not undertake to compensate everyone who is injured or whose property is damaged by the insured, but only those to whom the insured would be liable. In other words, the claimant must obtain or be entitled to obtain a judgment against the insured before the insurer is obligated to pay. In this connection, however, an insurer will investigate any claims made against its insured and defend any legal action; also, it reserves the right to settle claims without resort to judicial proceedings.

Most automobile insurance policies protect not only the named insured, but also family members and others who operate the car with the insured's permission. What is more, the insured person and his or her spouse usually are covered while operating someone else's car. Nevertheless, a prospective buyer should determine whether the policy being considered provides for such extended coverage, for deceptively low-priced policies often are limited in this respect.

There are several cogent reasons why an automobile owner should have ample amounts of both bodily injury and property damage liability insurance. Foremost, of course, is the underlying purpose of any insurance: protection against losses which might seriously impair an estate. Aside from this, liability insurance is required for all cars registered in certain states, while some others impose additional fees for registering uninsured cars. These extra charges are placed in a fund to indemnify persons whose claims or judgments against uninsured motorists cannot otherwise be satisfied. What is more, all states have some form of financial responsibility act.

Although the specific provisions of the various financial responsibility laws differ, most states require that whenever an accident occurs which results either in personal injuries or in property damage above a certain minimum amount (usually $50 or $100), each party must do one of three things: (1) establish that he has liability insurance in an amount prescribed by statute (generally 10–20–5); or (2) post security (cash or an indemnity bond) in an amount sufficient to satisfy any possible judgment against him; or (3) obtain and submit a written release from the other party. An owner or operator who fails to do any of these within a limited statutory period has his driver's permit suspended, usually until one year has elapsed without a lawsuit being commenced against him. Thus, even though he might have been entirely blameless, an uninsured motorist is in a vulnerable position. The cost of a bond or other evidence of financial responsibility might be prohibitive, while securing a release from the other party is often an impracticable alternative, for he might refuse to furnish a release unless a settlement favorable to him is agreed upon. Consequently, as a practical matter, the question is not whether to have liability insurance, but rather how much to have.

Automobile liability insurance usually is available in about whatever combinations and amounts a buyer desires, ranging from 5–10–1 to 300–500–100 or more. Probably the most popular coverage is 10–20–5, perhaps because these are the minimum sums required by the financial responsibility laws of most states. Translated, a 10–20–5 policy provides a maximum of $10,000 for bodily injuries to any one person, up to $20,000 if two or more persons are injured in the same mishap, and up to $5,000 for damages to another's property. If an insured becomes legally obligated for an amount greater than the limits of his insurance, payment of the excess is his own responsibility, of course.

In deciding what limits are adequate, a car owner would do well to consider the increasing frequency of sizeable judgments for personal injuries caused by the negligent operation of automobiles. Awards of $100,000 or more are no longer rare, especially in the larger urban areas. Consequently, carrying only minimum liability insurance seldom is prudent. This is especially evident when the costs for higher limits are compared with those for lower amounts: for example, if a particular insured were charged $70 for 15–30–5 coverage, he probably could buy 100–200–25 for less than $100. This last insurance coverage is the minimum most people should have.

Collision

The purpose of collision coverage is to compensate the owner if his car collides with another object or is upset. Whether the insured himself or someone else was negligent is immaterial, except that an insurer might refuse to continue doing business with someone whose driving record has made him a high risk.

Collision insurance can be purchased to indemnify an insured in full (although some companies no longer offer full collision), or for any amount above a specified minimum, such as $50, $250, or up to $1,000. If the latter type, which is known as "deductible collision," is used, the car owner would be self-insured to the extent of the deductible amount. Hence, if the car of an insured with $100 deductible were to sustain $800 damage, he would recover $700 of this sum from the insurer. Because a loss of $100 or so seldom would create a financial hardship, full collision coverage, which might cost 50% more than the premium charged for a $100 deductible, is an extravagance. Larger deductibles offer even greater savings, and in addition, the government would absorb part of any unreimbursed loss above $100 if an insured itemizes his income tax deductions: for example, if someone in the 36% tax bracket who has a $500 deductible were to "total" his automobile, he would be out-of-pocket only $356 minus whatever sum the higher deductible had saved him in premiums. Of course, if a car is not worth more than a few hundred dollars, there should be no need for collision insurance. Again, the sensible approach is to protect against the catastrophe and risk the nuisance.

Comprehensive

Any loss or damage to a car caused by something other than upset or collision can be protected against with "comprehensive" coverage. This provides indemnification for damages from such occurrences as fire, theft, hail, windstorm, vandalism, and falling objects. Hence, an insured would be compensated if his windows were shattered or his paint pitted by blowing gravel, if sugar or sand were placed in his gasoline tank by children, if his tires were slashed by delinquents, or if a tree were to topple over onto his parked car. It does not, of course, apply to thefts of personal articles, such as luggage or cameras, from a car. Similar to collision coverage, a buyer may purchase either full comprehensive or some deductible amount. The savings in premiums make the latter preferable in almost all situations, for full comprehensive might cost about twice as much as $100 deductible.

Medical Payments

This coverage is designed to compensate for medical, hospital, or dental expenses sustained by anyone injured while in, entering, or alighting from the insured's automobile, regardless of any fault or liability on the part of the insured. It is usually written in amounts ranging from a few hundred dollars up to $5,000. Each person so injured can collect up to the policy limit for expenses incurred within one year (or, under some policies, three years) of the injury. The cost is not great, normally no more than a few dollars, and the coverage is a worthwhile adjunct for car owners in states that do not have a "no-fault" law; in "no-fault" states, it is largely superfluous.

Uninsured and Underinsured Motorists

The purpose of uninsured motorists' coverage is to pay for *bodily injuries* that an insured, members of his household or passengers in his car might become entitled to recover from someone who is not insured or when inflicted by a hit-and-run driver. The protection also extends to bodily injuries caused by such a person to the insured and members of his family while they are pedestrians. Although this coverage is limited in most states to the costs associated with bodily injuries, in about one-fifth of the states, insurance is also available to protect against property damage up to $5,000 (with a $100 to $300 deductible). The bodily injury coverage, similar to the insured's bodily injury liability insurance, has two limits, such as $10,000 and $20,000; the first sum is the maximum amount payable for injuries to one person, and the second is the maximum for two or more persons injured or killed in the same accident. Many states require car owners to carry such insurance; but even if it is not mandatory, it is a sound buy and the cost is negligible.

In addition to "uninsured" motorists' coverage, protection

against "underinsured" motorists is available in most states. As the name suggests, this is designed to compensate an insured for bodily injuries in excess of the liability limits of the at-fault driver's policy.

Other Coverages

There are a number of other coverages designed to meet the needs or desires of particular car owners or operators. For example, because comprehensive insurance would not usually apply to the theft of items such as CB radios or non-permanently installed stereo equipment, an endorsement to an automobile policy may be purchased to cover these risks. The costs are high: perhaps 10% or so of the value annually.

For those who regularly use a car or cars they do not own, such as vehicles furnished by an employer, "Extended Non-Owned Automobile Coverage" is available. This is not needed if an insured uses another's car only occasionally, since the owner's policy would usually apply and, after its limits have been exhausted, the insured's own coverage would take over. In this connection, however, when renting a car for a short period, it's probably a good idea to pay the agency the additional fee charged for collision insurance: it would cover your deductible, as well as lessen delays or difficulties if the car were damaged.

If your peace of mind depends upon being protected against almost every imaginable financial hazard, about $10 or $12 a year will buy "Rental Reimbursement" coverage. This will pay up to $10 or so a day (exclusive of mileage charges) for up to thirty days to rent a replacement car when your vehicle is unavailable because of damages from some occurrence, such as a collision, covered in your policy. Ten or twelve dollars isn't much, and some drivers would think this coverage was not much either.

"No Fault" Systems

Historically, the basis for determining if someone who injures another is pecuniarily responsible to him has been whether or not the person causing the injuries was, in a legal sense, at "fault." To resolve this often difficult and frequently disputed question, the courts created the hypothetical "ordinary, reasonable, prudent man," against whose supposed conduct that of a defendant is measured. If a defendant's conduct fell short of that which the jury believes a reasonable man would have exercised under the same or similar circumstances, then he was negligent; and if such negligence was the "proximate cause" of harm to another and no valid defense (e.g., the contributory negligence of the victim) existed, there was "fault" and, hence, liability for the harm caused. When the harm is bodily injury, the extent of such liability might go well beyond the obvious costs of medical treatment and hospitalization, to include such other elements as loss of income (both current and in some cases prospective) and an amount designed to compensate the victim for his "pain and suffering." Bodily injury liability insurance, discussed above, provides financial protection for an insured in such a situation.

Although most people would not seriously dispute the fault concept, few would deny its practical shortcomings in an increasingly urbanized, impersonal, and vehicular society. Alarmed by congested court dockets, extensive delays in compensating victims, and a rapid escalation of premiums, in 1970 the Massachusetts legislature enacted a system to provide prompt compensation to persons injured in automobile mishaps, regardless of who might have been to blame. Since then, different versions of the "no-fault" concept have been adopted by about one-half of the states. So far, the results of this controversial approach have been mixed; nevertheless, various consumer and organized labor groups are still beating the drums for a federal law that would impose no-fault standards nationwide.

Basically, a "no-fault" (known as "Personal Injury Protection") system simply requires the injured person's own insurance company to pay, within specified limits, for certain types of damage (such as bodily injury expenses and loss of income) he suffers because of an automobile collision, regardless of whether he or the other driver was negligent. Minimum coverages are mandatory under most laws, and in two-thirds of the no-fault states, personal injury lawsuits are prohibited unless the medical costs pass a prescribed threshold level.

Apart from the merits or lack thereof in the "no-fault" concept, it is important for those who reside in states adopting it to understand generally what protection it does and does not provide. Because each of the systems so far enacted differs in specifics from the others, few generalizations would be accurate. But, without attempting to analyze the "no-fault" law of any particular state, the following threads are woven through most plans.

Medical Expenses

The victim's own insurance company pays for his medical and hospitalization costs and, in most states, for funeral expenses, up to a specified maximum amount, regardless of who might have been at fault. To recover expenses in excess of the statutory limit, an injured person may resort to traditional methods (litigation). In some states, an insurer may recover from the other party or his insurer for sums it has paid to its policyholder, assuming the other person would be liable; in other states, it may not do so.

Loss of Income

If personal injuries cause a person to lose wages, his insurer is required to compensate him; the amount payable is limited to a percentage of the income lost, up to a dollar maximum per week for a period of one year.

Personal Services

If an insured, due to his injuries, cannot perform essential personal services (such as housekeeping) for himself, his insurer will indemnify him in a limited amount (perhaps $10 to $15 a day) for a specified period (usually one year) for the costs of hiring someone for these purposes.

Pain and Suffering

Compensation for this frequently questioned yet often real component normally must be sought in a lawsuit, although most "no-fault" laws prohibit any recovery unless the medical expenses exceed a "threshold" amount (generally, several hundred dollars) or unless permanent or serious injuries have been incurred.

Death Benefits

Under most of the present laws, no provision is made for payment of any death benefit to the survivors of someone killed in an automobile accident; however, in a few states, payment of a sum set by statute is made if the deceased was the named insured.

Under most of the "no-fault" plans, the only payments made to a victim by his own insurer are those relating to the expenses incident to his bodily injuries. Consequently, property losses such as those contemplated by the collision and comprehensive coverages previously discussed are handled in the usual method. Also, because all of the laws permit suits for bodily injuries, including pain and suffering, if the injuries were sufficiently grievous or costly, an insured must continue to carry adequate liability insurance.

Costs of Automobile Insurance

Just how much a particular owner has to pay for his automobile insurance depends upon several factors. To begin with, in nearly all states, the rates insurers may charge are controlled by regulatory agencies. This does not mean, of course, that a person is just as well off buying from one company as another, for better selection of risks, more favorable loss experience, greater managerial ability, and other factors could make a significant difference. Also, as a general rule most of the small, unrated firms that sell by mail should be avoided, for in recent years a number of such companies, being unable to meet extraordinary losses, have ended up in receivership. What is more, their policyholders occasionally have been assessed to pay the defunct insurer's obligations.

The premiums that automobile insurers are permitted to charge depend upon the rating classification of the particular automobile and driver involved. Currently, for rating bureaus in most states, the rating of private passenger automobiles is based upon the "161 class plan." The main factors are:

- The *location* of the car. Each state is divided into "rating territories" which have a significant bearing on insurance costs. If you move from, say, Medicine Bow, Wyoming, to Boston, expect your new premium to be a shocker.
- The *age, marital status, and sex* of the named insured and other persons who will customarily drive the car. Several states have eliminated these criteria, and they are being hotly assailed elsewhere. Where they still apply, unmarried young men are charged the highest premiums, simply because as a group they are involved in a greater number of more costly accidents. In Denver, for

example, a 22-year-old bachelor might have to pay more than twice as much as his father for the same amount of liability coverage. On the other hand, women between the ages of 24 and 64 are a low-risk group, so they pay less.

- The *use* to which the car will be put: pleasure only, commuting to work, business, or farm use.
- The distance the car is *driven to work*. The cost varies according to whether the distance is less than three miles, less than ten miles, or more than ten miles.
- The *make* and *model* of the car.
- *Driver Training Course*. Premiums are lower for drivers through age 20 who have completed a recognized driver training course.
- The *age* of the *car*.
- The *driving record* of the insured and resident operators. Accidents and chargeable moving traffic violation convictions cause an increase in the premiums. Higher rates are charged on an increasing scale depending upon the number and severity of accidents and convictions.
- *How long the principal operator has been licensed to drive*. If less than three years, higher premiums apply.
- *Number of cars insured*. A premium reduction applies if more than one private passenger automobile is insured with the same company.
- Whether a student-operator is a "good" student (e.g., Dean's list or 3.00 GPA).

Assigned Risk Plans

Individuals with poor driving records are often unable to purchase the insurance they desire from a company of their choice. When this occurs, the only alternative is to obtain insurance under an assigned risk plan. These plans, which have been upheld by the Supreme Court, require automobile insurers, on an equitable apportionment basis, to insure those drivers who are unable otherwise to obtain insurance because of their poor records. In most states, the permissible premiums for such coverage, being commensurate with the greater risks, exceed by a wide margin the sums charged other policyholders. In addition, the maximum liability insurance available does not exceed 5–10–5 or 10–20–5 in most instances.

What To Do if You Have a Collision

Safeguarding personal assets from losses caused by the operation, use, or maintenance of a car does not stop with the purchase of adequate insurance, of course. For one thing, what is done in the event of a serious collision could have an important bearing on whether an estate will escape unscathed. Those things which are done or not done when the horns are blaring, the spectators gathering and the bumpers being disentangled might either facilitate or impede the settlement of claims, and in some situations can even determine whether protection really exists.

By and large, the things that an insured either should or should not do at the scene of an accident are simply those which common sense indicates. Yet under stress, many people overlook the obvious. For this reason, you should be familiar with the following suggestions, and try to follow them if the occasion ever arises when they are needed.

1. Never admit fault. Saying, "It was all my fault, but my insurance will cover it," could be tantamount to saying, "I'll personally pay for everything."
2. Promptly write down all pertinent facts, including:
    a. The make, model, year and license number of the other car or cars.
    b. The name, address and operator's number of the other driver and owner.
    c. The names and addresses of all occupants of the other car or cars.
    d. The extent of apparent damage to each car.
    e. The names and addresses of all witnesses.
    f. The precise location of the collision. (A simple sketch of the scene including locations and directions of the cars, place of impact, and distance of any skid marks, could be very useful later.)
    g. The time of the accident; road and weather conditions; visibility; and other relevant details. (If you have a camera handy, use it.)
3. Determine if there are any personal injuries, and if so, see to it that medical services are furnished as promptly as possible.

4. Notify your insurance company as soon as practicable. Most policies require such notice within a certain number of days. If there are serious injuries or extensive property damage, promptly telephone the nearest representative of your company.
5. Report the accident to the local authorities immediately. Many states also require a written report to be filed with state authorities, often within 24 to 48 hours, if there has been any bodily injury or if property damage exceeds a certain minimum, usually $50 or $100.

After the dust is long settled, remember that you still have some contractual responsibilities, for your policy obligates you to cooperate with the insurer. Among other things, this means that if you are later called upon to testify in a case arising from the collision, be there; otherwise, the insurer might claim that your breach of contract has relieved it of responsibility to indemnify you for any resultant adverse judgment.

In short, when your policy is issued, take a few minutes to read it and become familiar with its requirements. Then, if you do become involved in a collision, try to stay calm and follow the above suggestions.

PERSONAL PROPERTY INSURANCE

Until such time as a modest estate has been accumulated or a mortgage-free title to a house has been acquired, the principal assets of most people probably are their household goods and other personal property. In fact, although no single item may have cost more than a few hundred dollars, the aggregate value of an average family's furnishings, appliances, clothing, silverware, jewelry and other property is likely to be from two to three times its annual income. Obviously, the loss of all or of a substantial part of these assets would be a financially crippling experience. But again, insurance can eliminate or minimize the risk.

Whether a need for insurance actually exists depends, of course, upon how much of a financial hardship would result from the loss of personal property. Here, as with other forms of insurance, a sensible approach normally is to insure against the catastrophes and assume the risk of the inconveniences.

Floaters

There are several types of policies, most of them called "floaters" to mean that the insurance follows or "floats" with the property, regardless of where it is located.

Rather than discuss all, descriptions of two types will demonstrate the differences. The first is one for "scheduled" property, which provides "all risk" protection to the items insured. "Scheduled" means that items to be insured are actually identified in the policy, sometimes to include an appraisal or bill of sale. "All risk" means that, with the exception of a few named causes, the property is covered no matter what happens to it. Some of the *excluded* "perils" are nuclear war damage, vermin damage, wear and tear, and so on. The property for which this policy is designed includes jewelry, furs, cameras, musical instruments, stamp and coin collections, guns, and fine arts.

The second type of floater is for "unscheduled" property; that is, for the majority of your household goods. This policy insures against major hazards that could result in damage to or loss of your personal property. It covers property owned by you, your spouse, dependents who are residents of your household, and even somebody else's property when it is in your custody. There are some maximum limits prescribed in this floater for certain types of property and certain types of loss. Hence, it is more for general protection than for protection of specific or high-value items.

If an extensive loss of property were to occur, as sometimes happens when a house burns or a shipment of household goods is lost in transit, an owner usually has considerable difficulty remembering exactly what he had and establishing its true value. A periodically updated inventory can be of great assistance at such a time, but because constructing and maintaining such records is tedious, few people get around to doing it.

A far less onerous substitute for a current inventory would be photographs of your goods. Color shots of the contents of each room in your house, made with your instant camera (to avoid the risk of a theft ring having access to work done by a photo processing firm), could be worth thousands of dollars to you. These should be supplemented by close-ups of jewelry, silver, antiques, and other costly items. Particularly valuable articles should be appraised, of course, by a qualified person; in fact, the insurance company probably would require this or other proof of value before issuing the coverage. As an additional aid, note on the back of the photographs when and where the items were purchased or acquired and, if known, their costs.

Anyone about to move should spend some time compiling a photo inventory of his possessions. Obviously, such photographs should be kept separate from the property they depict: carry them with you if you are moving, and store them in a safe deposit box or in your office after you have arrived.

PERSONAL LIABILITY INSURANCE

Many people thoughtlessly neglect to protect themselves from becoming liable in a significant amount for injuries or property damage they inflict on others. Such liability could arise in any number of ways, of course: a babysitter might slip on a carelessly placed throw-rug and break her hip; a deliveryman might fall on an icy step and fracture his skull; a powermower might strike a hidden rock or metal object, causing it to kill or injure a neighbor; another golfer might be struck by a negligently driven golf ball; or the family dog might bite an innocent visitor. For a small sum (perhaps $20 to $25 a year for a $100,000 policy), comprehensive personal liability insurance will pay for all costs, including attorney's fees, incident to any claim or action brought against the policyholder, his wife, or children, except those resulting from the use, ownership, or maintenance of motor vehicles. And if an adverse judgment results, the insurer will pay it, up to the limits of the policy. Moreover, such policies also provide for payment of a small specified amount, perhaps up to $500, for medical costs or for property damage to others caused by the insured, regardless of his legal liability. Considering the nominal cost, and the frequent need for this coverage, most people should own personal liability insurance.

HOMEOWNERS' POLICIES

For a person who owns his residence, insurance against loss caused by fire and other perils is virtually indispensable. In fact, unless a house buyer has enough money to pay cash and does so, he will have no alternative to acquiring such insurance, for the lending institution which finances the purchase will require that its security interest in the property be protected. Hence, insurance that would indemnify the owner and the mortgagee in the event of a loss by fire, explosion, windstorm, smoke, hail, and similar perils is an almost integral part of home ownership. However, most policies do not include protection for losses from floods or earthquakes, so owners in areas where events of this nature might reasonably occur should obtain separate coverages for them.

Normally, the owner of a house will find that he can save money by buying what is known as a "homeowner's policy," which combines fire and extended coverage on his house and other structures on the premises, together with personal property insurance and personal liability insurance, instead of using separate policies.

In some circumstances, other forms of insurance closely related to a homeowner's policy might be advisable. For example, if an individual leases his house to another person, he can obtain fire, lightning, and extended coverage on the structure to protect his interests. Conversely, if he is a lessee, he can buy a renter's policy that will cover his personal property and potential personal liabilities for injuries to others. Condominium owners can buy policies to indemnify them for damages to the interior of their units, which usually are not covered by the condominium association's policy; they may also add other insurance to this, such as liability coverage for common-area losses (for example, a large judgment for personal injuries to someone on the grounds) that exceed the association's policy limits. (In the event of such an occurrence, the individual owners might be assessed to pay any deficiency.)

"UMBRELLA" COVERAGE

One of the fastest-growing types of insurance is "Personal Catastrophe Liability," which is more commonly referred to as an *"Umbrella"* policy. It is designed to add $1 million or more to the limits of other liability policies (such as automobile, boat, homeowner's, and personal liability), once these have been exhausted; also, it applies to some types of potential personal liabilities (such as a judgment for defamation) not usually covered by other policies. The cost for this supplementary protection might range from $50 to

$100 a year, depending among other things upon the coverage desired and the limits of the buyer's underlying liability policies. (Maintenance of minimum amounts of automobile liability and other insurance is required.) Although many less-than-wealthy persons might consider whether they need such coverage, the greater an individual's present and prospective assets, the more concerned he usually is about insulating them from unnecessary loss. An umbrella policy would help do so.

MEDICAL AND HOSPITALIZATION PROTECTION

With the continual escalation of costs for all types of medical care, the personal resources of most families would not be adequate to pay for severe and prolonged illnesses or major injuries. Fortunately, financial protection against such contingencies is now widespread.

For the elderly, the government's Medicare progam provides a substantial degree of assurance that the physical ravages of old age will not leave them impoverished. Millions of others are covered by plans sponsored by or available through their employers, and those in military service and their families receive comprehensive medical care at little or no cost.

Anyone who is not otherwise amply covered, though, should accord a high priority either to joining a health maintenance organization (HMO), such as the renowned Kaiser-Permanente plan in California, or to buying insurance that would pay for major medical and hospitalization expenses.

If insurance is purchased, the emphasis should be on obtaining coverage for *major* costs: occasional medical care for minor injuries or non-disabling illnesses seldom would do more than mildly strain a budget, so a high deductible is usually the better buy. On the top side, however, don't skimp: limits of at least $100,000 are not too much. Some other things to look for are provisions for a semiprivate room and payment of most of the costs if private nursing services are needed; reimbursement for a high percentage of hospital room costs, instead of a dollar limit; and—most importantly—a guarantee of renewability.

The rapidly-growing HMO's might offer some people an attractive alternative to insurance. For a monthly fee that averages a little under $100 a family nationwide (or only about 25% more than the average cost for family medical insurance), an HMO provides prepaid medical care, with an emphasis on preventive medicine, for its members. There are usually no additional charges; office visits are free; and generally the whole spectrum of medical services is available. Some of the larger HMO's even operate their own hospitals.

Health maintenance organizations have not yet been established in many sections of the country, but if one is nearby, consider it. Before deciding whether it would beat an insurance policy, check the plan carefully, to include the doctor/member ratio; the qualifications of its medical personnel; the services furnished; the days and times treatment is available; how far ahead it is necessary to make appointments for routine office visits; and the amount and quality of hospital care provided to members. In this connection, community reputation, especially among those in the medical profession, is often a reliable indicator, so ask around.

MAXIM ONE

Although we have done no more than survey the main types of insurance available, it should be apparent that almost anyone who tried to carry policies against all the financial risks to which he is exposed might end up with little or nothing to worry about, simply because he had spent all he has for premiums. Obviously, then, such an approach would be unrealistic, so choices must be made. You should be able to strike a balance between not enough and too much protection if you evaluate your needs objectively in light of the smart insurance buyers' maxim, which bears restating: *insure only when and in the amounts necessary to protect against financial losses you cannot afford to assume yourself.* In other words, self-insure to the extent you can comfortably do so, but buy insurance when the magnitude of the risk exceeds your means.

chapter 4
Big Brother Cares

Of all life's financial perils, none is quite so formidable as the risk of a premature death that would leave dependents without adequate means of support. And early in their married lives, when family responsibilities usually are the greatest, few people have accumulated personal estates of sufficient size to provide for their survivors' needs.

Life insurance is the obvious solution to this problem, at least until ample other assets have been acquired. But let's not get ahead of ourselves. Before trying to determine how much life insurance might be needed, you should have a basic understanding of the Social Security system, which now looms so large in almost everyone's estate planning.

THE IMPACT OF SOCIAL SECURITY

The Federal Insurance Contributions Act (FICA)—more commonly referred to as Social Security—encompasses a wide variety of programs, many of which are administered by the states with federal financial support. In addition to retirement income, these include disability benefits, hospital insurance for the aged and certain others, and supplemental medical insurance for those over 65.

For our purposes, the "social insurance" or "cash benefit" components have the most significance. These are lumped together under the awkward acronym, OASDI, which stands for Old Age, Survivors, and Disability Insurance. The basic idea is to provide, to a limited extent, income replacement when normal earnings cease because of retirement, death, or an incapacitating disability, so that the recipients may retain some degree of financial independence and not become burdens on families, friends, or other segments of society. Our attention will focus mainly on the benefits your surviving dependents would receive, in case you are not around to take care of them. In addition, because old age assistance is an important factor in estate building plans, we'll consider it also.

Before discussing who might receive what, though, a brief look at the system's background might help you to understand the nature of Social Security and to evaluate where it could be when you or your survivors need it.

THE FICA—BANE OR BLESSING?

Since the time it was spawned during the Great Depression of the 1930s, Social Security has mushroomed from a modest means of helping the elderly into a gargantuan welfare program. Soon after its enactment, the system was broadened to include benefits for family survivors as well as retired workers. Two decades later, disability benefits were tacked on, and in 1966 coverage was vastly increased by adding medical care for the aged. Successive Congresses boosted payments by some 70% from 1967 through 1972, then in 1972 tied the amounts of benefits to increases in both living costs and average wages occurring during a participant's working years.

Today, 93% of all people 65 and over are eligible for benefits, and 95% of all young children and their mothers are protected by the survivor insurance part of the system. Altogether, over 33 million people—one in seven throughout the nation—receive FICA benefits of one sort or another, and the ratio of recipients to workers (fast approaching four to ten) is constantly increasing. The staggering costs—now over $100 billion a year and expected to more than double by 1987—are financed by payroll taxes (currently totaling 12.26%) paid equally by workers and employers, and taxes paid by the self-employed.

Social Security is not a conventional insurance plan, of course, for (1) it is compulsory; (2) it is unfunded; and (3) the rights under it are statutory rather than contractual. Reduced to basics, *the FICA is the means by which the earnings of the working segment of society are levied upon to help support retired or otherwise eligible nonworkers.* Hence, it more closely resembles a form of "income redistribution" rather than anything for which a recipient has paid, although most people receiving benefits erroneously regard them as a return of funds they have previously contributed.

Collectivists praise the system as a humanitarian means of providing financial aid to all, and call for its continual expansion. Individualists, on the other hand, denounce it as a deprivation of personal liberty that is eroding our national character and slowly ruining the economy by stifling initiative and by draining huge sums from it that otherwise could be used for capital investment, which is essential for growth, employment, and prosperity. The truth probably falls somewhere between these two extremes.

Although most people acknowledge the fundamental merits of Social Security, and at least until recently its repeated expansion received broad public support, more and more informed citizens are becoming alarmed about its costs. For example, when the FICA was first enacted, the combined worker-employer annual tax was at most $60; by 1981, it will be $3,950, with no end in sight (see Table 4.1).

In spite of the staggering take, by 1975 the program incurred an operating deficit, and dire predictions of its eventual collapse were voiced. There is no way, of course, that the government would permit this, so in late 1977, major changes in the law were enacted. These were designed primarily to infuse additional billions of dollars annually into the system, so that its solvency could be assured. If the assumptions upon which the amendments were based (which include average annual increases of 5¾% in wages and 4% in living costs) turn out to be reasonably accurate, the fix should work—at least for the next two or three decades. If they turn out to be far wide of the mark, however, other measures will be required.

Regardless of Social Security's merits—or lack thereof—anyone trying to develop a long-range estate plan to provide for his or her future needs and those of their dependents must be aware of its impact. Although participants will have to pay more and more into the system during their working years, the payments most people eventually receive will represent an increasingly important part of their incomes. And in this highly uncertain world, at least one thing in addition to death and taxes seems inevitable: Social Security will be around, in one form or another, until the end of time.

SOCIAL SECURITY TAXES

First, the bad news: the tax bite for the financial security provided you by your government is indeed large, and if you suspect it's going to get even bigger, you're right. Also, because redistributing incomes ("takin' from them what has, to give to them what hasn't") is implicit in the system, those earning relatively more than others will pay more but receive proportionately less.

Figure 4.1 will give you a little historical perspective, as well as a rough idea of where taxes on wages are headed. Table 4.1 is more

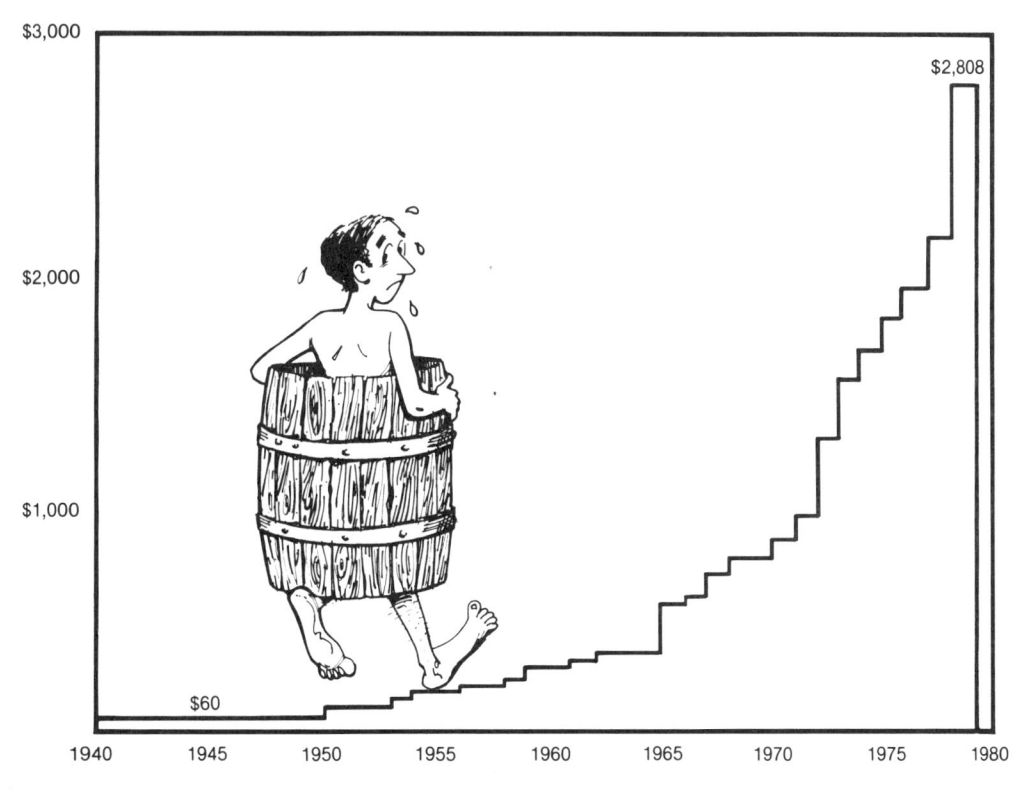

FIGURE 4.1. What Social Security Costs (combined worker and employer tax).

specific (see p. 51). Although projections well into the next century have been made, we won't bother with them: too much is bound to change, and you and your family might not even be here then, anyway.

WHO QUALIFIES FOR BENEFITS?

The Elderly

By far the largest group of Social Security recipients are the nation's "senior citizens"—its elderly. To be eligible for these benefits, a person must be "fully" insured by the time he reaches a specified age.

"Fully" insured means, for anyone who will become 62 after 1990, having worked in "covered employment" for at least ten years (forty quarters); those who reach 62 before 1990 do not need quite as much time.

When a "fully" insured worker reaches 65—or as early as 62, if he's willing to accept a reduction in benefits of up to about 20%— he qualifies for a monthly retirement check. (This, as well as any other Social Security benefit, must be applied for: none is paid automatically.) For those people who continue to work beyond 65, the amount they otherwise would have received at 65 is increased by 3% a year, up to age 72.

The amount a worker alone would be paid at age 65 is equal to his "primary insurance amount" (a term we'll explain later). If a 65-year-old worker has a 65-year-old spouse, their combined benefit is 1½ times the primary insurance amount, or slightly less if the spouse is between 62 and 65.

Surviving Dependents

The spouse and dependent children of anyone who was fully insured at the time of death are eligible to receive survivors' benefits, and so are those dependents left behind by a deceased who was only *"currently"* insured. All right, so here's another new term: "currently" insured. What does it mean, and how does it differ from being "fully" insured? Well, briefly, it is simply another category that entitles some people to some benefits, and it takes much less time to become "currently" insured than it does to become "fully" insured. How much less time depends primarily upon how old someone is when she dies. For example, if an unmarried woman born after 1929 were to die before she reaches 29, she would need only 1½ years of work credit to be "currently" insured; if the same person were to die when she is 40, though, 4½ years of coverage would be required.

In addition to a small ($255) burial allowance, the surviving family members of *either* a fully or a currently insured person are entitled to:

1. a monthly stipend for an unmarried, dependent child who is under 18 (or under 22, if a full-time student) or who became disabled before age 22. Payments stop when the child reaches 18 (22 for students) or is no longer disabled, or if he or she marries. Each eligible child would receive three-fourths of the deceased parent's primary insurance, provided the total amount paid to all family survivors does not exceed the "maximum family benefit" (MFB); this sum ranges from 150% to 188% of the primary insurance. (The child's benefit.)

2. monthly payments for an *unmarried* surviving spouse (or even a surviving divorced spouse, if the marriage lasted at least ten years) *who has an eligible child in his or her care.* These payments cease if the parent remarries, or when the child become 18. A surviving spouse with one dependent child receives one and one-half times the primary insurance; if there are two or more children, though, only the MFB is payable—which is one of the few examples of federal social legislation that does not reward prolificacy. (The mother's or father's benefit.)

In addition, if a decedent had been *fully* insured, his or her unmarried (unless remarriage occurs after 60), dependent spouse is entitled to benefits commencing at age 60 or, if disabled, at age 50. (The widow's or widower's benefit.) A surviving spouse of someone who was only *currently* insured does not qualify for this particular stipend.

The Disabled

Briefly, a covered worker who is unable to work because of a physical or mental condition that is expected to last for at least a year is eligible for a monthly benefit equal to the amount of his primary insurance. The age at which the disability occurs is not a factor, except to the extent that those who are 31 or older must have work credit for five of the ten years preceding the disability; younger people can qualify with less time.

HOW MUCH WILL BENEFICIARIES RECEIVE?

The FICA generally, as well as the regulations and rules implementing it, are of a complexity that would challenge a large firm of Philadelphia lawyers. This is especially so with respect to computing the specific amounts to which beneficiaries are entitled. The most significant revision in the 1977 law—apart from increasing taxes—was changing the benefit formula by introducing an indexing concept. What follows are the basics of calculating the amounts of benefits under this new system.

The Goal

One of the legislative purposes of the new approach in Social Security was to "stabilize" benefits, which means to tie the amount someone receives to a percentage of his prior earnings, indexed to reflect changes in general wage levels that occurred during his working lifetime.

What's the AIME?

One term with which you should be familiar is "Average Indexed Monthly Earnings," or AIME, for short. This is arrived at by first determining the "computation period," which is the number of years after 1950 (or after age 21, if later) up to the year the worker reaches 62, becomes disabled, or dies. The five years of lowest earnings or of no earnings are excluded, as long as at least two years remain.

The next step is to record the earnings upon which FICA taxes were paid in each of the computation years. Table 4.1 indicates the maximum sum taxed in any particular year (the wage base); wage credits cannot exceed the wage base, even though a worker might have earned more.

TABLE 4.1 *FICA Taxes on Employees.*

Year	Rate (%)[a]	Maximum Wages Taxed	Maximum Tax Paid[b]
1937–50	1.0	$ 3,000	$ 30
1951–53	1.5	3,600	54
1954	2.0	3,600	72
1955–56	2.0	4,200	84
1957–58	2.25	4,200	94
1959	2.5	4,800	120
1960–61	3.0	4,800	144
1962	3.125	4,800	150
1963–65	3.625	4,800	174
1966	4.2	6,600	277
1967	4.4	6,600	290
1968	4.4	7,800	343
1969–70	4.8	7,800	374
1971	5.2	7,800	406
1972	5.2	9,000	468
1973	5.85	10,800	632
1974	5.85	13,200	772
1975	5.85	14,100	825
1976	5.85	15,300	895
1977	5.85	16,500	965
1978	6.05	17,700	1,071
1979	6.13	22,900	1,404
1980	6.13	25,900	1,588
1981	6.65	29,700	1,975
1982	6.70	31,800*	2,131*
1983	6.70	33,900*	2,271*
1984	6.70	36,000*	2,412*
1985	7.05	38,100*	2,686*
1986	7.15	40,200*	2,874*
1987	7.15	42,600*	3,046*

[a]The rates paid by the self-employed are about 40% more than those assessed against wage earners.
[b]Employee's taxes only. Employers pay an identical amount.
*The wage base is fixed through 1981; the maximum wages subject to tax after 1981 are estimates.

The credited earnings for each year are then updated (indexed) by multiplying the actual earnings by the ratio of average wages in the second year before the worker reaches 62, becomes disabled or dies, to average wages in the applicable years. This ratio is expected to increase annually. But to illustrate, average annual wages were $10,002 in 1977, compared to $3,514 in 1956. Therefore, if a worker who earned $4,200 (the maximum then taxed) in 1956 were to reach 62 or become disabled or die in 1979, his indexed wage credit for 1956 would be:

$$(\text{Actual 1956 wages}) \times \frac{\text{Average wages in second year before entitlement}}{\text{Average wages in 1956}} = 1956 \text{ AIME}$$

or

$$\$4{,}200 \times \frac{\$10{,}002}{\$\ 3{,}514} = \$11{,}955$$

Similar adjustments are made for each year in the "computation period." This "updating" not only has eliminated many of the inequities in the previous, non-indexed approach (such as eligible survivors of relatively young people receiving considerably larger benefits than the survivors of older workers who had paid far more into the system over a much longer period), but it assures that benefits will be related to the standard of living that prevails when entitlement commences.

After the workers' indexed wages for all years in his or her computation period are computed, they are totaled, then divided by the number of years times twelve to obtain the average indexed monthly wage.

To be sure that you have been correctly credited with taxed earnings, ask for a copy of your earnings record every few years. You may obtain this simply by sending a signed postal card request, giving your name and Social Security number, to the Social Security Administration, P.O. Box 57, Baltimore, MD 21203.

The Primary Insurance Amount

Once a worker's AIME is known, his "Primary Insurance Amount" (PIA), which was mentioned earlier, can be determined. This is the important figure, because all benefits are multiples of the PIA, as shown in Table 4.2.

TABLE 4.2 Primary Insurance Payable to Beneficiaries.

Beneficiary	Amount
Worker at 65[a]	1 × PIA
Worker & spouse at 65[a]	1.5 × PIA
Surviving spouse at 65[b]	1 × PIA
Surviving spouse & 1 child	1.5 × PIA
Surviving spouse & 2 or more children	MFB[c]
1 child	0.75 × PIA
2 children	1.5 × PIA
3 or more children	MFB[c]
Disabled worker	1 × PIA

[a] Reduced benefits payable commencing at age 62. For those who work beyond age 65, benefits are increased by 3% a year, up to age 72.
[b] Reduced benefits payable commencing at age 60.
[c] The Maximum Family Benefit ranges from 1.5 to 1.88 times the PIA.

The simplest way to find the PIA for any particular average indexed monthly wage is to refer to current tables at your local Social Security office. But to give you an idea of the method used in the construction of the tables, the formula for someone who reaches 62, becomes disabled or dies in 1979 is:

90% of the first $180 of AIME; *plus*

32% of the amount between $180 and $1,085; *plus*

15% of the amount above $1,085.

For example, if someone had an AIME of $1,200, his PIA would be 0.9(180) + 0.32(905) + 0.15(115), which equals $468, or in his case about 39% of his AIME. This would be the amount of the monthly check if he commenced to receive benefits at age 65; if he has a wife the same age, their total benefit would be 1½ times the PIA, or $702 a month.

Because of annual changes in the ratio by which actual wage credits in previous years are multiplied to obtain an indexed wage, as well as yearly revisions of the "bend points" (the dollar amounts to which the 90%—32%—15% formula applies), there is no way to determine the precise dollar amount of any benefit commencing after the current year. Since the "replacement rate" (the percentage of

TABLE 4.3. Percentage of Average Indexed Earnings Replaced by Worker's Primary Insurance.

	Replacement Rate for Worker with		
Year	Low Earnings[a]	Average Earnings	High Earnings[b]
1979	57%	44%	34%
1985	55	43	26
1990	55	43	26
1995	55	43	27
2000	55	43	28
2010	55	43	30
2020	55	43	30
2030	55	43	30
2040	55	43	30
2050	55	43	30

[a]"Low" earnings were $4,600 a year in 1976, increasing thereafter by the same annual percentage as "average" earnings.
[b]"High" earnings are the maximum taxable under the system.

earnings that are "replaced" by the primary insurance amount) eventually will become "stabilized," though, you can approximate what percentage of your future earnings would be paid as a Social Security benefit in whatever particular year eligibility commences. These replacement rates are projected in Table 4.3 for workers with "low," "average," and "high" earnings.

Cost-of-Living Increases

The amount a beneficiary receives is adjusted upward in June of each year by whatever percentage the Consumers' Price Index has risen between the first quarters of the previous year and the present year, provided that an increase of 3% or more was registered. This cost-of-living adjustment is one of the few ways of assuring that inflation does not diminish the purchasing power of benefits paid to elderly people and others.

Reduction or Elimination of Benefits

Social Security benefits might be reduced or eliminated entirely if those otherwise eligible for them earn other income. Currently, if a beneficiary under 65 makes over $3,240 a year, or if someone between 65 and 70 earns more than $4,500 (a limitation that increases by $500 a year until it reaches $6,000 in 1982), the amount of his or her check will be reduced by $1 for every $2 earned above the threshold sum. Commencing in 1982, there will not be any reduction in payments to those 70 or over, regardless of the amounts earned.

You should also be aware of some other important limitations. (1) Income from sources other than earnings does not affect entitlement to Social Security benefits; hence, interest, dividends, or income from trusts or pensions will not decrease the amount paid. (2) If a surviving spouse is ineligible for benefits because of excess earnings, dependent children generally would still be able to collect their benefits. (3) Even if a husband and wife both work and pay FICA taxes, they are not entitled to retirement benefits based upon the earnings of both: only one entitlement, the larger, is payable.

OTHER SURVIVOR BENEFITS

As we have seen, almost—but not quite—everyone is a prospective recipient of Social Security benefits, because almost everyone must participate in the system, like it or not. Those not within its ambit are, in the main, employees at various levels of government. For example, the largest exempt group consists of the roughly three million federal civil servants who have their own program that, on a contributory basis, provides retirement, survivors and disability benefits for them. (A House-passed attempt in 1977 to force federal employees into the FICA was aborted in favor of a two-year study of the subject.) Similarly, large numbers of state and local workers—schoolteachers, police officers, sanitation workers, and the like—have been permitted to retain separate state-sponsored and other programs as substitutes for Social Security. They, too, might someday be compelled to join up.

It is no wonder that agonizing screams are usually heard when someone suggests that government employees should start paying more for less. By and large, the separate plans are far more attractive, because the benefits are pegged to what a participant has earned and paid for; in contrast, the FICA, as we have seen, is burdened with enormous social welfare costs, so on the basis of expected returns, it is a losing proposition for most people.

Apart from those people who have so far escaped the Social Security system, there are many others who are covered by it as well as by some other program or programs, usually provided by their employers. For example, in addition to whatever FICA survivors' benefits they might receive, the spouses of armed forces members who die while on active duty, whether in war or peacetime, are paid "Dependency and Indemnity Compensation" (DIC). The amount of DIC, which varies with the deceased's rank, ranges from about 70% of basic pay for a new recruit down to about 17% for high ranking officers; for survivors of officers in the middle ranks, the stipend amounts to about 25% of basic pay. Not much by itself, but if the survivors also receive Social Security benefits, the combined amounts often will replace a substantial proportion of a deceased person's income.

Also, the surviving dependents of members of the armed forces who have been in service long enough to qualify for retirement (20 years or more), as well as the survivors of retired members who had chosen to accept reduced pensions to participate, are entitled to payments under the "Survivors' Benefit Plan" (SBP). SBP participation assures servicemen that when they die, their families will continue to receive 55% of the retired pay to which they were entitled. An SBP annuity is reduced, however, by any DIC that might be payable, and also (except for limited categories of beneficiaries, such as a widow with two or more dependent children) by any Social Security benefit that is attributable to the deceased's military service.

Besides those in the military, millions of other people work for employers who, as part of the "fringes," have qualified retirement plans for their employees. Usually, these provide for annuity or other types of payments to dependents of deceased employees. The number and variety of plans defy cataloging, and it would be beyond the scope of this book to even try to do so. The point, though, is that if you don't already know, you should find out how much financial assistance would be available to your family from all sources, in case you were to die.

THE NEED TO KNOW

So where does all of this leave you? Well, perhaps a little less in the dark about all of those FICA taxes that are deducted from your pay, but also more aware of the importance of Social Security and other benefits for which you or your survivors someday might qualify.

For our present purposes, however, you should now be one big step closer to making an educated estimate of how much life insurance you need, which is what we'll take up next.

chapter 5

How Much is Enough?

Now that you know all—well, not all, but maybe more than you previously knew—about Social Security and other benefits your family might receive when you die, we're ready to tackle the basic question of how large an estate you need. The answer depends, of course, on numerous factors, not the least of which is who you ask: the figures that a stockbroker, a life insurance salesman, and a trust officer are likely to come up with probably wouldn't bear much resemblance to each other. What is more, not only are there wide variations among individuals (the family of a wealthy person would require far more to maintain its accustomed life style than the survivors of someone who had subsisted on welfare), but everyone's needs change significantly throughout life, a point we'll say more about later.

In this chapter, we will examine a relatively simple technique that will let you know whether or not you are even close. A general awareness of what you need should prevent you from being deluded by some of the inanities that are bandied about, such as "everyone should leave an estate equal to the total of all his future earnings." Reputable salesmen don't resort to such folderol, but sooner or later you will hear it, and when you do, you should be able to recognize it for what it is and act accordingly.

EXPENSES INCIDENT TO DEATH

Before attempting to estimate your estate requirements, you first should take into account the fact that any funds spent incident to your death would not be available to your survivors. These include last-illness and hospital bills, burial costs, and possibly the expense of moving your family to another location.

The incident-to-death costs are difficult to estimate in advance, principally because last-illness expenses might range from negligible to astronomical. And on occasion, unless ample medical and hospitalization insurance or some equivalent program exists, such costs could wipe out an otherwise ample estate. Disregarding this remote contingency, though, about one year's gross income should adequately cover the death-related expenses in all but the rarest cases, so we'll use that figure in our computations. If less is actually spent, so much the better.

CONSTRUCTING AN ESTATE PROGRAMMING CHART

Now for the big ticket item: how much would it take to assure that your family's income will continue at a satisfactory level? This sum can be approximated by spending a few minutes doing an exercise called "estate programming"—which is neither as complex nor as definitive as the term might suggest.

Initially, you simply estimate the monthly income you believe your survivors would need, assuming that you end up on a mortician's slab in the near future. Essentials such as housing, food, and clothing must be considered, of course, as well as other expenses (piano lessons, orthodontal work, or you name it) that, although not necessities, might contribute to the well-being and enjoyment of your spouse and children. Such an estimate is bound to vary with each family, of course. If your time and interest permit, you might work out the figure in detail. But unless there are special factors in your case, it's much easier to assume that the need will be 75% of your present monthly income. That is usually close enough.

Whatever monthly-income figure you use is based on present income and purchasing power, so it is not likely to remain realistic for long. This suggests that you should recompute your estate needs every two or three years. If you want to work out your requirements on a hypothetical basis at, say, five year intervals into the future, fine—but remember to factor in an inflation rate for all items. Any future erosion in the dollar, particularly on a long-term basis, will be a critical consideration when it comes to deciding what arrangements might be best for disposing of your estate, but we'll take that up later.

Getting back to present estate needs, the amount of monthly income you decide to provide your family is plotted on a piece of paper with the vertical scale representing dollars and the horizontal scale indicating years, commencing with the assumed year of death, which is labeled "0." Common graph paper is convenient for this purpose, but anything that's handy will do.

SOCIAL SECURITY AND OTHER SURVIVORS' BENEFITS

After you have entered your monthly income-for-survivors goal on the chart, the next step is to plot in whatever benefits your family might receive from the government or other sources.

At this point, it might help to illustrate the technique up until now. Let's assume that you are a husband and father in his mid-30s, earning $16,000 a year and fully covered by Social Security, with a 30-year-old wife, Irmatrude, and two children, Alpha, who is 8, and Omega, who is 2. If you decide that your family would require a monthly income of at least $1,000 (75% of current earnings) you would first draw a horizontal line at that point on your chart. This represents your goal. Next, you would enter the government survivors' benefits to which they would be entitled (see Chapter 4).

To keep everything simple, assume that your average indexed monthly wage (AIME) and primary insurance (PIA) are such that, as a widow with two children, Irmatrude would receive Social Security benefits totaling $700 a month for ten years, when Alpha is 18 (for programming purposes, disregard the prospect of continued eligibility beyond 18, as well as the automatic cost-of-living increases in benefits). Also assume that the amount of this benefit would then drop to $600 a month until Omega is 18, which is sixteen years after the "0" year. Then it would terminate until Irmatrude, at age 60, becomes entitled to $300 a month; this latter date would be 30 years from the assumed date of your death. After plotting these various sums, your estate programming paper should resemble Figure 5.1. (If there are other assured sources of income, enter these also.)

At this point, it is apparent that standing alone, the benefits provided by Social Security would not be nearly sufficient to meet your family's living expenses. For convenience, label and number the four different periods in which deficiencies are shown as "gaps." It then becomes graphically clear that to achieve your $1,000 a month goal during Gap 1, an additional $300 a month must be provided from some source. Similarly, Gap 2 requires $400, Gap 3 $1,000, and Gap 4 $700 monthly.

Determining the total number of dollars necessary to fill each of these gaps would be a matter of merely multiplying these monthly shortages by 12 times the number of years in each period. But this

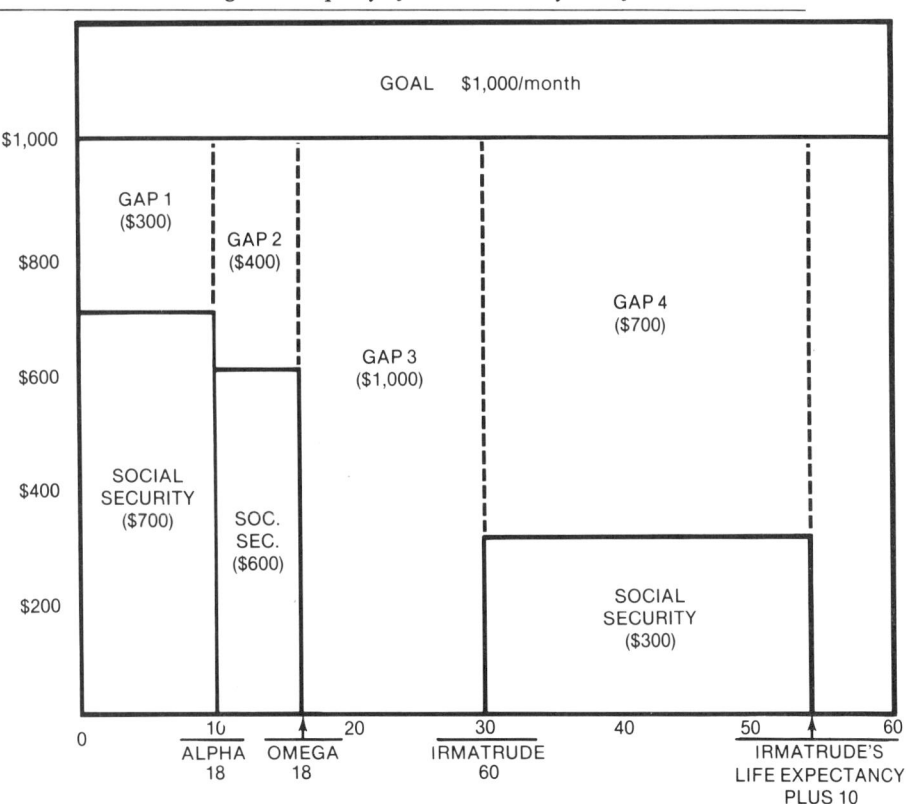

FIGURE 5.1. Plotting the Adequacy of Social Security Benefits.

would be almost as illusory as the "estate-equal-to-all-future-earnings" fallacy, for it disregards the time-value of money. In other words, all the funds to be used to supplement Social Security and other benefits need not be available at the time of death, but instead over an extended period, and until actually paid out, these funds could be invested and earnings from them added to principal. Hence, the inquiry should be: how much is needed at the assumed date of death to provide income to fill each gap *as it occurs*?

There is nothing difficult about determining this amount, and any reasonably bright sixth grader—or college freshman, anyway—who has access to *Present Value of Annuity* (PVA) and *Present Value* (PV) tables, and an explanation of how to use them, should be able to provide the answer. They may be found in most books of standard mathematical tables, but to save time, extracts are set forth in Tables 5.1 and 5.2.

FILLING THE GAPS

With PVA and PV tables, together with a pencil, scratchpad, and simple calculator, you are prepared to come up with a rough estimate of the principal sum your family would require to supplement its other monthly income. The procedure is to find out how much is necessary to fill each gap at the time it commences, then discount these sums to obtain a present value figure, then total these amounts. Returning to our illustration, we'll go through the exercise, step by step.

Gap 1

The shortage here is $300 a month, or $3,600 a year, for a period of 10 years. To determine how much would have to be available to the beginning of the period (year "0"), the annual deficiency of $3,600 is merely multiplied by some factor opposite "10" in the "years" column of the Present Value of Annuity table (Table 5.1).

The particular percentage column you use in the PVA table depends upon what rate of return you believe your estate would realize. This, in turn, depends not only upon what disposition you

TABLE 5.1. *Present Value of Annuity*

Years	.05 (5%)	.06 (6%)	.08 (8%)	.10 (10%)
1	0.9524	0.9434	0.9239	0.9091
2	1.8594	1.8334	1.7833	1.7355
3	2.7232	2.6730	2.5771	2.4869
4	3.5460	3.4651	3.3121	3.1699
5	4.3295	4.2124	3.9927	3.7908
6	5.0757	4.9173	4.6229	4.3553
7	5.7864	5.5824	5.2064	4.8684
8	6.4632	6.2098	5.7466	5.3349
9	7.1078	6.8017	6.2469	5.7590
10	7.7217	7.3601	6.7101	6.1446
11	8.3064	7.8869	7.1390	6.4951
12	8.8633	8.3838	7.5361	6.8137
13	9.3936	8.8527	7.9038	7.1034
14	9.8981	9.2950	8.2442	7.3667
15	10.3797	9.7122	8.5595	7.6061
16	10.8378	10.1059	8.8514	7.8237
17	11.2741	10.4773	9.1216	8.0216
18	11.6896	10.8276	9.3719	8.2014
19	12.0853	11.1581	9.6036	8.3649
20	12.4622	11.4699	9.8181	8.5136
21	12.8212	11.7641	10.0168	8.6487
22	13.1630	12.0416	10.2007	8.7715
23	13.4886	12.3034	10.3711	8.8832
24	13.7986	12.5504	10.5288	8.9847
25	14.0939	12.7834	10.6748	9.0770
26	14.3752	13.0032	10.8100	9.1609
27	14.6430	13.2105	10.9352	9.2372
28	14.8981	13.4062	11.0511	9.3066
29	15.1411	13.5907	11.1584	9.3696
30	15.3725	13.7648	11.2578	9.4269
31	15.5928	13.9291	11.3498	9.4790
32	15.8027	14.0840	11.4350	9.5264
33	16.0025	14.2302	11.5139	9.5694
34	16.1929	14.3681	11.5869	9.6086
35	16.3742	14.4982	11.6546	9.6442
36	16.5469	14.6210	11.7172	9.6765
37	16.7113	14.7368	11.7752	9.7059
38	16.8679	14.8460	11.8289	9.7327
39	17.0170	14.9491	11.8786	9.7570
40	17.1591	15.0463	11.9246	9.7791
41	17.2944	15.1380	11.9672	9.7991
42	17.4232	15.2245	12.0067	9.8174
43	17.5459	15.3062	12.0432	9.8340
44	17.6628	15.3832	12.0271	9.8491
45	17.7741	15.4558	12.1084	9.8628

TABLE 5.2. *Present Value.*

Years	.05 (5%)	.06 (6%)	.08 (8%)	.10 (10%)
1	.9524	.9434	.9259	.9091
2	.9070	.8900	.8573	.8264
3	.8638	.8396	.7938	.7513
4	.8227	.7921	.7350	.6830
5	.7835	.7473	.6806	.6209
6	.7462	.7050	.6302	.5645
7	.7107	.6651	.5835	.5132
8	.6768	.6274	.5403	.4665
9	.6446	.5919	.5002	.4241
10	.6139	.5584	.4632	.3855
11	.5847	.5268	.4289	.3505
12	.5568	.4970	.3971	.3186
13	.5303	.4688	.3677	.2897
14	.5051	.4403	.3405	.2633
15	.4810	.4173	.3152	.2394
16	.4581	.3936	.2919	.2176
17	.4363	.3714	.2703	.1978
18	.4155	.3503	.2502	.1799
19	.3957	.3305	.2317	.1635
20	.3769	.3118	.2145	.1486
21	.3589	.2942	.1987	.1351
22	.3418	.2775	.1839	.1228
23	.3251	.2618	.1703	.1117
24	.3101	.2470	.1577	.1015
25	.2953	.2330	.1460	.0923
26	.2812	.2198	.1352	.0839
27	.2678	.2074	.1252	.0763
28	.2551	.1956	.1159	.0693
29	.2429	.1846	.1073	.0630
30	.2314	.1741	.0994	.0573
31	.2204	.1643	.0920	.0521
32	.2099	.1550	.0852	.0474
33	.1999	.1462	.0789	.0431
34	.1904	.1379	.0730	.0391
35	.1813	.1301	.0676	.0356
36	.1727	.1227	.0626	.0323
37	.1644	.1158	.0580	.0294
38	.1566	.1092	.0537	.0267
39	.1491	.1031	.0497	.0243
40	.1420	.0972	.0460	.0221
41	.1353	.0917	.0426	.0201
42	.1288	.0865	.0395	.0183
43	.1227	.0816	.0365	.0166
44	.1169	.0770	.0338	.0151
45	.1113	.0726	.0313	.0137

have arranged (for example, a life insurance installment settlement option; a trust; a mutual fund withdrawal plan; or outright cash bequests to your spouse to manage), but also upon several variables that cannot be precisely measured (such as the yields and capital appreciation on funds held in trust or invested in securities). We'll discuss these matters in another chapter. Moreover, you might decide that a dispositive plan using two or more techniques is the safest. So about the best you can do for estate programming purposes is to select some conservative yield figure that, barring a major financial catastrophe, should be realized. To be on the conservative side, let's use a 6% rate.

As the period with which we are now concerned (Gap 1) lasts for 10 years, the factor opposite "10" in the "years" column and under ".06" (6%) is 7.3601. This simply means that if you invested $7.36 at 6% compound interest, you could withdraw $1 at the end of the first year and each of the following 9 years, and after ten years nothing would be left. Consequently, since the annual requirement here is $3,600, if you multiply 3,600 by 7.3601, you have the answer to how much is needed to "fill" Gap 1. The product is $26,496.36, or in round figures, $26,500. (The sum needed at the start of Gap 1 was not discounted, because the period commences at the time of death.)

Gap 2

One additional step is involved in determining the sum required at year "0" to fill Gap 2, which commences ten years later; this is to determine how much the funds might earn in this ten-year interval. But first, we have to go through a computation similar to that for Gap 1. Here, the dollar deficiency is $400 a month, or $4,800 a year, for a period of six years (from year "10" through year "16"). Going again to the PVA table, the factor opposite "6" and under the 6% column is 4.9173. Multiplying the annual shortfall of $4,800 by this factor produces an answer of about $23,600.

Now, here is where the second step comes in. An annual income of $4,800 for a six-year period would result from investing $23,600 at 6% compounded. But the six-year period with which we are concerned doesn't commence until ten years after the assumed date of death. Hence, the question becomes: if 6% annually is earned, what principal sum is necessary at the beginning of a ten-year period so that at the end of the period the principal and earnings would equal $23,600?

This is where the Present Value table is used (Table 5.2).

Referring to it, opposite "10" in the years column and below the 6% column you will find the factor 0.5584. This indicates that if you invested 56¢ at 6% compounded, after ten years you would have $1. Therefore, to find out how much it would require to have $23,600 after ten years, multiply 0.5584 by 23,600. The answer, $13,178.24 (rounded off to $13,200) is the sum needed in year "0" to fill Gap 2 on our chart.

Gap 3

The same steps used in determining the Gap 2 requirement are applied here. Additional income of $1,000 a month ($12,000 a year) is needed for fourteen years (from year 16 through year 30). Hence, again assuming a 6% yield, the factor 9.2950 is taken from the PVA table. Multiplying $12,000 (the annual requirement) by 9.2950 indicates that when the gap commences, $111,540 should be available. But as the gap does not start until sixteen years after year "0", $111,540 multiplied by 0.3936 (from the PV table), or about $43,900, is the sum that should be in the estate at year "0."

Gap 4

The same procedure is used for Gap 4, except that the termination date is not known. To estimate when this might occur (when Irmatrude might die), refer to the mortality table currently used by insurance companies to estimate the life expectancies of men and, as a rule of thumb, add three years (see Table 6.1 in the following chapter). Then, to avoid endangering an elderly widow's means of support if she doesn't cooperate with the actuaries, add about ten years.

At the assumed date of death (year "0"), Irmatrude would be 30. The life expectancy of a 30-year old woman is about 44 more years, or until age 74. To be safe, though, assume she will live until 84. Hence, Gap 4, which commences 30 years after year "0", would end 24 years later, or at the 54 year point on the chart.

The income shortage during these 24 years (from age 60 through 84) would be $700 a month or $8,400 a year. Taking the factors from the PVA and PV tables, 12.5504 times 8,400, which equals $105,423, should be available when the gap starts in 30 years, and 0.1741 times $105,423, or about $18,400 would be necessary at year "0" to produce it.

Minimum Net Estate Requirements

By adding the sums needed at the assumed date of death to fill each of the four gaps, the minimum amount your family would need to supplement its Social Security can now be estimated. In this case, $24,500 + $13,200 + $43,900 + $18,400, or a total of $100,000, should be provided for this purpose.

Remember, though, that this is no more than a rough planning figure, and that any number of circumstances, both foreseeable and unforeseeable, could alter it considerably. For example, if Irmatrude has some work skills, she might find employment; also, at age 30 her prospects of remarrying are reasonably good. So in a sense we have presented a worst-case situation. Nevertheless, it's a starting point, and most people fail to get even this far in planning for survivors' needs.

OTHER REQUIREMENTS

In addition to the basic need to have enough to pay your death-related expenses and to supplement your family's other income, your estate should be large enough to discharge your debts, to pay for the costs of administration and any death taxes that might be due, and assuming you have typical parental ambitions, to provide college educations for your children. Any number of other things—such as financial help for low-income parents, or funds to permit a widow who is not already qualified to obtain education or training for a job—might be appropriate considerations in particular cases. For our present purposes, though, disregard them.

Debts

Indebtedness will fluctuate, of course, but assume for our exercise that you have an outstanding real estate mortgage note with an unpaid balance of $35,000, secured by your residence bought a few years ago for $40,000 and now worth $100,000. If Irmatrude and your children would continue to occupy it after your death, they would be helped if there were an additional $35,000 in the estate to pay the mortgage. The monthly payments probably are not great—perhaps $350 or so. But on $1,000 a month, $350 plus related house maintenance and utility expenses might be stretching their income uncomfortably thin. If it came right down to it, of course, Irmatrude might sell the house for a $60,000 or so gain, but she and the children will still need some kind of housing. Since you're a considerate sort, let's add $35,000 to the estate you would like to leave.

College costs

Based upon current costs, four years in residence at a state college or university requires about $18,000 for tuition, room and board, books, incidentals, and travel; at a private school, the average figure is approaching $30,000. These costs are expected to increase significantly over the years. Of course, a fatherless child should be expected, through summer employment or otherwise, to contribute something to his or her own education, and there are alternatives, such as living at home while attending a community college. Moreover, providing basic subsistence income for your family obviously must have a higher priority. Nevertheless, you might want to earmark an additional amount to help with your children's educations. How much depends upon several factors, but let's settle now for $10,000 each. At 6% compounded, this would give Alpha about $18,000 and Omega about $25,000 by the times they are ready for college: not enough by then for all four years, but it might be enough to provide each with a decent start.

Death Taxes and Costs of Administration

An effort should also be made to approximate the potential shrinkage of assets that will be caused by the expenses of death taxes and estate administration.

Federal estate taxes would not be a factor for the size estate with which we are dealing, since it is well within the minimum $250,000 marital deduction plus the exemption equivalent, which is $175,000 for deaths that occur after 1980. As an estate grows, however, the federal levy becomes a consideration long before the

$425,000 threshold is reached. We'll discuss that subject in Chapters 9 and 10.

Aside from the federal estate tax, most states impose inheritance taxes or their own estate taxes on smaller sums. (In passing, the basic difference between an estate tax and an inheritance tax is that the former, which is levied upon the estate, taxes the right to transmit property on death, while the latter, which is levied upon the beneficiaries, taxes the right to inherit property.) How much, if anything, you should estimate for state death taxes depends upon where you live. If it happens to be in one of the few states, such as Nevada, that do not impose such taxes, the sum would be zero. If elsewhere, the amount would depend upon the tax laws and rate structure. These vary greatly. For example, there is no uniformity with respect to exemptions or credits; the valuations of various types of property interests differ; life insurance proceeds paid to a named beneficiary are exempt, in whole or in part, in about one-half of the states, but fully taxed elsewhere; and in community property states, only one-half the value of community assets are subject to taxation.

To give you some idea of state death tax costs, though, if a husband leaves his wife a $200,000 net estate, half of which consists of life insurance proceeds, state death taxes might be about $5,500 in New York, $400 in Missouri, or nothing in Hawaii. For our example, let's assume the levy would be about 2%, and add that amount to the other requirements.

An allowance should also be made for the incidental costs associated with transferring property to the quick from the dead, such as attorney's and executor's fees. If you have a relatively simple estate that is arranged in a manner to avoid judicial intervention, the costs of administration would not be large. They might be significant, however, depending upon a number of considerations, such as the nature of the property, whether it is located in more than one state, and the complexity of the distribution plans. For an estate of the size we're concerned with, 5% should provide an adequate margin in most cases.

GULP!

Based upon the computations we have gone through, to provide adequately for Irmatrude, Alpha, and Omega if you were to die in the near future, the size of your estate should be in the neighborhood of:

Death related expenses	$ 16,000
Income supplement	100,000
Indebtedness	35,000
College fund	20,000
Subtotal:	$171,000
Death taxes (2%)	$ 3,700
Costs of administration (5%)	9,000
TOTAL:	$183,700

Don't be discouraged by what, to most people, might seem to be an unreachable goal. First, if we have erred, it has been in the direction of providing more than enough. If you would feel more comfortable about it, eliminate important but secondary needs such as college costs and payment of the mortgage. What is more, the funds needed to supplement survivors' income would be considerably less if, as is becoming more common, some survivors' annuity

FIGURE 5.2. *How Much Is Enough?*

1. Capital needed to supplement survivor's income:

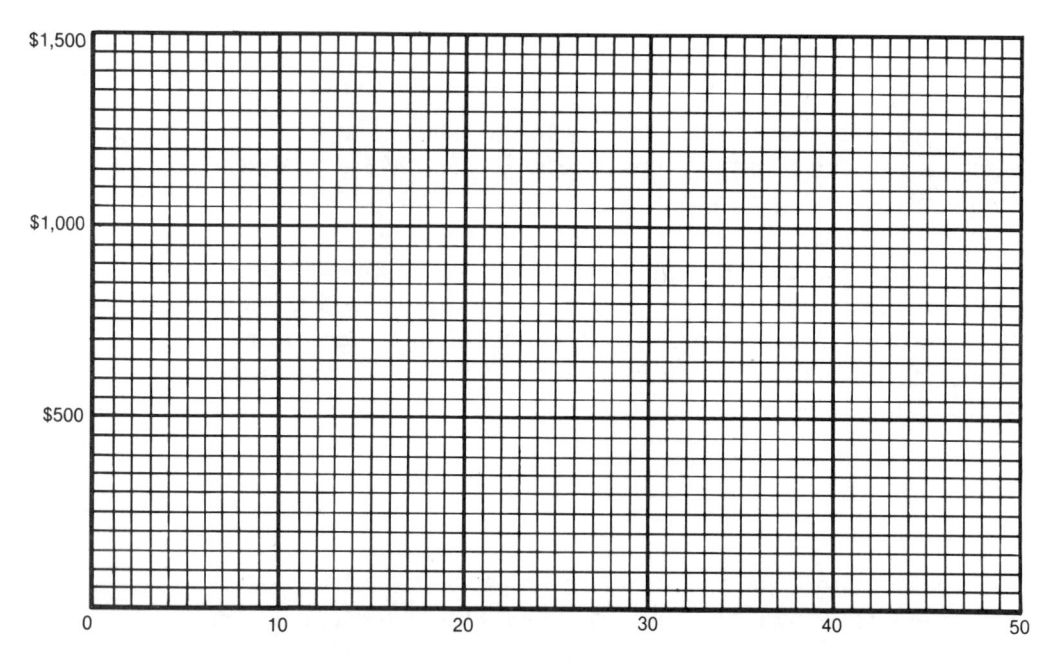

FIGURE 5-2. *(continued)*

	(a) Monthly require- ment	(b) Annual require- ment (12) × (a)	(c) Length of gap in years	(d) PVA factor (at 5%)	(e) Amt. needed when gap commences (b) × (d)	(f) Nr. of years before gap	(g) PV factor (at 5%)	(h) Amt needed at year 0 (e) × (g)
Gap 1								
Gap 2								
Gap 3								
Gap 4								
Gap 5								

                                                               Amount needed $ _____

2. Other requirements:
    a. Death-related expenses .... $_____
    b. Outstanding indebtedness
       (including mortgage note, if any) .... $_____
    c. College expenses .... $_____
    d. Other responsibilities (e.g., support of parent) .... $_____
    e. Death taxes .... $_____
    f. Administration costs .... $_____
3. Gross estate required (Total of 1 + 2) .... $_____
4. Do you need more than you now have?
    a. Estate Requirements (line 3) .... $_____
    b. Estate Assets

        Life insurance (face value) .... $_____
        Securities (present market value) .... $_____
        Savings .... $_____
        Real estate (present market value) .... $_____
        Other .... $_____
                           Total .... $_____
                           Deficiency (a minus b) .... $_____

in addition to Social Security were available. For example, if your employer provides a plan that would pay Irmatrude $250 a month, the amount required to fill the four "gaps" would be reduced by about $46,000.

Also, remember that estate needs constantly change as a person advances in age and family responsibilities; income (in real terms as well as in the number of dollars) normally increases; young children approach and eventually attain financial independence; the unpaid balance of a real estate mortgage decreases; and as each year passes, life expectancies and therefore total income supplement amounts decrease. For example, if the purchasing power of the dollar were to remain constant (it won't, but that's not the present point), estate programming estimates of future needs for the family situation used in our illustration probably would show a gradual increase (to perhaps $200,000 to $225,000) until children are on their own, then a gradual decline until retirement years, when a sharp drop would occur.

Don't take estimates of needs many years from now too seriously, though: they are of little value insofar as defining actual future requirements are concerned, simply because too many unforeseeable developments are bound to distort your assumptions.

ARE YOU THERE?

To determine what your present estate requirements might be, and whether you now have far too much or (join the club) far too little, spend a few minutes completing Figure 5.2. The results might surprise you. If an alarming shortfall is disclosed, however, please don't rush to the phone to contact your life insurance agent. Wait until you finish the next few chapters—they contain information that could help you reach your goal more easily and less expensively than you might think.

chapter 6
The Fundamentals Of Life Insurance

Entirely aside from the emotional impact accompanying the death of a father, the surviving wife and children are likely to experience a severe financial blow when the customary family income is suddenly terminated. Although the attendant economic hardship would be cushioned to a large extent by government survivors' benefits, maintenance of a satisfactory standard of living would require these to be supplemented by income from the decedent's estate. And unless or until personal assets (e.g., savings, securities, and real estate) are adequate, the only realistic way to meet this need is with life insurance.

Before buying any life insurance, however, an individual should have at least a rudimentary understanding of the types of policies available, their comparative costs, and their relative advantages and disadvantages. He should realize that life insurance can be used primarily for either of two purposes: *first,* solely to provide financial protection for survivors; or *second*, both for this purpose and as a means of accumulating funds for lifetime expenditure, in the event death is not premature.

The protective principle of life insurance is similar to that of any other type of insurance: a sharing of risks. Hence, for a relatively small contribution, a participant is assured that after his death, his beneficiaries will be indemnified to the extent of his policy's face value. The charge for such protection (the premium) necessarily must include at least two items of expense: the mortality cost, and the insurer's loading charge or overhead. If a particular policy provides more than pure insurance protection, an added charge is made for what might be considered a forced-savings account. At the outset, these basic costs will be considered.

MORTALITY RISK

Comprehensive death statistics enable insurance companies to predict with reasonable certainty the life expectancy of any group of

TABLE 6.1. Extracts from Commissioners Standard Ordinary 1958 Mortality Table (men[a]).

Age	Death Rate per 1,000	Expectancy in Years	Age	Death Rate per 1,000	Expectancy in Years
20	1.79	50.37	45	5.35	27.81
21	1.83	49.46	46	5.83	26.95
22	1.86	48.55	47	6.36	26.11
23	1.89	47.64	48	6.95	25.27
24	1.91	46.73	49	7.60	24.45
25	1.93	45.82	50	8.32	23.63
26	1.96	44.90	51	9.11	22.82
27	1.99	43.99	52	9.96	22.03
28	2.03	43.08	53	10.89	21.25
29	2.08	42.16	54	11.90	20.47
30	2.13	41.25	55	13.00	19.71
31	2.19	40.34	56	14.21	18.97
32	2.25	39.43	57	15.54	18.23
33	2.32	38.51	58	17.00	17.51
34	2.40	37.60	59	18.59	16.81
35	2.51	36.69	60	20.34	16.12
36	2.64	35.78	61	22.24	15.44
37	2.80	34.88	62	24.31	14.78
38	3.01	33.97	63	26.57	14.14
39	3.25	33.07	64	29.04	13.51
40	3.53	32.18	65	31.75	12.90
41	3.84	31.29	66	34.74	12.31
42	4.17	30.41	67	38.04	11.73
43	4.53	29.54	68	41.68	11.17
44	4.92	28.67	69	45.61	10.64

Courtesy of National Association of Insurance Commissioners

[a]The death rates and life expectancies for women are roughly those of men three years younger.

persons, and thus to determine what they must charge for the mortality risk. The 1958 Commissioners Standard Ordinary (CSO) Table, which reflects experience during the 1950–1954 period, is currently used by life insurers. In abbreviated form, it is set forth in Table 6.1.

The CSO tables are not, of course, precise measurements of actuarial expectations. Instead, they are constructed to provide companies with a margin of error in the event that a widespread epidemic or some other mass catastrophe were to radically distort the estimated results. Thus, while the 1958 CSO Table indicates a death rate of 1.93 per 1,000 for those 25 years old, the actual experience of 1969–1971 for the total population was a death rate of 1.47 for this group. Similarly, the actual death rate at age 30 was 1.55 compared to the table's 2.13, 3.14 compared to 3.53 at age 40, and 7.38 compared to 8.32 at age 50. The experience of insurance companies was even more favorable, because substandard risks or those whose life expectancies have been drastically reduced by illness or injury often are unable to buy insurance, at least without paying a substantial surcharge. Thus, the longevity of policyholders in general tends to surpass that of the populace as a whole. In 1960, for example, the mortality ratio (actual to expected deaths) of the nation's ten largest insurers was only 0.484. In other words, that part of premiums charged for the mortality risk was more than twice the actual mortality experience. Yet before the 1958 Table was adopted, the mortality risk charge was even greater, because for years insurers had based their premiums on the 1941 CSO Table, and before that on the American Experience Table of Mortality, which reflected death experience from 1843 to 1858. Although policy dividends will be considered later, at this point it should be noted that if savings due to favorable mortality experience are realized, policyholders of mutual companies normally have some of the excess charges refunded.

Disregarding the built-in safety factors, the 1958 CSO Table indicates that approximately 193 of every 100,000 individuals who have survived to age 25 will not be living one year later. Thus, if 100,000 persons at that age were to contribute $1.93 to a common fund, the aggregate amount, $193,000, would be sufficient to pay $1,000 to each of the beneficiaries of all 193 who do die. Similarly, at age 40 each participant would have to pay $3.53 to provide a $1,000 benefit for his beneficiary in the event he were to die within the year. And because the death rate increases with age, the mortality risk cost increases accordingly. For example, for those who survive to age 65, the charge would be an almost prohibitive $31.75 per $1,000 of insurance.

To prevent an annual escalation of cost, a level-premium method of computing mortality charges might be used. If it were, the cost for the mortality risk over a period of time (such as five or ten years, or until age 65) could be averaged and, after discounting to reflect present value, a constant or level annual charge made. The higher cost during the earlier years, together with earnings from the excess charge, would then offset the higher mortality risk of the later years. To illustrate, the death rates for persons 25 through 29 years of age, according to the 1958 CSO Table, are 1.93, 1.96, 1.99, 2.03 and 2.08. If these are added, the sum (9.99) divided by the number of years (5) would indicate that the mean death rate during this span of time is approximately 2.00 per 1,000 persons. Thus, an annual, level charge of $2 per $1,000 of insurance would pay for the mortality risk portion of a five-year policy. Similarly, the mean death rate per year over a ten-year period commencing at age 25 would be 2.13.

LOADING CHARGES

If premium charges were based upon mortality tables alone, the total fund accumulated would be depleted by the end of the year, assuming the actuarial expectations were accurate. Necessarily, therefore, insurance companies must include in their premium calculations an additional charge for expenses. This factor, which is known as a *loading charge*, pays for agents' commissions, executive and other salaries, training programs for new salespeople, costs of issuing and servicing policies, advertising, and many other items of overhead. In a typical year, for example, out of every dollar received by life insurance companies (of which about 78 cents comes from premiums and 22 cents from investment income), about 23 cents is required for operating expenses, taxes, and other costs, including 7 cents for agents' commissions and 10 cents for home and field office expenses; of the balance, about 56 cents is paid to policyholders or beneficiaries and 21 cents is added to policy reserves, or special reserves and surplus.

FORCED SAVINGS

The amount of any premium in excess of the cost of the mortality risk plus the loading charge is not essential, of course, to pay for the insurance itself. However, an added charge is an important ingredient of every permanent or cash value form of life insurance. The bulk of these overpayments, which in a sense constitute forced savings, are accumulated in reserves which the insurer is required by law to maintain, and a portion might be added to the insurer's special reserves or surplus account. These reserves are invested by the insurer, mostly in fixed-dollar assets such as corporate or government bonds, and real estate loans. By and large, most insurance companies maintain reserves considerably in excess of those required by law, so that they and their policyholders may be assured of their continued solvency and ability to meet claims in the event of almost any contingency.

The insured has certain rights with respect to his policy reserve, or at least that portion of it known as "the cash surrender value," which will be considered later. For the present, however, you should understand that on the insured's death, his beneficiaries are not paid *both* the face value of the policy and his savings, but just the face value, for *the amount of true life insurance provided by any cash value policy is the difference between the face value and the policy reserve.* This lesser sum is all the insured has paid for, of course.

Because of its savings feature, cash value life insurance is often regarded as a means of building a lifetime estate, for it may serve not only as a means of providing for survivors' needs, but also as a savings medium for later use by the policyholder. The advantages and disadvantages of the noninsurance aspect of cash value policies will be discussed in Chapter 8.

To summarize up to this point, however, and at the risk of oversimplification, if p represents the amount paid for a life insurance policy (the premium), m the cost of the mortality risk for the insured for the period covered, l the insurer's loading charge and s the sum paid for the policy's savings account:

For *term* insurance, $p = m + l$
For *cash value* insurance, $p = m + l + s$

TYPES OF LIFE INSURANCE POLICIES

Although there are only two basic types of insurance policies, term and cash value (including whole life and endowment), the variations and combinations offered can baffle even a normally discerning buyer. Hence, we shall briefly consider the fundamental nature of the principal contracts and a few of the more common modifications.

Term

Term insurance is the closest thing to pure life insurance available, for, similar to automobile, fire, or other casualty insurance, it simply provides financial protection in the event of death and does not include any savings plan. Instead, the premium pays for only two things: the *mortality risk* and the *loading charge*. Hence, it is the lowest cost type of individual life insurance sold. Term policies written by commercial insurers are in effect for limited periods of time, such as 1, 5, or 10 years, or from the date of issue until the insured reaches age 65 or 70. Because mortality risk increases with age, the longer the "term," the greater the premium. For example, at age 25, a 5-year, $10,000 renewable and convertible term policy might cost $40.30 a year. If at the end of the initial 5-year term, the insured renewed this coverage for another 5 years, he would pay $43.90 a year. If he continued to renew his policy each time a successive 5-year term expired, he would have to pay $50.90 a year between ages 35 and 40, $63.90 a year between 40 and 45, $86.62 a year between 45 and 50, $122.70 a year between 50 and 55, and $179.10 a year from 55 to 60.

Instead of buying and renewing a 5-year term policy, he might have purchased, at the outset, a term-to-65 policy for $78.70 a year. The higher initial costs for the longer term policies result, essentially, from averaging the mortality risks over the period of the policy. If the insured does not die prematurely, the costs in the later years of the period are less than those charged for shorter term coverage at the same age.

The principal characteristics of term insurance are that it is inexpensive, provides temporary protection (e.g., for 5 or 10 years, or until age 65 or 70) rather than lifetime coverage, builds up no cash value, and costs progressively more as the insured becomes older. Thus, it is particularly suited for individuals with low incomes and substantial insurance needs, and for those who prefer to separate their life insurance from their savings programs.

Individual term policies usually provide for convertibility, which simply means that the insured can exchange his term coverage for a cash value policy if he later elects to do so. The premium for the cash value insurance would be based on the policyholder's age at the time of conversion, of course. Term insurance may also be renewable, which permits the insured, regardless of his insurability, to extend the policy in the same amount for the same period upon the expiration of the original policy, but at a somewhat higher cost due to the greater mortality risk as he ages.

Term insurance is available in either: (1) level or straight term, in which the face amount remains constant, or (2) decreasing or reducing term in which, as the name suggests, the death benefit declines during the policy period. A common example of the latter is mortgage redemption insurance, which is designed for persons who borrow to finance house purchases, securing their purchase money notes with mortgages or deeds of trust. If an insured were to die before his note had been paid, the insurance proceeds would satisfy the unpaid balance. As the amount of indebtedness is continually decreased by monthly payments, the amount of insurance in force would decrease correspondingly.

Whole Life

Whole life insurance, which is also referred to as straight life or ordinary life, is the lowest cost form of cash value insurance available. For a level, fixed premium for as long as the insured lives or until some very advanced age such as 99, when most whole life policies mature, the insurer contracts to pay the face value to the beneficiary whenever the insured dies. Thus, while term insurance provides protection for a limited segment of an insured's life and usually is not written beyond age 65 or 70, whole life is in effect for an entire lifetime. And while the premium for term pays for the *mortality risk* plus the *loading charge*, the higher premium for whole life contains an *additional* component for its *savings* feature. Thus, after its first or second year, a whole life policy has a cash value. As we shall consider shortly, the insured may withdraw this cash value by surrendering his policy; he may borrow all or most of it from the company; or he may use it to acquire extended term insurance or a paid-up whole life policy in a smaller face amount. In effect, similar to any form of life insurance other than term, *a whole life policy combines decreasing term insurance and increasing cash value in such a manner that the total always equals the policy's face value.*

Endowment

Similar to whole life, an endowment policy combines decreasing term coverage with cash value. However, the cash value accumulates at a much faster rate, so that if the insured survives the endowment period, which often is 20 years or until age 65, he is entitled to the face value of the policy. If he were to die before then, his beneficiary would receive this sum following his death. The premiums are much higher, of course, than those for a corresponding amount of whole life. For example, at age 35 a 20-year endowment might cost about 120% more than whole life, and an endowment-at-65 policy might cost about 50% more. Because *the primary purpose is to accumulate savings*, with the secondary emphasis on protection, those who require or desire maximum protection for minimum cost seldom find endowments suitable to their needs. Nor are they generally advisable unless or until a prospective buyer has all the other assets or insurance his survivors would require.

Miscellaneous Forms of Life Insurance

The three policies discussed above represent the underlying forms of life insurance upon which numerous other policies are based. The following represent some of the principal variations.

Group Life Insurance. In recent years, the most phenomenal growth in life insurance has occurred under group plans, which were first introduced in 1911. Since 1940, when the total amount of group life in force was about $15 billion, it has tripled every decade to reach over $904 billion, or 42% of all life insurance in force, by 1975. Group life is used mainly by employers, usually at their own expense, to provide life insurance for their employees. Over 97% of the group insurance in force is term insurance. The widespread use of this means of financial protection is further evidenced by the more than 380,000 master policies in force and by the more than 100 million individual certificates under these master policies.

Because of substantially reduced selling and administration costs, group term is about 15% to 40% less expensive than most individual term policies. If you are in the market for additional term coverage, first check with your employer to see if an increase in limits (at your expense) might be available. If it is not, then consider whatever might be offered through the professional or trade associations to which you belong or which you could join.

Association Life Insurance. Association insurance, which is almost always term, resembles group life insurance in many important respects. An organization representing a group of people who have some common bond (such as public employees, members of professional societies, trade unions) purchases a master policy from an insurance company. Those members of the group who desire the coverage may obtain it by paying premiums directly to the association, which uses the money it receives to pay for the master policy. Most master policies, which are issued for one-year periods, are noncancellable by the insurer except for failure of the association to pay premiums, and most are guaranteed renewable, although a change in mortality experience could result in an increase in premiums. Here again, wholesale purchasing reduces the cost, so *association insurance generally is significantly less expensive than individual term.*

Servicemen's Group Life Insurance (SGLI). Commencing in World War I, members of the armed forces have been able to obtain inexpensive term life insurance from the government through a variety of successive programs. Currently, Servicemen's Group Life Insurance (SGLI) is available in multiples of $5,000, up to a maximum of $20,000. The cost is $3.00 a month for the full amount, or a net cost of $1.80 a year per $1,000 of coverage.

Although SGLI entitlement ends with separation, it may be converted into a five-year non-renewable term policy known as Veteran's Group Life Insurance (VGLI). Currently, the cost for those under 35 is the same as for SGLI; above that age, $20,000 coverage is available for $6.80 a month ($4.08/$1,000/year). When VGLI expires, an insured who desires to do so may convert it into a commercial whole life policy without a medical examination.

Deposit-Term Insurance. "Deposit-term" insurance is not a separate form of life insurance, but rather merely an individual term policy for which a buyer pays an initial "deposit" in addition to his regular premiums. Generally, the amount of the deposit is $10 for each $1,000 of insurance under a ten-year plan. If the policy is kept in effect for the period of the plan, twice the sum deposited would be paid, tax free, as a guaranteed cash value. This equals a 7.2% compounded annual return. If the policy lapses or is surrendered before the end of the period, however, some or all of the deposit would be forfeited.

The premiums for deposit-term usually are significantly less than those charged for the same amount of individual term, since lapse rates, and hence the company's costs, are less. In some cases, however, these savings are not passed on to buyers; consequently, be sure to make some cost comparisons before buying. Also, weigh the chances that you might not be able to or wish to continue the insurance for the necessary period of time.

Limited-Payment Life. With whole life, both protection and premiums cover an entire life span. With limited-payment life, however, protection is for a lifetime but premiums are paid for only a specified period, such as 20 or 30 years. Depending on the insured's age, the cost for a 20-pay policy might range from about 100% more (at age 22) to 25% more (at age 55) than for a corresponding amount of whole life, because the reserve must accumulate much more rapidly. Thus, *a limited-payment policy is, in effect, whole life which is paid for within a specific number of years instead of over a lifetime.* Normally this type of coverage would not be practical for a young married man whose primary need is for maximum protection at low cost. A limited-payment policy might be attractive, though, for those who want cash value insurance but prefer to have it paid for prior to their retirement, assuming the total of all their life insurance and other assets would be adequate for survivors' needs, and that they have sufficient income to afford the increased costs. Sales of limited-payment life policies have declined substantially in the last decade.

Modified Life. A modified life policy can be deceptive. At the outset, it is partially or all term insurance, then after the first three or five years, it automatically becomes whole life. The premium during the initial period is considerably more than for term, but somewhat lower than that which would be charged for the same amount of whole life. Thereafter, however, the cost becomes more than it would have been had whole life been purchased initially. While this approach might be superficially appealing to a young person who wants permanent insurance but cannot afford the premiums for the amount of coverage he needs, many buyers fail to appreciate fully the fact that the cost will increase substantially after the first three or five years, or else they overestimate their future abilities to meet the higher costs. Normally, the same objective can be achieved at less expense by buying convertible and renewable term insurance, which the insured can later convert into cash value coverage if his income permits.

Educational Policies. Educational or juvenile policies are primarily designed to provide for the future financial needs of young children. Generally, they are written as either a 15- or 20-year endowment or a limited-payment life policy. The idea is that the policy will serve as a savings account, with the proceeds of an endowment or the cash value of a limited-payment policy available to provide for college costs or other needs when the child grows older. The popularity of this type of insurance has decreased markedly in recent years, as more and more salesmen and prospects alike have recognized that usually the premium dollars would be better spent insuring the life of the father, for if the child were to die, the financial consequences would be minimal, but the wage earner's death would create economic hardships for his survivors. Also, because the return on the cash value portion of such policies has not been competitive in recent times with that obtainable from commercial banks, savings and loan associations, government savings bonds, or elsewhere, and as spiralling college costs have required larger and larger sums, the former allure of educational policies has been badly tarnished. In this connection, Harvard's tuition had remained unchanged in the 19 years preceding 1948, but since that time it has been increased on several occasions and is now more than five times greater than it was then. Similarly, the tuition at colleges such as Cal Tech, Stanford, and Yale is around $5,000 a year. If living expenses (perhaps $1,500 to $2,000 or more a year for room and board), books, fees, transportation, and a modest spending allowance are considered, the total cost of a four-year education at one of the better private schools now approaches $30,000. At a state university, this sum might be about $18,000. When a child born today reaches college age, the four-year expense could be $83,000 and $47,000 respectively, assuming an inflation rate of 6% a year.

Family Income Policies. A family income policy combines decreasing term insurance for a 10- to 20-year period with some form of permanent insurance, usually whole life. In its most common form, if an insured were to die during the "family period," his beneficiary would receive $10 a month until the end of the period for each $1,000 of permanent insurance, and she would then be paid the face value of the permanent portion of the policy. Some family income policies, however, permit the beneficiary to receive the face value or commuted value on the insured's death. And under some policies, an insured who does not die prematurely may add more cash value insurance in the future, regardless of his insurability. After the family period terminates, the insured still has his permanent policy and, as the term coverage no longer exists, his premium is reduced.

Family Plan Policies. A family plan policy usually consists of whole life insurance on a husband, and smaller amounts of term coverage on his wife and each child, generally irrespective of the number of children he might have. For most average-income families, insurance on the wife until her children are self-supporting is quite sensible, for her premature death could place an inordinate financial burden on her surviving husband.

Minimum Deposit Insurance. Before 1964, a few insurance companies and salesmen specialized in minimum deposit insurance, or what is sometimes called executive plan insurance. Tax savings were, and to a lesser extent still are, the principal feature. Briefly, under a minimum deposit plan an insured would buy a whole life policy, but instead of paying the full premium he paid only the difference between the policy's cash value, which he borrowed annually, and the stated premium. He had to pay interest on the aggregate sum borrowed, of course, but repayment of the principal was not contemplated. Instead, the money released was available for what the policyholder anticipated would be more profitable investment elsewhere. Usually, part of the package consisted of one-year term insurance in the amount of the indebtedness. For example, under a minimum deposit arrangement, at age 35 a $100,000 whole life policy might cost $1,900 a year, and its first year's cash value might be $700. The insured would pay $1,200 and borrow the cash value from the insurer to pay the difference. Similarly, in each successive year the insured's out-of-pocket expense would be the difference between the premium and each year's increase in cash value, plus the interest on the cumulative sum owed. After about 20 years, the combined cost of the premium and the interest might be about $1,800, but approximately $1,400 of this would be interest, which previously was deductible for tax purposes.

The law now prohibits income tax deduction of interest on loans to pay insurance premiums. However, certain exemptions are granted (e.g., if the amount of interest is $100 or less, or if any four of the first seven annual premiums are not paid with borrowed funds). These restrictions have imposed a severe limitation on the sales potential of such arrangements. However, if the interest paid qualified for deduction, after 20 years the net cost to the insured in the above example would be about $1,000, assuming he were in the 50% bracket. And while his indebtedness on the policy would have reduced his actual coverage to about $70,000, at age 55 he could buy a $30,000 one-year term policy for around $470. In any event, the advantage of any minimum deposit plan is definitely limited to high-bracket taxpayers. Hence, unless a prospective buyer is in at least the 50% tax bracket and believes he will be there or in a higher bracket in the future, he is not likely to benefit from this otherwise superficially appealing scheme. What is more, the comparative costs of most policies sold for such purposes are quite high.

Annuities. In a sense, an annuity is the converse of permanent life insurance. Instead of periodically paying premiums, a portion of which will be accumulated as a policy reserve, an annuitant pays a lump sum to an insurance company, which then distributes a specified amount to him, usually on a monthly basis. In effect, an annuitant acquires a fixed income either for his life or for a certain portion of it, and on his death nothing remains of the sum he paid for the annuity, unless the contract guaranteed payments for a minimum number of years that had not then elapsed. From an economic perspective, their main appeal is limited to healthy septuagenarians.

Retirement-Income Policies. A retirement-income policy simply combines decreasing term insurance with an increasing cash value that, at a specified age (usually 65), is automatically converted into an annuity to provide the policyholder with a lifetime income, usually with a 10-year certain guarantee. ("How we retired in 15 years with $300 a month.") In other words, it is tantamount to buying an annuity on an installment plan and having insurance in the event the purchaser dies prematurely. Most retirement-income policies are constructed to provide for monthly payments of $10 per $1,000 of insurance. But since more than $1,000 is required to purchase an annuity which will pay $10 a month at the ages at which most such policies mature, the cash value actually has to exceed the face value at that date. However, if a policyholder dies after the cash value exceeds the face value but before the maturity date, his beneficiary receives the larger amount.

A retirement income policy has serious limitations, not the least of which is the probability of continual erosion in the dollar's purchasing power. Another drawback is cost: depending upon the purchaser's age, such a policy might be two to three times as expensive as the same amount of whole life. Also, when the payments start (assuming the insured lives to that age), a buyer might not need them, but might want life insurance for which he or she is not then eligible. Hence, anyone whose aim is to accumulate funds to supplement income many years in the future is likely to be more successful if insurance is separated from savings, or if whole life is purchased. If an annuity is desired when retirement age is reached, the insured might then be in a better position to purchase one that would provide more income than would be available from a retirement-income policy bought at a younger age.

Variable Annuities. Unlike a conventional annuity, which pays the annuitant a fixed number of *dollars* periodically, a variable annuity, the assets of which are invested primarily in common stocks, is designed to provide the investor with the value of a fixed number of *units* each month. Unit values will fluctuate, of course, with the investment results of the company.

The sales of these plans were given considerable impetus by the Employee Retirement Income Security Act of 1974. Among other things, ERISA permits employees who are not covered by a regular pension plan to set aside, tax-free, up to 10% of their pay (to a maximum of $1,500 a year) in an Individual Retirement Account (IRA); also, the maximum amount a self-employed person can contribute, tax-free, to a Keogh Plan for his retirement was increased to $7,500 annually.

IRA and Keogh investments are not restricted to variable annuities, of course, but may be made in any number of other ways. Their big appeal, obviously, is that the earnings used for such purpose are not taxed until they are paid out to the owner, when presumably he will be in a lower tax bracket.

Always anxious for new business, life insurance companies, mutual funds, savings and loan associations, banks, brokerage firms, and others have been heavily promoting their services for tax-deferred savings. Currently, over 50 life insurers operate variable annuity funds that have attracted over 1.6 million participants; the largest (Aetna Variable Fund) has assets approaching $500 million. To manage their investments, most life insurers have organized their own funds, but a few have tied in with already-existing mutual funds.

An individual who qualifies for an IRA or Keogh Plan usually would be well advised to take advantage of the opportunity they offer, if he can afford to defer some current income until later years. Whether he prefers a variable or a fixed-dollar annuity (or some combination of both) to, perhaps, a savings and loan association's time deposits or a no-load mutual fund (or both) is up to him. The obvious advantage of the latter, however, is that he would not have to pay any commissions on the sums invested; if he buys a variable annuity, he will be charged an average of about 8% of the amounts he pays (his premiums).

The promotion of variable as well as fixed-dollar annuities has spilled over recently to include not only persons who are eligible for IRA's or Keogh's but also those who are not. Because those in the latter category would have to pay after-tax dollars for premiums, most of the attractiveness of such plans is lost. Although the earnings on the sums paid in would not be taxable until received by the annuitant, the usual 8% commission presents a formidable deterrent to prospects who prefer to invest their surplus funds in other ways, some of which (e.g., municipal bonds) provide actual tax avoidance on yields, rather than merely tax deferral.

Variable Life Insurance. The latest "product innovation" is variable life insurance (VLI). This is designed to appeal to the increasingly large number of people who, having witnessed their dollars continually shrink in purchasing power, have become disillusioned with the dismal results of using cash value life insurance as a method of saving and who have sought refuge in non-fixed dollar assets (e.g., stocks, mutual funds) or in other savings media which provide higher yields.

Similar to whole life insurance, a VLI policy would have a fixed premium (perhaps 10% or so higher than for whole life) and a guaranteed minimum death benefit. The cash value, however, would fluctuate with investment results and, if the stock market rises, the insured's beneficiary could receive more than the policy's face value.

The extent to which VLI might make inroads on conventional, fixed-dollar life insurance sales remains to be seen. In early 1973, the Securities and Exchange Commission (SEC) rejected the insurance industry's assertion that such policies were outside of the federal securities laws. Hence, the policies are securities which must be registered; salesmen must register as broker-dealers; the separate VLI account of an insurer is treated as an investment company; and those who provide investment advice relating to issuance of the policies are subject to the laws regulating investment advisors. However, VLI accounts were exempted from the complex regulatory requirements of the Investment Company Act, and also from the limitations imposed on salesmen's commissions. In late 1976, though, the SEC issued a regulation restricting salesmen's commissions to no more than 50% of the first year's premium and to 9% of total premiums over a 20-year period. To date, sales of variable life insurance have not lived up to early expectations, and the once avid interest of many insurers appears to have cooled, due largely to the expense of developing programs and to the tight regulations imposed by state regulatory agencies.

Adjustable Life. In their never-ending quest for new business, a few companies have recently introduced what is called "adjustable" life insurance. The basic idea is to permit a policyholder to change at any time the amount of his coverage, its length, and the premium he pays, and even to swap whole life coverage for term, if he so desires. The concept isn't bad, but because of the additional cost imposed for these privileges, a potential customer should examine alternate less-expensive ways to achieve the same goals.

Coupon Policies. Although coupon policies are not widely sold, you should know enough about their nature and purpose to avoid becoming ensnared in the event someone suggests you buy one. The reason few people are exposed to these strange arrangements is that many state insurance commissioners, recognizing that the incidence of deception among naive buyers is quite high, have prohibited their sale. Usually, the type of salesman who handles coupon policies is not averse to deliberately representing them as investments rather than life insurance. In fact, unless he has more than average perception, an innocent prospect might not even realize that the salesman is talking about life insurance. Instead, he often is led to believe he is being offered an opportunity to acquire some type of profit-sharing, equity investment. The policies themselves, which are embellished with coupons to resemble corporate bearer bonds, help lend some credence to this iniquitous misrepresentation.

Actually, *a coupon policy is nothing more than cash value life insurance for which a substantial surcharge is made so that the company can guarantee payment of the coupons when they become due!* In effect, then, the buyer pays much more than the insurance itself would otherwise cost him, in return for which he becomes entitled to have part of the overcharge refunded to him. Fortunately, ethical insurers and salesmen so deplore the deception which customarily accompanies the sale of such policies that they have caused effective action to be taken in most states to eliminate or minimize their use.

Before proceeding further, it might be helpful to graphically illustrate the structure of the basic policies and a few of the modifications we have considered. At this point, comparative costs or advantages are not a concern. Instead, the purpose is simply to demonstrate the fundamental nature of the several policies and to show how the different forms of cash value life insurance variously combine true insurance (the insurer's net risk) with policy reserves to produce the face value at any given time (see Figure 6.1).

PARTICIPATING AND NONPARTICIPATING POLICIES

Life insurance companies are operated as either stock or mutual companies. Similar to any corporation, a stock company is owned by investors who provide the capital, elect the directors, and hope to share in any profits or to realize capital gains from their investments. The customers of a stock company are its policyholders, who do not share in profits unless they have purchased a "participating" policy. A mutual company, on the other hand, is theoretically owned by its policyholders, who ostensibly are entitled to share in its profits. All policies issued by mutual companies are participating (par), while the majority of those written by most stock companies are nonparticipating (NP).

FIGURE 6-1. Basic Policies.

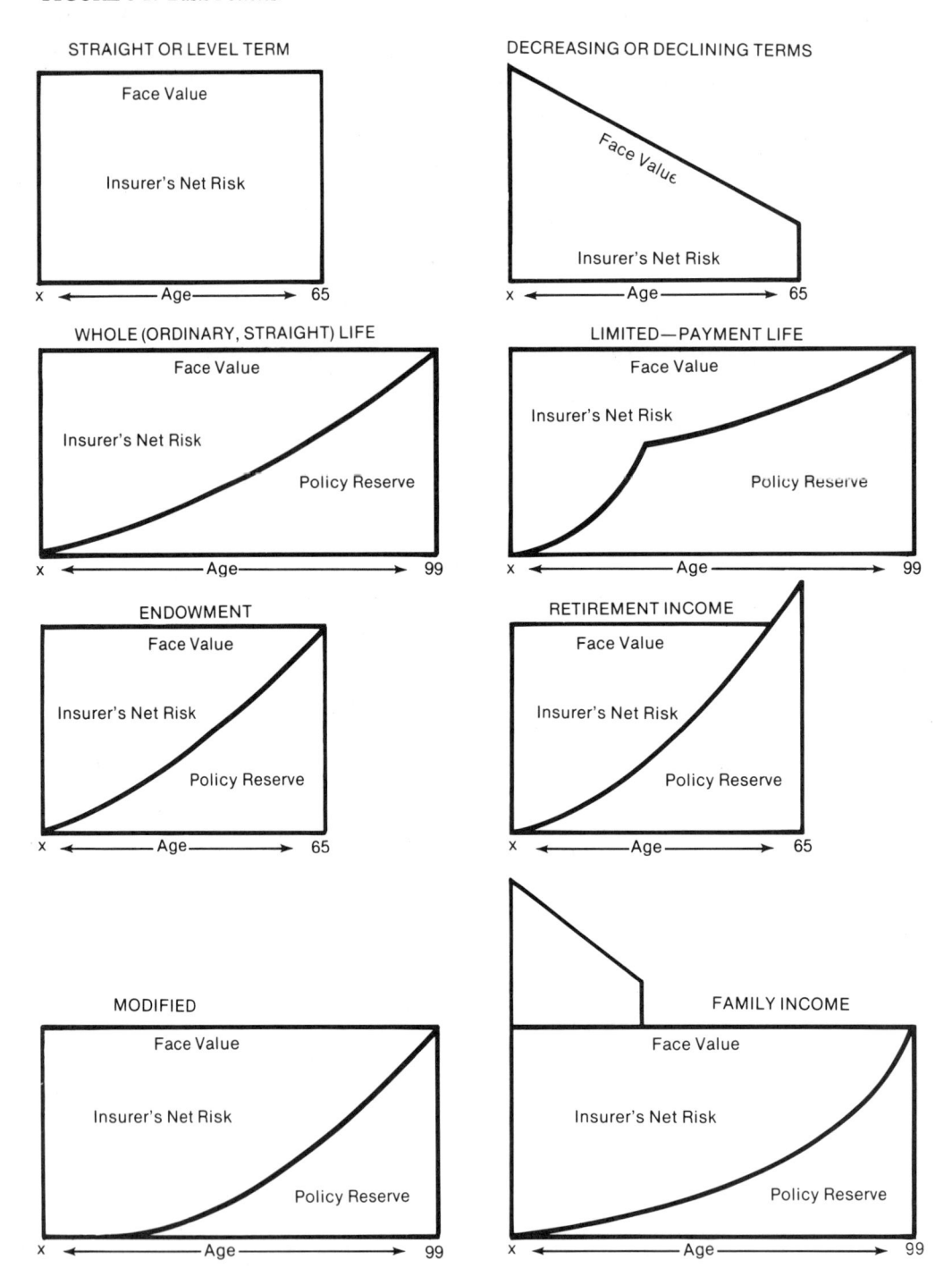

Insurance Company Investments

Many people misunderstand the nature of a policyholder's interest in the income and assets of his insurance company. The $18 billion-plus a year that, industry wide, the life companies earn on their $300 billion-plus assets, represents about one-fifth of their total income. These huge assets, which are held primarily to meet future obligations to policyholders, together with the billions of dollars annually added to them, are an important source of the new capital needed in our economy. The life companies invest their funds in various ways, but over 90% are in fixed-dollar uses (government securities, corporate bonds, mortgages, loans). In recent years, the net rate of return has exceeded 6%, compared to an average of about 4.5% in the 1960s and 3.5% in the 1950s.

What does all this mean to a typical policyholder? Essentially, simply assurance that the financial means exist for his insurer (if he has purchased a policy from a reliable firm) to meet its contractual obligation to pay his beneficiary when he dies, and if he owns a participating policy, that a higher than anticipated yield on investments might result (in the discretion of a company's directors) in a somewhat larger "dividend," thereby reducing the cost for his coverage. What it does *not* mean is that he has any indirect equity interest in the firms which obtain financing from his insurance company, or that he might realize any capital appreciation or benefit from such investments, other than through the assurance of solvency and possible reduction in net premiums. Elementary, right? Of course—but consider the impression probably created among masses of uninformed viewers by the nationwide TV campaign sponsored a few years ago by one of the largest mutual life companies: in a series of inane commercials, an ebullient policyholder frenzily chortled to enraptured bystanders about all the interests he held in construction, mining, transportation, and other industries *because he was a policyholder*! Although the insured in the commercial might be regarded as a prime candidate for the white-coated boys with the butterfly nets, a few salesmen are not above indulging in similar insinuations. So, *caveat emptor.*

Costs of Par vs. NP Policies

The gross premium for a participating policy is considerably higher than that for nonparticipating insurance (e.g., at age 25, a participating whole life policy would cost a buyer about 50% more). Part of this overcharge, as well as some of the insurer's investment and underwriting profits, are distributed to policyholders as "dividends." In this connection, however, do not confuse a "dividend" on an insurance policy with a dividend paid a corporate shareholder. The former is more in the nature of a rebate of an overcharge, while the latter normally is a share of earnings. Thus, insurance dividends are not taxable income, for the Internal Revenue Service recognizes that they are not true dividends but a partial return of the premiums paid.

An insured has several options with respect to any dividend to which he is entitled: he can take it in cash, leave it with the company to pay interest, use it to buy a paid-up addition to his policy, or apply it toward payment of his next premium. Nationwide, about equal percentages of policyholders do each. Normally, after a participating policy has been in force for several years, the annual premium minus the "dividend" will be less than the annual premium for a nonparticipating policy issued at the same age.

PRINCIPAL CONTRACTUAL PROVISIONS

One of Jerry Marcus' cartoons depicts a salesman asking a bewildered looking couple, who are examining a policy, "Of course it's complicated—would you trust an insurance policy you could understand?" Jokes of this nature abound about "fine print" provisions in insurance policies, which are designed to be both comprehensive and explicit. If an insured understands the terms and carefully reads the maze of verbiage, he should have an adequate understanding of what he has purchased. Nevertheless, the judge's observations in a case before the Kentucky Court of Appeals are not without some validity:

> Ambiguity and incomprehensibility seem to be the favorite tools of the insurance trade in drafting policies. Most are a virtually impenetrable thicket of incomprehensible verbosity. It seems that insurers generally are attempting to convince the customer when selling the policy that everything is covered and convince the court when a claim is made that nothing is covered. The miracle of it all is that the English language can be subjected to such abuse and still remain

an instrument of communication. (*Universal Underwriters vs. Travelers Ins. Co.,* Ky. Ct. App., March 20, 1970).

We shall briefly consider a few of the more important standard provisions, and the significance they have.

The Entire Contract Clause

This merely provides that the policy and the application for it constitute the entire agreement between the insured and the insurer; that any statement made by the applicant will be treated as a representation rather than a warranty; and that only certain executives of the company can modify the policy or waive any of the company's rights. Thus, neither the company nor the insured can unilaterally change the policy. The premium cannot be increased, nor can restrictions be added, even if the insured were later to engage in a more hazardous occupation or go to war. Moreover, once the contestability period has expired (usually 1 or 2 years), the company cannot invalidate the contract due to either inadvertent or deliberate misrepresentations that the policyholder may have made in his application. Conversely, the insured cannot change any provision without the company's consent. Hence, if he wishes to name another beneficiary, he may do so only by submitting his request and the policy to the insurer, who would make the change by endorsement.

Misstatement of Age

This clause provides that if the insured has misstated his age in applying for insurance, the value of the policy will be equal to the sum that could have been purchased for the same premium at the insured's true age.

Suicide

The suicide clause provides that if within a stated period (either 1 or 2 years) the insured takes his own life, his beneficiary is entitled only to a return of the premiums paid for the policy. This clause is designed to discourage despondent persons from buying large sums of insurance and then promptly committing suicide, which would distort actuarial expectations and place an inequitable burden on other policyholders.

War or Civil Disturbance

Because the standard mortality tables are not weighted for the increased hazard of warfare, riots, insurrections, and other civil disturbances, some companies include a clause to relieve them of their obligation to pay the face value of the policy if death were to result from such occurrences. For obvious reasons, any member of the armed forces should be careful to avoid buying a policy that contains such an exclusion.

Aviation

Due to the somewhat greater risk of death in aircraft, most policies contain an exclusionary clause that, similar to the war clause, limits the insurer's liability to return of the premiums paid if death results from any aircraft accident in which the insured was a pilot, crew member, student, or instructor, or in which he had any duty in connection with the aircraft. To avoid this standard exclusion, flying personnel may obtain aviation coverage for a higher premium. The amount of the added cost depends upon such factors as the policyholder's age and experience, the type aircraft he flies, and his geographical location.

Double Indemnity

For a small additional charge (perhaps 70 cents to $1.25 per $1,000 of whole life insurance at age 25), most insurers will include a double indemnity or accidental death clause in the contract, which entitles the beneficiary to collect twice the face value if the policyholder's death is accidental and not within certain specific exclusions. Although those who consider all life insurance as a gaming vehicle might regard this potential windfall as a worthwhile wager, a sound insurance program should be geared to the needs of survivors, not upon the particular manner in which the insured dies. Consequently, a double indemnity clause seldom is a desirable adjunct of life insurance.

Waiver of Premium

The purpose of a waiver of premium clause is to relieve an insured of the burden of continuing to pay premiums in the event he becomes totally disabled. The disability must be such as to terminate his earning power, and it must exist continuously for a minimum period, often six months, before the waiver becomes operative. Also, the benefit does not pertain to injuries or illnesses which existed before the policy application was made, nor does it apply to self-inflicted injuries or, with some policies, to disabilities resulting from war. Some companies include waiver of premium benefits within their basic premium charges, while others charge an additional nominal amount (from 20 cents to 50 cents a year per $1,000 of whole life insurance at age 24).

NONFORFEITURE PROVISIONS

The rights of an insured with respect to the reserve or cash value of his permanent life insurance were mentioned previously. The standard provisions, which all permanent policies are legally required to include, permit a policyholder who decides to terminate his coverage after the first or second year to obtain cash, paid-up whole life insurance, or extended term insurance for his policy's reserve. These benefits will be considered separately.

Cash Surrender Value

After the first or second anniversary of any cash value life policy, an insured may elect to surrender it and be paid the policy's surrender value. If he cancels his insurance before then, the policy is said to lapse, and he recovers nothing. Since the 1930s, when a few companies were unable to promptly meet requests to pay cash surrender values, insurers have included clauses that permit them to defer paying the cash value for a six-month period. But barring another severe economic depression and collapse of the real estate and securities markets, this contractual moratorium need not concern policyholders, for resort to it would be rare. However, policies issued by some companies specifically provide that the insured is entitled to his policy's cash value only after his premium payments have been in default for a certain length of time. Thus, if an insured who pays premiums annually were to ask for his cash surrender value in mid-year, the company might refuse to pay it until several months later when the premiums are in default.

Just how much the cash surrender value of a particular policy might be depends, of course, upon several factors, including the amount of the premium and the interest rate used (depending upon the insurer, this ranges from 2½% to 3½%). Every cash value policy includes a table enabling the insured to determine the sum to which he is entitled at various times. These tables are usually constructed so that if the policy is surrendered before its twentieth year, the cash value would not actually be the full policy reserve, but a smaller amount due to a surrender charge imposed by the company. Although critics have sharply assailed this practice, using a not entirely valid analogy of a bank deducting a charge if savings are withdrawn before 20 years have elapsed, the importance of this non-forfeiture right is demonstrated by the fact that about 20% of all benefit payments made by insurance companies, exclusive of policy dividends, constitute payments of cash surrender values.

Extended Term Insurance

If an insured stops paying premiums for a policy that has a cash value, and if he does not within a stated period of time otherwise direct how the cash surrender value will be used, an automatic extended term clause will result in the insurer applying the cash value to buy term coverage, in the same face amount as the permanent policy, for the number of years and days indicated in a schedule which is a required part of every cash value policy. The extended term option might be desirable for a policyholder who, for reasons not anticipated when he purchased his coverage, is unable to continue paying premiums. A few salesmen, though, sometimes suggest that an insured who is interested only in maximum protection for minimum cost should buy a cash value policy and, after 4 or 5 years, stop paying premiums and obtain extended term coverage for another 10 or 12 years. They reason that the total premiums paid, divided by the total period for which the insurance is in effect, will result in a lower cost per $1,000 of insurance per year than if term insurance were purchased separately. In actual dollar outlay, this often is true. But the sophistry lies in the fact that no mention is made of the insured's loss of use of the difference in premiums between the permanent and term policies, nor of the fact that the insured might die long before the extended term period expires. When these are considered, buying permanent coverage for the purpose of later obtaining extended term is more expensive.

Paid-up Life Insurance

The insured's third option is to use his cash surrender value to have his policy continued, in a lesser amount, as paid-up insurance for the balance of his life. The amount of such insurance to which a policyholder would be entitled depends upon his age, the cash value of the policy, and the insurer. Again, this can be determined from a schedule incorporated as a part of every permanent policy.

POLICY LOANS

Although not one of the nonforfeiture benefits, another right available to the owner of a cash value policy is to borrow all or most of the cash value from the company. As previously mentioned, the insured will be charged interest (on policies now being written, the rate ranges from 5% to 8%, but in most states it is 6%), for if the company had not lent the money to him it could have invested it elsewhere, and in the meantime the policy will continue to accrue additional cash value, just as if the loan had not been made. And although the company's risk is nonexistent, as the amount of any indebtedness would be deducted from the face value of the policy if the insured were to die before repayment, loans of only a few hundred dollars seldom are profitable because of costs incident to processing and servicing them.

The principal advantage of a loan provision to a policyholder is that in the event of severe financial need, the insurer may be his only loan source. And although most policies permit the company to defer making a loan for up to six months from the time the policyholder requests it, he can expect a reasonably prompt response from most insurers, barring either a widespread economic collapse or a particular insurer's financial instability. Moreover, he need not repay the principal if he is unable or elects not to do so.

TABLE 6.2. Non-Forfeiture and Loan Values.

End of Policy Year	Cash or Loan Value	Paid-up Insurance	Extended Term Insurance (Years—Days)
1	0	0	0
2	$ 91.10	$ 360	3–146
3	184.70	700	6–207
4	280.80	1,040	9–154
5	379.50	1,360	11–336
6	480.80	1,680	14–24
7	584.60	1,980	15–323
8	691.10	2,280	17–152
9	800.10	2,570	18–256
10	911.80	2,860	19–282
11	1,026.20	3,130	20–242
12	1,143.30	3,400	21–144
13	1,262.90	3,650	21–364
14	1,385.20	3,900	22–174
15	1,510.00	4,150	22–313
16	1,637.40	4,380	23–55
17	1,767.40	4,610	23–134
18	1,899.80	4,830	23–187
19	2,034.70	5,040	23–219
20	2,172.00	5,250	23–231
At age 60	4,931.20	7,950	19–68
At age 65	5,721.20	8,420	17–59

A representative table, illustrating the nonforfeiture values and loan values of a $10,000 nonparticipating whole life policy, purchased at age 22 for an annual premium of $114, is shown in Table 6.2.

DEATH BENEFIT PAYMENT PROVISIONS

Few policyholders ever give much attention to the "optional methods of settlement" provisions in their policies or to how changing circumstances might alter their selections. Consequently, on occasion some option utterly unsuited to their survivors' needs might be specified, thereby causing needless future hardships. A typical policy would enable the insured to have the proceeds paid his beneficiaries in any of the following manners:

Lump Sum

The first option is a lump sum or cash settlement, which entitles the beneficiary to the face amount of the policy, less any outstanding indebtedness, when the insured dies. The beneficiary may be anyone, of course, including an individual, a trustee, or the insured's estate.

Limited Installments

This option enables the insured to provide for the payment of equal periodic installments to his beneficiary for a specified term, such as 10, 20 or 30 years. The advantage is that a financially irresponsible person could not rapidly dissipate the proceeds, but the perils are that the beneficiary's needs might extend well beyond the term selected and inflation might diminish the purchasing power of the payments to a dangerous level.

If a limited-installment-for-a-fixed-period option were selected, the beneficiary of a $50,000 life insurance policy might be paid, under a liberal schedule, about $290 a month for 20 years. This amounts to a yield of about 7% on the principal sum, but at the end of the period, payments would cease and nothing would remain of the $50,000.

Life Income

Under a life-income option, the proceeds are used to purchase a life annuity for the beneficiary. If she were to die soon after the insured, the balance of the principal would be forfeited. On the other hand, if the beneficiary were to live an exceptionally long time, she might collect far more than the face amount of the policy.

A more popular variation of this option would provide a smaller guaranteed income to the beneficiary for a specified term (such as 10, 15 or 20 years) and, if she survives that period, for the balance of her life. If she died during the years-certain period, the payments would continue to someone else (a contingent beneficiary) for the remainder of the term. Under a current representative schedule, a life-income-with-20-years-certain annuity would provide $3.89 a month for each $1,000 of insurance to a 50-year-old widow, $4.58 a month if she is 60, and $5.24 a month if she is 70. Hence, if an insured with a $50,000 policy dies when his wife is 60, she would receive $229 a month. Although there is no danger of her outliving this income, a significant drawback is the likelihood of continual inflation.

Another rather apparent shortcoming of a life-income option is that the yield from the principal sum (the life insurance face value) in most cases is less than that available in recent years from the interest alone paid on high-grade, long-term corporate or government bonds. For example, if a 60-year-old widow were to receive a life income with a 20-year-certain guarantee, the amount she would be paid would be less than 5.5% a year, and upon her death or after 20 years, whichever is later, nothing of the insurance proceeds would remain for her survivors. If, instead, she had been paid the face value in cash and invested it in highly secure bonds, at current yields she would receive significantly more income than the insurer's payments would provide, and the principal would be intact on her death. Alternately, if she were not concerned with leaving anything for her survivors, she might also spend a small amount of the principal each year and thereby have two or more times the income payable under a life-income option.

Proceeds Left with Company

Under this option, the insurer retains the proceeds, invests them as it does with its other reserves, and pays the beneficiary interest only for a specified number of years or for her lifetime. How long the funds might be left with the company, and whether the beneficiary may withdraw all or part of the principal, depend upon the terms of the policy, state law, company practices, and the choice made by the person who selected the option. If the guaranteed yield is 3½%, a beneficiary would receive at least $2.92 a month for each $1,000 of insurance proceeds, and probably more if the company's earnings so permit. Often policyholders who select this method of settlement also include a spendthrift clause to protect the beneficiary against either herself or her creditors.

Selecting the Best Option

What settlement option is best depends to a large extent, of course, upon the situation and needs of the beneficiaries *after the insured dies.* And since this obviously cannot be determined ahead of time, only an unusual combination of circumstances would suggest that an insured select any option other than lump sum payment. Aside from the real and clear risk of inflation, the most significant limitation of any installment option selection by an insured is that it is a premature decision. In other words, the beneficiary will be stuck with what he has chosen, although it may be wholly unsuited to the circumstances that then exist. For example, an insured may be killed in an automobile collision and his wife-beneficiary may die a few hours, days, or weeks later from the same cause; or, because of extraordinary medical expenses or other reasons, the beneficiary may need a large sum of money at one time, rather than small installments over many years. If freeing his wife from managerial responsibilities is the insured's paramount concern, a simple trust (see Chapter 9) could not only reduce the risk of the diminishing value of dollars, but also provide for invasion of the principal to meet any contingency. Under the rigidity of most installment options, though, the beneficiary would be helpless. At times, however, an elderly beneficiary with a very small estate may be compelled, as a practical matter, to take a life-income option, simply because she cannot prudently assume the risk of living too long.

Income taxes are one factor which should not be either overlooked or overstressed in deciding whether to leave insurance proceeds with the company. Under current laws, the first $1,000 a year of interest paid to a surviving spouse is exempt from income taxation. Just how much this saving is worth depends primarily on the amount of the beneficiary's taxable income. However, if tax saving is a controlling consideration, a higher return might be realized if the insurance proceeds were invested in tax-exempt state or municipal securities. Moreover, for those in the lower tax brackets, the greater yields obtainable elsewhere would usually amount to more after taxes than the interest paid by an insurer.

In summary, although the gaps in survivors' income disclosed by an estate programming chart can be neatly filled with periodic payments under an installment settlement option, a flexible trust arrangement could be expected to achieve superior results. Similarly, for an insured who either doubts his survivors' abilities to manage large sums productively or desires to relieve them of this burden, a trust normally would be more advantageous than freezing insurance proceeds under an installment option.

SELECTING A LIFE INSURANCE COMPANY

In a sense, most policyholders do not buy life insurance, but instead have it sold to them. And seldom is much serious consideration given to the company the salesman represents. Any discerning prospect should realize that the value of the policy he buys depends upon the financial stability of the company which issues it. Hence, he should deal only with salesmen who represent reputable concerns.

The difference in stock and mutual companies was discussed previously. Less than one-tenth of the nation's almost 1,800 insurance companies are mutual, but these account for over half of the total life insurance in force. What is more, the five largest companies in terms of assets are all mutuals: Metropolitan Life Insurance Company, Prudential Insurance Company, Equitable Life Assurance Society, New York Life Insurance Company, and John Hancock Mutual Life Insurance Company. Only 3 of the 15 companies with assets over $3 billion are stockholder-owned: Aetna Life Insurance Company, Travelers' Insurance Company, and Connecticut General Life Insurance Company. There are, of course, many large and highly-regarded firms besides those in this select group.

Although many of the other companies have assets that are negligible compared to those of the industry giants, at times well-managed, smaller companies are able to compete effectively by using reinsurance to hedge against large losses. For example, a small insurer might set a $10,000 limit on the risk it will carry on any one person; thus, if it issues a $25,000 policy, it would reinsure $15,000 with another insurer.

Obviously, a prospective buyer should not decide from which company to buy insurance on size alone, for a small or medium firm which earns a high net rate of interest, has a low expense ratio, and insures only the most favorable mortality risks might offer more attractive rates than a larger, less efficiently operated company. Nevertheless, he should be certain that the company is adequately financed, for insolvency among small insurers is not unknown. In this connection, a buyer should be generally aware of the requirements for forming insurance companies in the different states. For example, the standards in New York and California are high. On the other hand, in previous years the requirements in Arizona and

Louisiana have been less stringent. There may be nothing wrong with a company headquartered in a minimum-capital state, but before purchasing anything as important as life insurance, a prudent buyer should ascertain that the company has a reasonable degree of financial stability. *Best's Life Insurance Reports,* which any salesman should be willing to show a prospect or which is available in most libraries, is a ready reference for such an inquiry.

THE "COST" OF LIFE INSURANCE

Although the typical buyer is concerned with what he must pay for life insurance, he is not likely to have much awareness of *relative* costs. However, a prudent purchaser will try to determine what offers the best value. While it is true that the actual cost of life insurance cannot be precisely measured prospectively, due to the number of variables and assumptions that must be made, various ways to approximate costs have been developed. These can be helpful, provided their limitations are understood, and they are not used for other than comparative purposes.

Until a few years ago, the typical life insurance sales pitch usually included a reference to a policy's "net cost," which in most cases was determined by what is called the "traditional" method. More recently, another technique, known as the "interest-adjusted method," has come into vogue. As an informed buyer, you should be familiar with both.

The "Traditional" Net Cost Analysis

The method once commonly used to illustrate the "net cost" of an insurance policy is to add the premiums a prospective purchaser would have to pay over a period of years (usually 20), then subtract the cash surrender value at the end of the period as well as, for a participating policy, the sum of the projected dividends plus the terminal dividend (if any). The result might then be divided by the number of years used in the illustration and the face value of the policy (in thousands) to show what is claimed to be the annual cost per $1,000 of insurance for the period used. For example, if a 25-year-old prospect were considering a $10,000 whole life participating policy for which he would be charged a $177 annual premium, the following representation might be made:

Premiums for 20 years (20 × 177)	($3,540)
Dividends over 20 years	$1,258
Cash value at end of 20th year	$2,893
Net Cost:	$ 611 Profit!

A common refinement of this method is to provide a prospect with a computer printout summarizing the pertinent data year-by-year. This purportedly will show that the policy's "cost" progressively declines and that after several years, the annual increase in cash value plus the estimated dividend (if the policy is participating) exceed the premium: ergo, thereafter the insured will have "free" insurance as well as a "profit," "credit," or "net gain" each year! In such a wonderland, Alice might indeed exclaim about how things become curiouser and curiouser.

If the "traditional" method's results were used for no more than to demonstrate the *relative* differences between similar policies, it might be defensible. However, few salesmen make much effort to disabuse prospects of the erroneous idea that life insurance will cost less and less as time goes by, which the data as usually presented seems to imply. Moreover, seldom will the results be related to the "net cost" of competitors' policies, unless the comparison would be favorable. Although the "traditional" net cost analysis apparently bemuses large numbers of prospective buyers, it is often used in so illusory a manner as to smack of misrepresentation. Some of the more glaring deficiencies are:

1. The loss of use of money is ignored. (If the policyholder, rather than the insurer, had the cash value, he could invest it in any number of ways; how much he might realize would depend on several factors, but a 4% to 5% net return should be a minimum expectation.)
2. The practice of some companies of ballooning dividends in later years is disregarded, because of the inherent, fallacious assumption that as long as the same total sum is received over the same period, when the dividends might be paid is immaterial.
3. By ignoring the value of the use of money, a participating policy will appear to cost less than a similar nonparticipating type; also, policies with larger premiums and cash values will seem to be less expensive than policies with lower premiums and cash values.

4. With participating policies, the assumption is that current dividend scales will not be changed. They will.
5. Other questionable assumptions are that the policyholder will survive to the end of the period (over 18% of those who purchase and retain policies die within 20 years), will not surrender or otherwise terminate the policy prior thereto, and will surrender it at the end of the period.

The "Interest-Adjusted" Method

Because of mounting criticism of the "traditional" method and the uses made of it, the Institute of Life Insurance appointed a special committee which, in 1970, recommended substitution of the "interest-adjusted" method of computing and comparing costs. In June 1973, the National Association of Insurance Commissioners proposed a regulation banning use of the "traditional" method and requiring disclosure of the "interest-adjusted" cost. After strenuous resistance by some insurers, most reliable companies today use the latter almost exclusively.

Essentially, the interest-adjusted approach differs from the traditional method simply by recognizing that the use of money over a period of time is worth something. Under the formula used to calculate an interest-adjusted cost, the first step is to determine what the yearly cost of $1,000 of insurance would be worth if it had been accumulated at some compound rate of interest (5% is now commonly used) for some particular period (say, 20 years). This merely requires multiplying the annual premium for $1,000 of coverage by 34.719, which is the factor that represents what $1 a year at 5% would amount to after 20 years. Next, if the policy is the "participating" type, the value of the dividends (also accumulated at 5%) is subtracted; so, too, the cash value at the end of the 20-year period and the terminal dividend (if any) are deducted. The result is then divided by the same factor used earlier (34.719) to obtain the "Interest-Adjusted Surrender Cost Index" for the particular policy.

You could readily calculate the interest-adjusted cost of any policy for which you have the required data, but don't bother: the information is not difficult to obtain elsewhere. So before you decide to buy any life insurance from anyone—even your struggling cousin, whom you would like to help—*please* write the Publications Unit of the New York Insurance Department, Agency Building, One Empire State Plaza, Albany, NY 12223, for a free copy of its

Consumer Shopping Guide for Life Insurance. Also, drop by your local public library to peruse the current edition of Best's *Flitcraft Compend* or the National Underwriting Company's *Cost Facts on Life Insurance—Interest Adjusted Method.* If you would like to pursue the subject in even greater depth, try Belth, *Life Insurance—a Consumer's Handbook* (Bloomington, IN: Indiana University Press, 1973), as well as *The Consumers Union Report of Life Insurance* (Orangeburg, NY: Consumer Report Books, 1977). The money you save will be your own!

    Similar to other cost indices, the interest-adjusted method does not purport to precisely measure actual costs, but instead, it is designed to provide a basis for comparing the relative costs of different policies. What it does disclose can be shocking to anyone who has naively assumed that there really isn't any great difference between life insurance companies (which is equivalent to having thought that because both were regulated railroads, the Penn Central must have been as well-managed and profitable as the Southern Pacific).

    If, for example, you were a 25-year-old man, one of the nation's largest insurers would charge you $186 a year for a $10,000 participating whole life policy; another prominent company would sell you a similar policy for $174. The one dollar a month difference sounds insignificant, but if you compare the interest-adjusted costs you would learn that the first policy's was $6.12 for each $1,000 face value of insurance, while that for the second policy was only $2.12. That's right—the first policy costs almost *three times as much* as the second, considering not just the admittedly negligible difference in premiums, but more importantly, the differences in cash values and in the amounts and timing of dividends. So if someone really did what the formula assumes (bought a policy, lived at least twenty more years, kept it in effect, then surrendered it for its cash value), the total cost differences would be several thousands of dollars—not just a measly twelve dollars a year.

    Table 6.3 will give you a little broader view of how great the differences in costs really are between different life insurance companies. Except for the two non-participating policies illustrated, there isn't all that much difference in the annual premiums, and even the cash surrender values after twenty years seem reasonably close. The dividends that the participating policyholders might receive (not shown in the table) would vary by several hundred dollars, which could make a difference. But putting everything together, the relative

TABLE 6.3. *Interest-Adjusted Surrender Cost Indices (20th year costs for selected $10,000 whole life policies purchased at age 25).*

Company	Annual Premium	Par/NonPar	20th Year Cash Value	Interest-Adjusted Cost Per $1,000
A	$126.90	NonPar	$2,250	$6.21
B	$170.60	Par	$2,880	$3.10
C	$156.20	Par	$2,550	$4.08
D	$135.20	NonPar	$2,900	$2.66
E	$142.80	Par	$2,732	$2.94
F	$158.40	Par	$2,250	$9.25
G	$175.60	Par	$2,700	$1.85

costs are shown in the far right column. And yes, it's true: if you don't know what you're doing, you could pay more than four times as much as you should for the same amount and type of coverage.

OTHER COST ANALYSES METHODS

Various other ways exist to approximate the comparative costs of life insurance, and more are forthcoming. Presently, a task force appointed by the National Association of Insurance Commissioners has been trying to develop a new method that will provide even greater reliability. In the meantime, though, the Federal Trade Commission has announced its own investigation of the life insurance industry, having as its primary aim requirements for more uniform cost and value disclosures, to permit buyers to decide how to get the most for their money.

One of the most accurate techniques yet devised is the *Level Price Method* proposed by Professor Joseph M. Belth of Indiana University in 1966. Briefly, it involves computing a yearly price, calculating a yearly amount of protection, and then arriving at a level price. The ILI committee that recommended use of the interest-adjusted method considered the Belth approach but rejected it for several reasons, including the belief that it was too complicated for widespread use and understanding.

There is, however, a simple approach that will provide at least a rough guide to the relative attractiveness of various policies for an informed and discriminating buyer who wants life insurance primarily for its financial protection. In this connection, both the "traditional" and the "interest-adjusted" methods can be mildly deceptive, since they are predicated on an assumption that an insured will survive for 20 years or until age 65. Statistically, 1 in 14 men who are age 30 will not live to 50, and 1 in 5 will die before reaching 65. Hence, unless you have delusions of immortality, some consideration should be given to what insurance costs would be if you were to fail to make it into the senior citizen category.

Similar to Professor Belth's method but without either its detail or precision, this technique involves separating the actual insurance from the savings element, calculating the price for the insurance and then determining what the protection itself would cost *if the insured were to die during the year in question.* I suggest you make similar computations for several different times in the future (yearly data are not necessary), then compare the results for different policies.

The only figures necessary are the annual premiums and the cash values at various times, both of which are set forth in policies and in Best's *Flitcraft Compend,* and the dividend scales for participating policies. A policy's end-of-year cash value is subtracted from the face value to determine the net insurance; next, to estimate the cost, what the beginning-of-year cash value might have earned during the year (if the policyholder had the use of it) is added to the annual premium and the dividend (if any) is subtracted. For these purposes, the net yield the policyholder might have realized from the cash value might be assumed to be a conservative 5%. The cost is then divided by the net insurance (in $1,000) to arrive at a cost per $1,000.

To illustrate this approach, assume you have a $20,000 participating whole life policy, which has a present cash value of $4,000. Your annual premium is $320 and you expect to receive a dividend of $120 for the coming year. The first step is to find out how much *actual insurance* you have; this is merely a matter of subtracting the $4,000 cash value from the $20,000 face value. The result is $16,000. (Your beneficiary would be paid the full $20,000 if you died, but keep in mind that part of this sum—the cash value—would be your "savings.")

Next, determine how much it would cost you to continue the policy for another year. Easy, you say: $320 (the premium) less $120 (the dividend), or just $200. Think again. What if you had use of the $4,000 cash value? It could easily net 5%, so by not having it available, in effect it has cost you at least 0.05(4,000), or another $200, for the year. Adding this $200 hidden cost to your $200 visible expense will give you a truer idea ($400) of how much the insurance would really cost if you died before the year is out.

Finally, to produce a death-cost index, simply divide the total

TABLE 6.4. *Cost of Insurance if Death Were to Occur at End of the Policy Year.*

A. Actual Insurance in Force
    Face value (FV)................$_____
    Cash value (CV)................$_____
    Net Insurance (FV minus CV) ....$_____

B. Cost for Insurance Component
    Annual premium ....$_____
    Dividend (if any) ....$_____
    Net cash cost (premium minus dividend) ......$_____
    Loss of use of cash value (0.05 × CV)........$_____
    Total cost (net cash cost plus loss of use of CV) ....$_____

C. Cost per $1,000 of Actual Insurance
    Total cost (B) divided by net insurance (A) in $1,000 ......$_____

TABLE 6.5. *Death-Cost Index of Different Policies.*

If the method outlined in Table 6.4 is applied to three non-participating policies (a 20-pay life, a whole life, and a 5-year renewable term), each issued in the amount of $25,000 to a 25-year old man by the same insurance company (one of the largest and lowest-cost firms in business), the results would show:

		\multicolumn{4}{c}{*Policy Year at Time of Death*}
Type of Policy	*Annual Premium*	5	10	20	*Age 60*
20-pay life	$512	$23.18	$30.91	$65.53	$57.43
Whole life	$376	$16.57	$21.99	$43.72	$75.32
5-year renewable-and-convertible	$103 (to age 30) to $459 (to age 60)	$ 4.92	$ 6.15	$12.28	$28.67

To further illustrate relative differences in costs, consider the following "association" term coverage, keeping in mind that most term policies are not available beyond age 65 or 70.

Association term	$32 (to age 30) $375 (to age 60)	$ 1.54	$ 2.16	$ 5.29	$15.00

cost ($400) by the amount of actual insurance, in thousands (16). The result is $25. So, you grunt, is $25 per $1,000 good, bad or indifferent? By itself, of course, the figure is none of these. Its significance would become clear, though, if you made similar calculations for other policies you own or might be thinking about buying. Table 6.4 outlines the steps to follow, and Table 6.5 shows what the comparisons look like at various ages for a few representative policies.

Remember that the death-cost index method is concerned only with the *relative* costs for the *pure insurance* components of different policies, assuming that death occurs in the particular year you consider. Obviously, rarely does anyone know when he will die. Consequently, an appropriate collateral inquiry would be (in the words of the insurance salesman in a Rea cartoon), "What if, God forbid, you should live to a ripe old age?" Or, what if you actually did surrender your policy for its cash value at some future time, such as the usually-illustrated 20-year point or age 65?

If you eliminate the possibility of an early death from consideration, then other factors (such as how much the difference in premium costs would be worth to you) must be entered. The basis for comparison then depends principally upon the relative attractiveness of life insurance versus other uses of savings. This subject will be explored in Chapter 8, after we consider the fundamentals of various investment alternatives in Chapter 7.

chapter 7
The Fundamentals Of Investments

The financially mature person, who has avoided unnecessary indebtedness and saved a reasonable portion of his or her income, soon will be confronted with the problem of how best to invest the surplus funds.

Before considering any type of investment, however, an adequate cash or cash equivalent reserve should be established for unforeseen emergencies. Four to six months' pay is probably sufficient for most people. Another essential is ample life insurance to supplement survivors' benefits if death is premature. In some cases, home ownership should also have priority over other investments.

After meeting these requirements, the next decision that must be made is what to do with the remainder of the savings. This decision necessarily depends upon several factors. The most important of these are the savings objectives, which might be to finance children's college educations, to supplement retirement income, and to accumulate an estate sufficient to provide for survivors' needs. Other significant considerations are age, family responsibilities, other assets, stability of employment, earnings prospects, and the adequacy of future retirement income. Also, any investment decision necessarily will be influenced by personality factors: some people are not emotionally capable of coping with the inevitable fluctuations in the securities markets; others may have undisciplined spending habits and require some sort of forced saving in their investment planning.

Obviously, then, any investment program must be tailored to the needs of the individual who must determine, among other things, how much weight to accord safety of principal, yield, liquidity, convenience, capital appreciation potential, and protection against inflation. An elderly person, for example, normally is most interested in high yield coupled with low risk, while a young person might be more concerned with growth of capital and protection of purchasing power.

WHAT IS AN INVESTMENT?

In a generic sense, an investment is any use of money for income or profit. For clarity, however, a distinction should be made between lending and investing. One who lends money is a *creditor*. He expects to be paid for the use of his money and eventually to have his principal returned. An *investor*, in the sense in which that term is used in this book, usually seeks both current income and profit from an increase in his principal.

Figure 7.1 shows some of the more common uses to which savings might be put. Although both fixed-dollar and non-fixed dollar assets are represented in the estates of most people, the fundamental differences between the two should always be kept in mind.

In the creditor category, it is convenient to distinguish between "savings-account" creditors and others. Savings-account creditors receive only income in the form of interest for the use of their money. Other creditors receive not only interest but, depending upon market conditions, might profit or lose from their holdings.

FIXED-DOLLAR ASSETS

"Savings Account" Creditors

Government Savings Bonds. As obligations of the federal government, the widely held Series E and less familiar Series H bonds are among the safest of all uses of money, at least insofar as

FIGURE 7-1. Possible Uses of Savings.

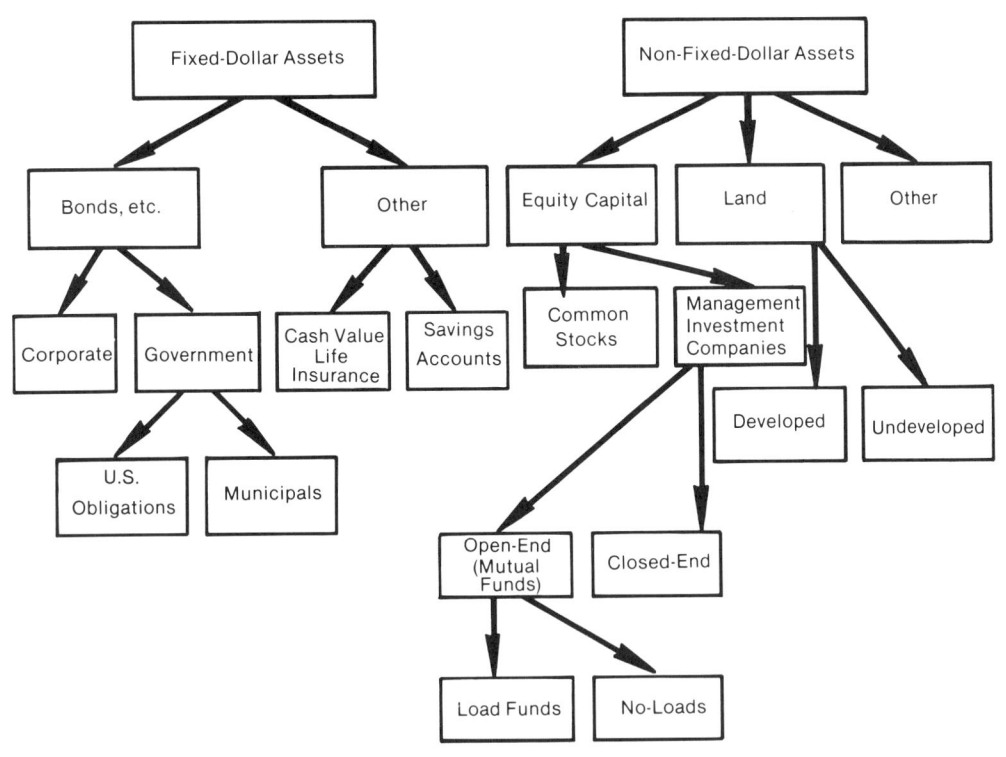

safety of principal is concerned. In January 1980, two new series—the EE and HH—will be introduced by the Treasury as replacements for the E's and H's. Although the terms of the new issues differ somewhat from those of the present bonds, they serve essentially the same purposes.

The EE's will be sold for one-half their face values, with the minimum denomination bond being $50. At maturity, which requires more than 10 years compared to 5 years for the E's, they may be redeemed for face value, so like their predecessors, the average annual yield will be 6½%. (To spur sales, the interest on savings bonds was increased from 6% to 6½% effective June 1, 1979; under present law, the Treasury could pay as much as 7% if it elected to do so.) An owner of an EE may redeem it anytime after six months from purchase, but if he does so before maturity, his yield would be less than 6½% because, similar to the E's, interest accrues on a graduated scale (less in the early years, more in the later years).

For many people—especially lower-income wage earners who otherwise might have difficulty in saving any of their income and young workers at the beginning of their careers—government savings bonds are a sound and practical way of accumulating something. Aside from the relative painlessness of automatic saving through payroll deduction, the E's and EE's offer unsurpassed safety, since they are guaranteed by the government, registered to the buyer, and will be replaced if lost, stolen, or destroyed. (For reissuance of missing bonds, notify the Bureau of Public Debt, Division of Loans and Currency, 536 South Clark Street, Chicago, IL 60605.) In addition, the earnings on federal obligations are exempt from state and local income taxation, and the owner has the option of paying federal income taxes either on the interest as it accrues, or deferring payment until he redeems his bonds.

Another appeal of the E's and EE's is that they may be used conveniently for the purpose of building a secure, tax-free education fund for a young child. All the buyer has to do is to have the bonds registered in the child's name as owner, with a parent normally listed as the beneficiary, then for the first year only file an income tax return in the child's name, reporting the accrued interest. Thereafter, no returns are necessary unless the child's income exceeds $1,000, and when he or she is ready for college, the bonds may be redeemed without incurring any tax liability.

Despite these advantages, the bonds do have some serious drawbacks. During periods of high interest rates, such as we have experienced with only brief respites over the last several years, other government securities pay more. In recent times, in fact, the returns on the E's have not even equalled increases in consumer prices. Nevertheless, stripped of the specious appeals to "patriotism" or other noble causes that often are used to encourage their purchase, savings bonds do have some merit for some purposes, although they would be an utterly dismal choice as the crux of a long-term estate accumulation plan.

Series HH bonds, which serve a different purpose than the EE's, can be purchased in minimum denominations of $500. Instead of being sold at a discount, the buyer pays face value, and receives interest twice a year at a steady 6½% rate, which is treated as current income for federal tax purposes. HH's may be bought for cash, of course, but they also may be acquired in exchange for Series E or EE bonds; in the latter case, any earnings that previously had been deferred from income taxation may continue to be deferred. Actually, the opportunity to postpone further the payment of taxes on interest that has accrued in E or EE bonds is about the only sound reason for considering the otherwise unappealing HH's: as long as Treasury notes of similar maturities (10 years) yield more than 6½% (over 9% was common in mid-1979), money can be put to far better uses elsewhere.

"Passbook" Accounts. Commercial banks, savings and loan associations, savings banks, and credit unions all accept money from savers, usually with little or no minimum requirement as to the amount deposited. Withdrawal at any time is customarily permitted; until then, the funds earn interest. There are some important differences among these institutions, though, and how they calculate interest (concerning the latter, see Appendix A).

Commercial banks, which use most of their funds for business loans and investments, are currently authorized by the Federal Reserve Board to pay up to 5¼% interest on passbook accounts. Normally, a commercial bank is the safest non-governmental repository for savings, and over 95% of all banks participate in the Federal Deposit Insurance Corporation (FDIC), which insures individual accounts up to $40,000. Although a bank may require 30 days' notice before withdrawal, there should not be any delay in getting your money out, barring a financial or other catastrophe. A principal disadvantage, apart from the low yield, is that most banks do not credit interest on passbook accounts more often than quarterly, and some only semiannually.

The funds in *savings and loan associations* are used almost exclusively for home loans secured by mortgages or trust deeds on real property. Because such investments are somewhat more risky than those of commercial banks, their earnings and their return on deposits are generally higher. Currently, S&L's and savings banks may pay a maximum of 5½% on passbook accounts. Daily compounding, which is commonplace, increases this yield to 5.39% annually.

Withdrawal of funds on demand is usual, but an association might require notice of up to six months, for unlike the creditor relationship a depositor has with a bank, in most states an individual does not actually "deposit" money in an S&L; instead, he purchases what in effect are shares in a type of mortgage investment fund. Hence, the S&L does not "owe" him the amount in his account, but rather he has an interest in the association's assets, which are long-term and of low liquidity.

If an association's accounts are insured by the Federal Savings and Loan Insurance Corporation (FSLIC), individual accounts of $40,000 or less will be paid in cash or transferred to another association. An extensive delay in recovering savings might be expected, however. Some associations not participating in the FSLIC carry other forms of insurance, which might or might not afford sufficient protection. In recent years, accounts in most S&L's and savings banks have been practically as safe as those in commercial banks, although in isolated cases, depositors in uninsured or inadequately insured institutions have lost money.

A *credit union* is a cooperative organization of persons who have a common bond of occupation or association, such as employment by a government agency or by a large company. Its funds are used primarily to make short-term, personal loans to members for purposes such as purchasing automobiles, furniture, or other personal property. Currently, most federally chartered credit unions pay at least 6% interest (dividends) on deposits (share accounts), and some state-chartered organizations pay up to 9%. Also, most credit unions furnish, without charge, a type of group term life insurance that, up to a $2,000 limit, doubles the savings of members who die. A credit union member is not a creditor, but a shareholder, similar to a person who purchases shares in a S&L. Shares (deposits) in federally chartered credit unions are insured up to $40,000, so the risk of loss in them is slight, although a credit union obviously does not have the degree of security of either a commercial bank, an insured savings and loan association, or a savings bank.

Time Deposits. If you are reasonably sure that you won't need to withdraw your savings from a bank or a thrift institution before a particular time, you might consider a time deposit instead of a passbook account, since the former pays much more. Time deposits (sometimes loosely called certificates of deposit) are usually available for periods ranging from 90 days up to seven years. The 90-day accounts pay ½% more than passbook accounts, and the longer, fixed-term certificates yield up to 7.5% at commercial banks and 7.75% at the thrift institutions. If the interest is compounded daily, 7.75% represents a first-year return of 8.06%.

When savers withdraw funds from banks and thrift institutions to seek higher yields elsewhere, some segments of the economy—especially housing—suffer. Such an outflow is called "disintermediation," which translated means, essentially, to take money from a place that serves an intermediary function between those who have funds to lend and those who borrow them. In May 1978, when rapidly rising money market rates presaged widespread disintermediation, the Federal Reserve Board permitted commercial banks, as well as S&L's and savings banks, to remain competitive by selling two new types of time deposits at higher rates than they previously could offer.

The first type of deposit is an eight-year certificate with a maximum annual rate of 7¾% at commercial banks and 8% elsewhere, which is ¼% more than had been authorized on six- or seven-year deposits. Compounded daily, 8% actually yields 8.33% over the first year. There is no minimum denomination required for these "8-for-8" certificates.

The second and more interesting type is a six-month "money market certificate" (MMC), sold in minimum amounts of $10,000 with interest pegged to the average rate paid at the most recent auction of 26-week Treasury bills. Since new T-bill rates change weekly, the yields on MMC's (which usually remain the same throughout their six-month lives) depend upon when they are purchased. Both commercial banks and thrift institutions currently pay the same rate, although the thrifts are authorized to pay ¼% more if the rate on new T-bills falls below 9%. Initially, most savings and loan associations offered daily compounding of interest; this practice has been prohibited since March 1979, however, to slow down the massive inflow of funds into these certificates. Hence, unless the restriction on daily compounding is lifted or unless T-bill rates fall below 9%, there is no difference in yields between MMC's sold by banks and by thrift institutions.

Mainly because of the high yields and convenience, MMC's met with enthusiastic acceptance at first, and despite the recent restrictions, their yields are competitive with most short-term, fixed-dollar alternatives. If you have $10,000 that you won't need for six months and would like a piece of this action, there are far worse places for your money. You should be aware, though, of three unadvertised factors. (1) The actual yield on T-bills is slightly more than on MMC's, since T-bills are sold on a discount basis (less than face value is paid, and a buyer receives face value on maturity); therefore, the actual yield is always higher than the discount rate. For example, if a 26-week, $10,000 Treasury bill is sold for $9,550, the annual rate of return is 450/9,550 times 2, or 9.42%, but the discount rate (which is what is paid on a MMC) is only twice the difference between 100 and 95.5, or 9%. Also, a few banks and institutions reserve the right to change yields in accordance with changes in T-bill rates. Avoid them. (2) If you are from a state with high personal income taxes, proceed cautiously. Even if your yield is, say, 9.6%, it could be reduced by as much as one-fifth—or to less than 8% (for example, if you are from New York City and have taxable income of over $25,000). Treasury issues, on the other hand, are not subject to state or local taxation, so the rate of return on a new T-bill purchased at the same time would be 9.6%. Interest on both is taxed by the federal government. (3) A stiff penalty (loss of three months' interest if the certificate matures in a year or less, and six months' interest if its maturity is longer) is imposed if, for whatever reason, you find it necessary to redeem your certificate before its maturity. A similar penalty is required on other time deposits, also.

Permanent Life Insurance. Buying any form of cash value life insurance is tantamount to acquiring financial protection against premature death plus, in a limited sense, opening a savings account. The return on that part of the premium which constitutes available savings (the policy's cash surrender value) is usually 2.5% to 3%. Remember, though, that if a policyholder dies while the policy is still in effect, his beneficiary would not receive both the face value of the policy plus its cash value, but only the former.

Normally, unless an insured has an endowment or retirement income policy, he does not contemplate ever withdrawing his savings. However, as previously discussed, most insurers will lend a policyholder his cash surrender value. He has to pay the company interest, of course, just as he would have to pay a bank if he borrowed from it rather than withdraw his savings, but he has no obligation to repay the principal. What is more, because cash value insurance combines decreasing term insurance with a type of savings account, the face value of his policy would be reduced by the amount of any indebtedness if a policy loan were outstanding at the time of death.

Other Creditor Relationships

A creditor status also is created with the purchase of a bond, which is an obligation to pay a principal amount at some stated future date, and interest at a fixed rate during the life of the bond.

Although most bondholders have the same investment purposes—safety and income—as those who lend their money to banks, savings and loan associations, or credit unions, all bonds (except government savings bonds) fluctuate in price. Government bonds and top-rated corporates sell in line with prevailing money rates, which, of course, continually vary. The prices of other bonds reflect not only current money rates, but also the obligor's credit standing. Therefore, a bond might be sold or redeemed for more or less than it cost. The principal types of bonds available include:

Government Securities. These are the safest of all fixed dollar investments. Aside from Series E and H savings bonds, they include Treasury *Bonds* which are long-term obligations, Treasury *Notes* which are issued for periods of 1 to 7 years, and Treasury *Bills* which have maturities of up to one year, although usually they are sold for 13 or 26 week periods. Yields depend upon current money market rates, and in recent times the bills have ranged from 3.5% in early 1971 to 9.93% in mid-1974. Generally, the less volatile, longer term bonds return the most and short term bills the least. The minimum denomination of bills normally is $10,000, but notes are available for as little as $1,000.

New bills are sold almost every Monday throughout the year, and new notes may be offered about once a month. You may place an order through your bank or broker, but to save the $25 or so commission it would cost, you may apply in person or submit by mail a "non-competitive" bid on forms available from the nearest Federal Reserve Bank. Once issued, government securities are traded over-the-counter at prices which may be more or less than their cost.

Several types of quasi-governmental obligations also are available, such as Federal National Mortgage Association ("Fannie Mae") notes and debentures, Government National Mortgage Association ("Ginnie Mae") pass-throughs, Federal Land Bank Bonds and others. However, none is likely to be of much interest to most individual investors.

Municipal and State Bonds. Local and state governments also issue bonds for various purposes. Some are "general obligations" of the insurer, which places its taxing power behind them; others are "revenue" bonds, such as those issued to construct turnpikes, airports, sports arenas, or other facilities, which depend upon revenues generated by the facility. Most are quite secure, but some are of dubious value. The returns reflect current market rates as well as the bond's rating, which may range from gilt-edge to perilous. The interest rates on the better municipals are less than those of United States obligations, but their appeal is that the earnings are *exempt from federal income taxes.* Also, all but seven states exempt income from in-state bonds owned by a taxpayer, although most states tax earnings from out-of-state bonds and tax-exempt funds.

Tax-exempt interest is something that should not be dismissed lightly. With ever-increasing family incomes, reflecting the decrease in the dollar's purchasing power and the sharp rise in the number of wives who work outside the home, more and more people are moving into income tax brackets that make tax-free earnings attractive. Table 7.1 shows how much of a taxable yield is required at different income levels to equal various tax-exempt yields.

Prior to the introduction of unit trusts in 1961 and municipal bond funds in 1976, smaller investors seldom ventured into this market. Direct purchases can have some drawbacks: municipal bonds usually are issued in minimum denominations of $5,000; selection of appropriate issues requires some degree of expertise; diversification is difficult unless large resources are available; if the issue is subject to refunding and interest rates decline, the holder might lose an attractive yield; safeguarding the bonds themselves and clipping coupons might be an inconvenience; maturities of most new issues are quite long (often 20 to 40 years); and there is no ready market for most issues, particularly those of obscure school districts and other government entities, so if a holder wanted to sell before maturity, he might have difficulty in finding a buyer. These disadvantages can now be avoided by buying either unit trusts or muni-funds.

Unit trusts. Many of the larger brokerage firms sponsor municipal bond trusts in which units are sold, usually for $1,000 each. The trust's holdings, a package of investment grade tax-exempt securities, are established before the initial offering, and are retained until maturity or redemption. Hence, a buyer receives a fixed yield over a long period of time. Unit holders are mailed interest checks each month, and the sponsor maintains a market in the units so that a holder may sell (at what could be more or less than his cost) at any time. A sales commission of around 4% is charged, but there are no management or redemption fees. Anyone interested in this type of investment should contact his brokerage firm, or write the

TABLE 7.1. Equivalent Taxable Yields from Tax-Exempt Income (under Revenue Act of 1978).

Taxable Income		Tax Bracket	Equivalent Taxable Yield of Tax-Free Yield of:			
Single Return	Joint Return		4%	5%	6%	7%
	$11,900–16,000	21%	5.06%	6.33%	7.57%	8.86%
$10,800–12,900	$16,000–20,000	24%	5.26%	6.58%	7.89%	9.21%
$12,900–15,000		26%	5.41%	6.76%	8.11%	9.46%
	$20,000–24,600	28%	5.56%	6.94%	8.33%	9.72%
$15,000–18,200		30%	5.71%	7.14%	8.57%	10.00%
	$24,600–29,900	32%	5.88%	7.35%	8.82%	10.29%
$18,200–23,500		34%	6.06%	7.58%	9.09%	10.61%
	$29,900–35,200	37%	6.35%	7.94%	9.52%	11.11%
$23,500–28,800		39%	6.56%	8.20%	9.84%	11.48%
	$35,200–45,800	43%	7.02%	8.77%	10.53%	12.28%
$28,800–34,100		44%	7.14%	8.93%	10.71%	12.50%
$34,100–41,500	$45,800–60,000	49%	7.84%	9.80%	11.76%	13.73%
	$60,000–85,600	54%	8.70%	10.87%	13.04%	15.22%
$41,500–55,300		55%	8.89%	11.11%	13.33%	15.56%
	$85,600–109,400	59%	9.76%	12.20%	14.63%	17.07%
$55,300–81,800		63%	10.81%	13.51%	16.22%	18.92%
	$109,400–162,400	64%	11.11%	13.89%	16.67%	19.44%
$81,800–108,300	$162,400–215,400	68%	12.50%	15.63%	18.75%	21.88%
Over 108,300	Over 215,400	70%	13.33%	16.67%	20.00%	23.33%

company that started it all: John Nuveen & Co., Inc., 61 Broadway, New York, N. Y. 10006, for an explanatory booklet and prospectus of a current offering.

Muni-Funds. Another way relatively small investors may participate in the municipal bond market is through purchase of shares in a municipal bond mutual fund. These did not exist before October 1976, when legislation was enacted permitting investment companies to pass tax-free interest through to their shareholders. The muni-funds serve many of the same purposes as the unit trusts, but there are significant differences. Most muni-funds are no-load (i.e., no sales commission), but they charge management fees that range from about 0.4% to 1% of net assets a year. Initial purchases can be made for as little as $1,000 to $2,500, with no minimum necessary for additional purchases. Also, the muni-funds are "managed," which means that bonds are bought or sold whenever the fund believes it would be advantageous to do so. Hence, instead of being fixed, the yields vary.

Whether portfolio switches and varying yields are an advantage or disadvantage depends to an extent upon future interest rates and bond markets. If rates are high at the time of purchase and later decline, a unit trust might lock up a good return; conversely, if rates are low and later increase, a skillfully managed muni-fund might fare better. Of course, if interest rates on municipals collapse suddenly, massive redemptions by both muni-fund and unit trust holders might require sales of the best bonds in their portfolios, leaving only the more illiquid. Also, if what had once been an investment grade issue loses its attractiveness (once upon a time, even New York City's obligations were thought to be sound), shrewd muni-fund managers might detect the situation in time to avoid a large loss, but a unit trust would be locked-in. Nothing, of course, is risk-free.

Muni-funds also offer some services not available from the trusts. At the shareholder's option, his earnings may be reinvested automatically in additional shares; redemptions by telephone are permitted; and if the sponsor is a multi-fund, transfers between its muni-fund and its other funds may be readily made. More information may be obtained by writing or telephoning some of the funds. More than a score are available, including:

Fidelity Municipal Bond Fund
P.O. Box 832
82 Devonshire Street
Boston, Mass. 02103
(800–225–6190)
Dreyfus Tax-Exempt Bond Fund
600 Lincoln Boulevard
Middlesex, N.J. 08846
(800–325–6400)
Scudder Managed Municipal Bonds
175 Federal Street
Boston, Mass. 02110
(800–225–2470)

Rowe Price Tax-Free Income Fund
100 East Pratt Street
Baltimore, Md. 21202
(800–638–1527)

Corporate Bonds. As evidence of indebtedness, bonds rank ahead of preferred or common stock in a corporation's capital structure. A corporate bond may be issued in either registered or bearer form. If registered, the owner's name is recorded with the issuer, who sends the owner a check whenever interest is due, which normally is semi-annually. Bearer bonds are not registered, and to receive interest payments the holder must clip a coupon attached to the bond and send it in for payment. Some corporate bonds are traded on securities exchanges, but most are bought and sold over-the-counter. Prices continually fluctuate, of course, depending upon money rates and the issuer's credit standing, but these fluctuations usually are small compared to those of the issuer's common stock. The yield on most corporate bonds is more than on government bonds, and in recent times returns of 8% to 10% have been common on high quality issues.

Prices of bonds are quoted as a percentage of face value, so a price of 88 for a $1,000 bond means it costs $880. Because interest is paid on the face value, a $1,000, 9% bond pays $90 a year, regardless of its market price. Thus, if it were purchased at 88, the current yield would be over 10%, and the yield to maturity even higher. Most bonds are issued in amounts of $1,000 and may be bought or sold through brokerage houses for a commission of $5 or $10 per bond.

The principal advantage of bonds is that funds used to purchase them are safer than if invested in the issuer's equity capital. However, as with any fixed-dollar asset, their greatest drawback in a long-range investment program is that they do not afford any protection against inflation. Since the late 1950s, the current yield on bonds has been more than that of high-quality common stocks. Despite this, bonds in general are still rejected, except for short-term purposes, by a formidable number of investors, who realize that the true return, after allowing for the year-after-year increase in the cost of living and after income taxes, is far below the apparent return. This unattractiveness is readily apparent in the case of higher income individuals. For example, a person in the 50% income tax bracket immediately loses half of the return from a bond purchased at par which has a 9% coupon; then, if 6% is lost by increased living costs, his net return would be negative. Similarly, even for a single person earning $12,000 a year, the real return would be less than 1%.

Because of these considerations, long-maturity bonds are of questionable value in any estate-building program. For elderly persons, some widows, and others who need a secure, high income from their investments, however, bonds can be superior to keeping funds in savings institutions.

Alternately, shares in one of the "income" investment management companies or in one of the newer, intermediate-term bond funds might be considered. Fidelity Thrift Trust, P.O. Box 832, Boston, MA 02103, and Dreyfus Intermediate Bond Fund, 600 Lincoln Blvd., Middlesex, NJ 08846, are examples of the latter. With the average maturities of their holdings less than seven years, they are designed for those who seek higher returns than a money market fund might provide, without running the risk of very long-term, fixed-dollar investments.

Keep in mind, though, that bond prices fluctuate. For example, some bonds issued in the mid-1960s with then-competitive yields of 5% or so were selling at half their face value a decade later. Simply stated, when long-term interest rates increase, the prices buyers are willing to pay for already issued bonds decrease; conversely, if interest rates decrease, bond prices go up. The lesson should be clear: *never* buy long-term bonds when credit is plentiful and interest rates are low.

Convertible Bonds. Various other types of corporate obligations are available, but except for convertible bonds or debentures, most are of little interest to private investors. In theory, *convertible debentures* can be an ideal investment. Because they are a corporate obligation, convertibles afford greater safety than the common stock of the issuer, and they also provide a current return, which many growth stocks do not. Also, due to the conversion privilege, they appreciate with the common stock once the conversion point is reached. To illustrate, if a corporation issues 6% debentures which are convertible into its common stock at the rate of one share of common for each $50 face value of debenture, a $1,000 debenture could be exchanged at the holder's option for 20 shares of common stock at any time before maturity or before the corporation redeems the issue. If the common is selling at $40 when the debentures are issued, the conversion privilege would not be of any immediate value, of course, other than as a future call on the common. However, if the common stock were to go to $60, the debenture would be worth at least $1,200. Conversely, if the common were to decline 50% to $20, the debenture would not likely go down as much, for it then would tend to sell in line with what it would be worth as an obligation of the issuer.

Convertibles, then, can serve as a hedge against a declining market, as well as a means of participating in any advance of the common stock. These advantages are well known, of course, so a buyer must be particularly selective in what he buys and how much he pays. Initially, of course, only those convertibles of companies whose common stock is attractive for appreciation potential should be considered. Next, as a rule of thumb to prevent paying an excessive premium, no more than some small percentage above conversion value should be paid, and the debenture should be selling at a price not too far removed from its par value. Bargains are not easily found in this type of investment, but when they are discovered the rewards can be attractive.

Money Market Funds. From late 1973 to early 1975, a combination of double-digit inflation, a tight money supply, and a high demand for funds caused short-term money rates to reach unprecedented levels. However, the high returns—which often ranged from 9% to over 12%—generally were available only to those institutions or individuals with $100,000 or more to lend. Persons of more limited means usually had to settle for what (after taxes and loss of purchasing power) amounted to negative yields from savings institutions.

To enable the man-on-the-street to participate in the more attractive yields, a number of "money market" or "cash equivalent" mutual funds were organized. These funds, most of which require initial investments of $1,000 to $5,000 but permit additions of much smaller sums, soon attracted billions of dollars from small savers and others. By providing a needed service, they appear to have carved out a permanent niche for themselves in the financial marketplace.

No sales commission or redemption fee is charged by most of the funds, which earn their income from management fees that commonly are 1% a year. Their holdings consist of high-grade, short-term obligations (e.g., large denomination certificates of deposit issued by the nation's biggest and strongest banks, commercial paper of the largest corporations, bankers' acceptances, and government securities). Dividends are declared daily and may be automatically reinvested for a compounding effect. Most funds offer plans that permit a shareholder to have all or part of his investment redeemed and transferred to his bank account within one business day, and also to write checks of $500 or more against his fund account.

Although the 11% to 12% returns of 1974 are a thing of the past, many individuals who have a few thousand dollars reposing in a conventional savings account might do well to consider a money market fund instead. Because of the nature of their holdings, the money placed in shares, although not insured, is highly secure, and as long as the yields (which fluctuate daily) equal or exceed the 5¼% to 6% paid by banks, savings and loans, or credit unions, the funds have the advantage.

About 50 or so money market funds are available. A few of the larger ones are listed below. A postal card or toll-free telephone request for a prospectus and information booklet will provide more detailed information.

Dreyfus Liquid Assets
600 Lincoln Blvd.
Middlesex, N.J. 08846
(800) 325-6400

Fidelity Daily Income Trust
P.O. Box 832
82 Devonshire Street
Boston, Mass. 02103
(800) 225-6190

Rowe Price Prime Reserve
100 E. Pratt Street
Baltimore, Md. 21202
(800) 638-1527

Scudder Managed Reserves
175 Federal Street
Boston, Mass. 02110
(800) 225-2470

Table 7.2 will give you a quick comparison of some of the more common fixed-dollar uses of savings. The early-1979 rates shown may be quite different now, of course.

TABLE 7.2. Approximate Yields on Representative Fixed-Dollar Uses of Savings (May 1979).

	Average Annual Yield (%) Banks	Thrifts	Minimum Deposit or Purchase	Maturity	Remarks
Banks & Thrift Institutions					
Passbook Accounts	5.39	5.65	None	None	Fully taxable. Indicated yields assume daily compounding.
Time Deposits	5.92	6.18	None	90 days	*Returns on 6-month money market certificates (MMC's) are pegged to discount rates at weekly T-bill auctions.
	9.62*	9.62*	$10,000	6 months	
	6.18	6.72	None	1 year	
	7.75**	8.00**	None	4 years	**Returns on 4-year savings certificates at the thrifts are 1% less than the average 4-year rate for Treasury securities and 1¼% less at banks.
	8.04	8.33	None	8 years	
Government Obligations					
Savings bonds					
Series E	6.50		$18.75	5 years	Tax on Series E interest may be deferred until bonds redeemed. Exempt from state/local income taxation.
Series H	6.50		$500	10 years	
Treasury Issues					
Bills	10.03		$10,000	13 weeks	
	10.28		$10,000	26 weeks	
Notes	9.83		$1,000	1 year	
	9.25		$1,000	5 years	
Bonds	9.31		$1,000	15 years	
	9.15		$1,000	25 years	
Municipal Bonds					
High quality	6.27		$5,000	15–20 years	Exempt from federal income taxation.
Medium quality	6.85		$5,000	15–20 years	
Mutual Funds					
Tax-exempt bond funds	5.77		$1,000	None	Exempt from federal income taxes
Money-market funds	9.83		$1,000	None	Fully taxable.
Bond funds	8.36		$1,000	None	Fully taxable.

NON-FIXED-DOLLAR ASSETS

Equity Capital

All corporations have common (or capital) stock, and some also have preferred stock. Both classes are known as equity capital, and the owner of either type, unlike a bondholder, owns part of the business.

Preferred Stock. As the name suggests, the preferred stock of a company has priority over the common stock in certain respects. The dividend on the preferred is fixed and must be paid before any dividend can be paid on the common. Most preferreds are cumulative, which simply means that if a dividend is not paid when due, it accumulates so that at the next dividend date the stockholder is entitled to the usual dividends for the two periods. Also, the preferred has a prior claim against assets if the corporation is liquidated. However, the preferred shareholder generally has no vote. Because of their fixed dividends and priorities, preferred stocks are safer than the common stock of the same corporation, and the prices of preferreds are relatively more stable. Preferred stocks rank just below bonds of the same corporation in security, and usually yield more.

Straight preferred stock has the same major disadvantage of other fixed dollar investments: no protection against the decreasing purchasing power of the dollar. Hence, for long-term estate building purposes, there usually are better uses for savings. One of these is *convertible preferred stock,* which is a relatively conservative way to participate in the growth of a business.

Convertible preferred, similar to convertible debentures, may be exchanged for common stock at a predetermined rate, so it will advance with the common once the conversion point is reached. Also, due to its greater safety and fixed return, it tends to decline less than the common in weak markets. Because of these advantages, convertibles generally sell at prices above their current conversion values. In periods of market weakness, some high-grade convertible preferreds might sell at prices at which their dividend yields are 10% or more; although in many cases the depressed common stocks into which the preferreds might be converted would have to double or more for the conversion privilege to equal the preferred's market price, they nevertheless can provide an attractive investment for long-term buyers.

Common Stock. At the bottom of the corporate totem pole in terms of safety of principal, but at the top in terms of capital gain potential is the common (or capital) stock. As owners of the business, common stockholders have a voice in certain corporate matters and elect the directors, who in turn appoint the management. After all prior charges are met (e.g., bond interest, preferred dividends), the common stockholders participate in any distribution of earnings. Whether earnings are distributed depends, of course, on the directors' decision, and not all corporations pay dividends. Some may have insufficient or no earnings, while others may be expanding so rapidly that the directors prefer to reinvest all earnings in the business.

The recent average return has been about 5.9% on high-quality industrial stocks and about 8.9% on utilities. Many medium-grade stocks yield more, while the return on some speculative commons, which all but the most experienced trader should avoid, might be even greater. There is nothing static about common stock dividends, of course. In favorable years disbursements may be increased, and in poor years they may be decreased or eliminated. The long-range trend has been upward, however, with only sporadic declines. While dividends are not unimportant, especially for those who depend upon such income to meet living expenses, investors concerned with long-term estate building should not be especially influenced by current return, for their primary goal is capital appreciation over a period of years.

Options

In 1974, the Chicago Board Options Exchange (CBOE) inaugurated the first organized market in options. Previously this had been known as put and call trading, and was a relatively obscure practice. Since then, the buying and selling of what are now simply called "options" has become the fastest growing segment of the securities business. Currently, call options on more than 200 stocks are traded on the CBOE, American, Pacific, Philadelphia, and Midwest Exchanges, and the number is continually growing. Put option trading in a few stocks commenced in mid-1977.

A call option entitles the holder to buy ("call") 100 shares of a particular stock at a specified price (the "striking price") within a certain period of time. Conversely, a put option permits the holder to sell ("put") stock at a predetermined price within the option period. The striking prices as well as the expiration dates are set by the exchange listing the option. Options at several different striking prices for the same stock may be available, since the exchange will issue a new class of options of 5, 10, or 20 point intervals (depending upon the price at which the stock is trading) whenever there has been a significant change in the stock's price. The expiration dates are fixed at 3 month intervals out of 9 months in the future. The prices (called "premiums") at which options are bought and sold result from competitive bidding on the exchange floor. The more time remaining before the expiration date, the more an option will trade at, of course, as the chances of an appreciable advance are that much greater.

Neither certificates nor contracts are actually issued, for transactions are merely entered in the exchange's and the broker's computers. All trading is reported on a ticker system as it occurs, and the financial press publishes all activity for the previous day (see Figure 7.2).

Writing Options. Options may be used for purposes ranging from rank speculation to staid conservation. Sellers who own the stock against which the option is written (the "underlying stock") might have a tax motive (e.g., to convert what would otherwise be a short term and hence fully taxable gain into a long term gain), but usually they seek to decrease risks and increase income. For example, if someone owns 100 shares of a particular stock at $75 a share, he might sell ("write") a 6-month option against it with a striking price of 80. For this, he might receive $9 a share, or a total of $900 minus commissions. If the stock were to fail to reach the striking price before the option expires, he would still have his 100 shares plus the premium. He might then sell another option on the same shares, further reducing his investment risk.

If the stock were to go above the striking price, however, the option probably would be exercised, which would then limit the seller's gross gain to $1,400 (the $900 premium plus the $500 difference between the striking price and the cost for the stock) on his $7,500 investment. Thus, he would realize an 18% gain over a 6 month period, which isn't all that bad—unless the stock happens to

FIGURE 7.2 *Options Trading Table.*

Option	&	price	Aug	Nov	Feb	
C Data		...30	9	8¾	a	38⅜
C Data		...35	4¾	5⅝	5¾	38⅜
C Data		...40	1 11-16	3⅛	3¾	38⅜
GnDyn	o	...32	11-16	b	b	29¾
GnDyn	o	...36	3-16	b	b	29¾
Gn Dyn		..30	1¾	2¾	3½	29¾
Gn Dyn		..35	¼	⅞	1⅜	29¾
Gen Fd		...25	4¼	a	5⅝	29¼
Gen Fd		30	a	1¼	a	29¼
Gen Fd		35	1-16	a	a	29¼
Hewlet		...80	16⅛	18½	20⅞	96½
Hewlet		...90	8¾	11¼	13	96½
Hewlet		...60	3	5⅝	a	96½
H Inns		...15	5¼	5⅝	5⅞	20
H Inns		...20	1¾	2⅝	3¼	20
Honwll		50	19⅝	b	b	69¾
Honwll		60	10⅝	11¾	a	69¾
Honwll	p	...60	3-16	13-16	1⅜	69¾
Honwll		...70	3⅛	4⅝	5¾	69¾
Honwll	p	...70	2 11-16	3¾	4¼	69¾
Honwll		...80	¼	1 5-16	2¼	69¾
Honwll	p	..80	10⅝	a	a	69¾
In Flv		20	a	a	2⅜	20⅜
In Flv		25	1-16	5-16	9-16	20⅜
Manv		...20	a	4⅞	5⅛	24⅜
J Manv		...25	¾	1¼	1⅞	24⅜
MGIC		25	1⅞	2⅞	a	25
Mobil		65	11¾	a	b	75¾
Mobil		70	7	a	a	75¾
Mobil		80	⅞	2 1-16	3	75¾
N Semi		...15	10	a	b	25¼
N Semi		...20	6	6½	7⅜	25¼
N Semi		...25	2⅜	3½	4	25¼
N Semi		...30	13-16	1 9-16	2¼	25¼
Occi		15	6⅝	6⅝	7⅛	21½
Occi		20	1⅞	2⅝	3⅛	21½
Occi		25	¼	11-16	1	21½
Raythn		...40	7¼	a	a	47⅛
Raythn		...45	2¾	a	a	47⅛
Raythn		...50	9-16	1½	a	47⅛
Rynlds		50	a	7¼	a	56⅜
Rynlds		60	⅜	⅞	a	56⅜
Slumb	o	.53⅜	22⅝	a	b	76
Slumb	o	..60	16¼	a	b	76
Slumb	o	.66⅝	9¼	a	b	76
Slumb	o	.73⅜	4	6	b	76
Slumb		...60	15¾	a	17	76
Slumb		.70	6⅞	8¾		76
Slumb		.80	1¼	2¾		
Skyl			1		15-16	
Sk					⅛	

Courtesy of Associated Press Newsfeatures

double in the same period. Another risk is that within the call period, the stock might advance to, say, 95 (at which point the option seller could have sold his shares for a $2,000 gross profit), then decline to, say, 50 by the time the option expired.

Options may be sold "naked" (without owning the underlying stock) as well as "covered." This is roughly akin to shorting a stock the seller does not own, and reeks with risk even though protective stop orders may be used. (Or as Daniel Drew, one of the colorful financiers of an earlier day, put it, "He who sells what isn't his'n, must buy it back or go to pris'n.")

Buying Options. Options might be bought to limit dollar risks or to increase leverage. In the example above, whoever bought the option might have instead used his $900 to buy 12 shares of the stock. If the stock then advanced from 75 to 100, his gain would be $300 or about 33% less commissions. However, if he thought the stock would advance sharply over the near term and instead purchased the option (which he could resell later rather than exercise), a move from 75 to 100 would mean a profit of close to $1,100 or about 122%. That's leverage. Of course, if the stock never reached the striking price, he would be out his entire $900, but this would be the full extent of his loss regardless of how far the price declined. Conversely, if he had invested $7,500 to buy 100 shares and the stock dropped drastically, his loss would have been much greater.

Option traders use numerous sophisticated techniques such as hedges and spreads (including such esoteric types as "perpendicular," "butterfly," and "sandwich") to enhance their chances of success, and there is even a means of using options as tax shelters. All of these are beyond the purpose of this book, but a small or inexperienced investor should realize that he would be up against some heady competition. Moreover, unless he has adequate capital to move in and out frequently, the commissions alone could soon eat him up.

A sure way to rapid riches, option buying isn't, for over any extended period of time, the odds favor the sellers. But even they can lose on balance despite the premiums they pocket, if they stick with it long enough. Thus, anyone lacking considerable experience and ample reserves who might be tempted to play in this newest game in town would do well to heed the caveat in the prospectus that "no investor should commit any amount of money to the purchase of options unless he is able to withstand (a total) loss." The prerequisites suggested for anyone thinking of trading options include (1) an interest in and experience with stocks; (2) a thorough knowledge of how the options markets function; (3) a sizeable investment portfolio (at least $50,000, and preferably $100,000 is recommended, of which no more than 5% to 10% should ever be in options); and (4) the temperament to sustain wipe-outs, which might be expected in four out of five call option purchases (see, generally, *Business Week,* March 7, 1977, pp. 77–82).

To learn more about this market, write the Chicago Board Options Exchange, LaSalle at Jackson, Chicago, IL 60604, for free copies of the booklet, "Understanding Options," and the prospectus of the Options Clearing Corporation. Also, you should study some of the better books on the subject, such as Henry K. Clasing, Jr., *Dow Jones—Irwin Guide to Put and Call Options* (1978), and the more advanced Gary L. Gastineau, *The Stock Options Manual* (1975).

Obtaining Investment Information

Before launching any investment program, a prospective investor should obtain as much information concerning securities as his time and interest permit. Perhaps the best place to start is the financial pages of your newspaper. If you read these daily, after a while you will become somewhat conversant with the securities markets. In addition to reading the financial news and columnists, you might pick out a few stocks and follow their daily progress, which is recorded in the stock exchange tables (see Figure 7.3).

Reading these is not difficult. For example, if you were interested in Disney, you could tell from Figure 7.3 that its high for the year had been 47⅛ and its low 33. Following the name of the company, the current annual dividend (48¢ a share) is shown. The next figures are the yield (1.4%), then the price-earnings (PE) ratio (the price of the stock divided by its earnings per share for the preceding twelve months), which in the illustration is 11. The next

FIGURE 7.3. *New York Stock Exchange Table.*

52-Week High	52-Week Low	Stocks	Div.	Yld. %	P-E Ratio	Sales in 100s	High	Low	Close	Net Chg.
83	48	Datapnt		....	14	190	76¾	76⅜	76¾	+ ½
18	13⅜	Dayco	.50 b	3.4	3	28	15	14⅝	14⅝	− ½
84	65½	Dayc pf	4.25	5.4	...	z100	78	78	78	+ 3
43	33¼	DaytHd	1.60	4.1	3	524	39¼	39⅛	39⅛	− ¼
18¼	14⅝	DaytPL	1.74	11.2	8	88	15½	15¼	15½	+ ⅛
81¾	68	DPL pf	7.48	10.6	...	z180	70¼	70¼	70¼	+ 2¼
83	71½	DPL pf	7.70	10.6	...	z50	72¾	72½	72½	+ ½
79	72	DPL pf	7.37	10.1	...	z200	73⅝	72⅝	72⅝	− 1⅛
38⅝	30¼	Deere	1.60	4.7	7	527	34½	34	34⅜	+ ¼
14½	12⅛	DelmP	1.38	10.6	7	132	13⅛	12⅞	13	+ ⅛
58	36½	DeltaAir	1.20	2.9	6	128	41	40⅝	40⅞	+ ⅜
8½	5⅜	Deltec	2.50 c	....	21	10	6¼	6¼	6¼	......
15¼	7⅛	Deltona		....	17	14	11¼	11⅛	11⅛	+ ⅛
21¾	17¾	DenMf s	1.00	5.2	8	10	19¼	19¼	19¼	......
35	17¾	Dennys	.88	4.8	6	16	18½	18⅜	18⅜	− ⅜
25½	13¾	Dentsply	.88	5.9	9	27	15	14⅞	14⅞	......
17⅜	10¼	DeSoto	1.00	10.0	8	63	10¼ d	10	10	− ¼
16¾	13⅜	DetEd	1.60	10.7	7	198	15⅛	15	15	− ⅛
97	81	DetE pf	9.32	11.1	...	z150	84	84	84	......
83¾	67¼	DetE pf	7.45	10.6	...	z2300	72⅜	70¼	70¼	− 1¼
27½	24½	DE pfF	2.75	11.0	...	13	25	25	25	......
27½	24⅝	DE pfB	2.75	10.9	...	2	25⅛	25⅛	25⅛	+ ¼
24⅛	19¾	DetE pr	2.28	11.3	...	5	20½	20¼	20¼	− ¼
23¾	16	Dexter	1.00	5.0	8	9	20	19⅞	20	......
14⅞	9	DiGior	.48	3.8	8	139	13	12¾	12¾	+ ⅛
25	15½	DialCp	1.20	5.6	7	23	21⅞	21¼	21¼	......
40⅜	30	DiaInt	2.20 b	6.4	8	40	34¾	34⅜	34½	− ¼
29⅛	19	DiamS	1.48	6.8	7	397	21¾	21½	21⅝	......
25¾	14¾	Diebold	.60	2.4	13	61	24¾	24½	24⅝	+ ⅛
58¼	44⅜	DigitalEq		....	14	410	52⅜	51¾	51¾	− ¾
14⅛	7	Dillingm	.52	4.0	7	860	13⅝	12¾	12⅞	− ⅝
26¾	20½	Dillingm pf	2.00	7.5	...	13 u	27¼	26½	26½	......
34¾	27½	Dillon	1.32 b	4.3	10	8	31	30¾	31	+ ⅛
47⅛	33	Disney	.48	1.4	11	566	34½	34⅜	34½	+ ⅛
5½	1⅞	DivrsfdIn		....	9	123	4⅝	4½	4½	− ⅛
6½	2⅝	DivrsMtg		....	...	176	5⅛	4⅞	5	+ ⅛
20¼	13⅞	DrPeppr	.68	4.4	13	105	15½	15¼	15½	......
119	65½	DomeM g	.96	....	...	254 u	123	119½	121⅜	+ 2½
40	36½	DomeM wi		....	...	165 u		40½	40½	+
	3⅛	DonLJ		9	11	29		½	3⅜	...
		Donnly			9				25⅞	−
		Dor			6				16⅜	

Courtesy of Associated Press Newsfeatures

figure is the number of shares in hundreds (56,600) traded on the day in question. The next series of figures represent the high, low and closing prices at which the stock sold. These are followed by the change from the closing price on the preceding day. In this example, the difference was plus ⅛, or 12½¢ more than the price at which Disney closed the day before.

Going beyond the daily newspapers, far more comprehensive information can be obtained from reading *The Wall Street Journal,* which is published daily in four regional editions, and other periodicals such as *Barron's,* which is published weekly. Most experienced investors regard these two publications as indispensable. Also, studying some books on investments is suggested for those who wish to acquire a rudimentary understanding of securities. The classic is *Securities Analysis* by Graham, Dodd, and Cottle, but it is somewhat heavy for beginners. At the outset, you probably would do better with Venita VanCaspel, *The New Money Dynamics* (1978), and Louis Engel, *How to Buy Stocks* (6th ed., 1976), which is widely available in paperback. Going further, you might enjoy—as well as profit from—Gerald M. Loeb, *The Battle for Stock Market Profits* (1971). If bonds interest you, read Hugh C. Sherwood, *How to Invest in Bonds* (1974).

Reputable brokerage firms might be asked for their recommendations. The larger houses publish a plethora of investment information and advice, which usually is free to customers. Additionally, advisory services, which may cost $50 to $200 or more a year, are available. You may read the better ones, such as Standard and Poor's *Outlook, Moody's,* or *United Business Service,* in your broker's office or in larger public libraries.

If you want information about a particular company, you can write the company for a copy of its annual report or look it up in *Moody's* or *Standard and Poor's.* One of these reference sets is maintained in most large libraries, brokerage offices and banks.

Selecting Securities

The type of securities you buy for estate building purposes obviously should be suited to your objectives and personal situation. Too often, people who should own growth stocks invest instead in high yield issues or cyclicals, such as motors or metals, and people who should own safe securities buy highly speculative stocks in promotional companies.

A person who depends on investment income for part of his living expenses certainly should be conservative and seek both high yield and safety. Straight bonds, preferred stock, or high-quality common stock in blue-chip industrials or electric utilities might be the best places for his funds. Other investors may try to amass fortunes through short-term trading or by buying very speculative securities or options in hope of realizing large capital gains. Success requires not only extensive knowledge and considerable experience, but a fair amount of pure luck. The rewards can be high, but so is the risk; therefore, anyone who wants to match his skill with that of professional traders, or speculate on the future of promising but unseasoned small companies, must be prepared to accept sizeable losses.

Most young people are in the early stages of building an estate. By and large, they probably will do best by concentrating the bulk of their investment funds in the common stocks of good quality growth companies and leaving them there. But growth is an elusive term, and finding a genuine growth stock that sells at a reasonable price requires considerable effort or competent advice. A few securities salesmen are prone to refer to almost anything they want to sell as a growth stock. But most security analysts probably would agree that the growth label should be reserved for those companies which have been able to compound their earnings per share (EPS) by 10% or more a year with reasonable consistency over a period of several years, and seem likely to continue to do so into the foreseeable future.

Stocks in such companies normally sell at a high price-earnings ratio. Hence, if a true growth company is currently earning $1 a share, it might cost $15 to $20 or more, although it is unlikely to pay much, if any, cash dividend; at the same time, a company in a cyclical, static, or declining industry might also earn $1 a share and pay a 60 cents dividend, yet sell for only $7 or $8. Over the years, however, growth stocks have justified their higher multiples by outdistancing the general market, although they are not immune to sharp declines in bear markets, or to taking a backseat to high-yield industrials and utilities over extended periods of months or even years.

TABLE 7.3. Compound Growth Rates.

Rate	3 Years	4 Years	5 Years	10 Years
2%	1.06	1.08	1.10	1.22
4%	1.12	1.17	1.22	1.48
6%	1.19	1.26	1.34	1.79
8%	1.26	1.36	1.47	2.16
10%	1.33	1.46	1.61	2.59
12%	1.40	1.57	1.76	3.11
14%	1.48	1.69	1.93	3.71
16%	1.56	1.81	2.10	4.41
18%	1.64	1.94	2.29	5.23
20%	1.73	2.07	2.49	6.19
22%	1.82	2.22	2.70	7.30
24%	1.91	2.36	2.93	8.59
26%	2.00	2.52	3.18	10.09
28%	2.10	2.68	3.44	11.81
30%	2.20	2.86	3.71	13.79
40%	2.74	3.84	5.38	28.93
50%	3.38	5.06	7.59	57.67
60%	4.10	6.55	10.49	109.95
70%	4.91	8.35	14.20	201.60
80%	5.83	10.50	18.90	357.05
90%	6.86	13.03	24.76	613.11
100%	8.00	16.00	32.00	1,024.00

Although many factors other than a company's growth rate must be carefully weighed when making an investment decision, the historical importance of growth in estate accumulation programs is such that you should understand how it is determined. To approximate the growth rate of any company is a simple exercise, given a record of earnings per share (EPS) over the past several years (which can be found in financial publications such as S&P's Stock Reports) and a compound growth table (see Table 7.3).

IBM, for example, has been regarded as a premier, established growth company for some time. Over the most recent five-year period, its annual EPS grew from $2.70 to $5.32. If 5.32 is divided by 2.70, the result is 1.97. Under the five-year column in Table 7.3, the closest figure is 1.93. Going across to the rate column (and not bothering with interpolation) indicates that the percentage compounded EPS growth rate was over 14%.

Or consider Intel, a much smaller company still in an early, rapid growth phase. Although the firm is no more than several years old, it has become a leader in the burgeoning and highly volatile semiconductor industry, with sales expanding from $23 million in 1972 to over $400 million in 1978. Dividing 1978 EPS of $2.16 by the 50¢ per share earnings of five years earlier results in 4.32, which in turn means that its growth rate exceeded 30%. Such a torrid pace is not likely to be sustained indefinitely, for as a company becomes larger and matures, the rate at which its earnings increase is bound to decline. Also, of course, with smaller, less entrenched companies that lack the financial, marketing, and other strengths of the giants, an important consideration is whether they can continue to grow at all.

While no single investment approach can assure unqualified success, the prospects for *long-term* gains could be considerable for investors who buy shares in proven firms within industry groups that have the potential for growing at a rate in excess of the economy as a whole. Table 7.4 illustrates some of the industries and companies within them which might be considered. In virtually every example, the firm is involved in many activities other than the principal one listed; also, the risk levels vary significantly from company to

TABLE 7.4. Representative "Growth" Stocks.

Electronics & Business Eqmt.	Leisure Time	Medical	Miscellaneous
COMPONENTS	ENTERTAINMENT	PHARMACEUTICALS	ENERGY
Texas Instruments	Disney	Merck	Schlumberger
Intel		Pfizer	Geosource
Nat'l Semiconductor	SELF-HELP	Eli Lilly	Hughes Tool
Advanced Micro Devices	Black & Decker	Shering-Plough	Atlantic-Richfield
			Phillips Petroleum
COMPUTERS	FRANCHISERS	MED. SUPPLIES & EQMT.	Superior Oil
IBM	McDonalds	Johnson & Johnson	
Burroughs		Becton-Dickenson	PUBLICATIONS
Digital Equipment		Baxter Travenol	Dow Jones
Data General			Dun & Bradstreet
Amdahl		COSMETICS	Prentice-Hall
		IFF	
INSTRUMENTS			CHEMICALS
Hewlett-Packard			Air Products & Chem.
Perkin-Elmer			Dow Chemical
Beckman			Stauffer Chemical
Tektronix			
			OTHERS
OTHERS			Coca-Cola
Datapoint			Emery Air Freight
Four-Phase Systems			Levi Strauss
Spectra Physics			MMM
Sony			Millipore
Wang Laboratories			Philip Morris
			Proctor & Gamble
			Raychem
			Tandy

company. Obviously, mention of a particular firm as representative of its industry is not intended as a recommendation.

Where Securities Are Bought and Sold

While most people have heard of Wall Street, relatively few understand how the securities markets operate. The principal market place is the New York Stock Exchange, where currently more than 2,000 issues are listed. To qualify for listing, a company must meet stringent standards. The companies whose stocks are traded on the New York Exchange (the "Big Board") account for over two-thirds of the net profits earned by all companies in the country, and they pay almost three-fourths of all dividends.

The Exchange itself does not, of course, own or sell securities or set prices. Instead, it is a two-way auction market where bidders attempt to buy the shares they want at the lowest possible prices, and sellers try to obtain the highest prices for the shares they offer. Those who actually do the buying and selling have "seats" on the Exchange. There are 1,366 of these. About half are held by members of commission houses, and about one-fourth belong to specialists. A specialist's function is to maintain a fair, orderly and close market in the one or more stocks for which he is responsible. This often requires him to risk his own capital by buying at higher prices or selling at lower prices than the current bids or offers for a particular stock.

The nation's second largest securities market is the American Stock Exchange (the "Amex" or "Curb"), which also is located in New York's financial district. Its listing requirements are less strict than those of the New York Stock Exchange. There also are several regional exchanges throughout the nation, such as the Midwest Stock Exchange in Chicago, and the Pacific Coast Stock Exchange in San Francisco and Los Angeles. The principal options trading center is the CBOE in Chicago.

Not all stocks are traded on securities exchanges, however. In number of transactions and in dollar volume, the vast over-the-counter market dwarfs that of all exchanges. Trading in unlisted (over-the-counter) securities is by negotiation rather than auction. Sometimes a broker makes a market in particular stocks, in which case, acting as a principal rather than as an agent, he will buy the securities himself or will sell them from his holdings. If he does not make a market in the particular security a customer wants to buy or sell, he will buy it from or sell it to another dealer who does. There is no common meeting place similar to that provided by the exchanges. Rather, over-the-counter negotiations are conducted over a complex teletype and telephone network. Current bid and ask prices for all but the more obscure companies are readily available to brokers through the computerized NASDAQ quotation system.

Although many highly speculative issues of dubious value are traded over-the-counter, so are many staid and high quality stocks, such as those of virtually all investor-owned life insurance companies and banks. And while it has been a fertile area from which a number of companies have gone on to achieve prominence or pre-eminence in their fields and return large profits to their early stockholders, most novice investors should stay out of the over-the-counter market, where substantial losses as well as gains can occur. There are always ample opportunities elsewhere.

Over the next few years, an entirely new type of stock market is likely to evolve. Because of the great strides made in data processing and communications over the past several years, Congress in 1975 directed the Securities and Exchange Commission to establish a national marketing system to meet certain legislative goals. A board was appointed whose studies could lead, in time, to an electronic linking of all markets. In the meantime, the National Association of Securities Dealers (NASD) has already launched a method (the Consolidated Quotation System) to provide bid and asked prices of NYSE stocks traded over-the-counter and on other exchanges. What all this portends is a possible demise of the regional exchanges; large brokerage firms dealing with retail customers from their own inventories of actively traded stocks; and greater assurance that investors will obtain the best prices available for the securities they desire to buy or to sell.

Doing Business with a Broker

Once you are ready to invest, you will need the services of a brokerage firm. Someone may recommend one to you, or you can refer to a telephone directory or advertisements in the financial pages of a newspaper. Usually, doing business with a member firm of the New York Stock Exchange is preferable to dealing with a non-member firm.

Opening an Account. Opening an account with a stockbroker is no more complex than opening a savings account. You will be asked if you are over 21 (the age of contractual capacity), your address, occupation, and the name of your bank. If you know what you want to buy, simply tell the representative (customer's man) assigned to you what it is, how many shares you want, and whether you want to buy it at the market price (the best price currently obtainable) or place a limit order (not more than certain price). When your order is executed, you will be billed. Payment is due within 5 business days. Your stock certificate will be mailed to you if you wish, or most brokers will keep it for you. After opening an account, you probably will conduct most of your future securities business by telephone.

Commissions. Since 1 May 1975, when "fully competitive" rates for all stock transactions replaced minimum fixed commission schedules, different brokerage firms have charged different amounts to execute orders for customers. Lacking the financial clout to force reductions, however, those engaging in transactions involving only a few hundred dollars may have to pay from 3% to 6%. As the size of an order increases, the commission decreases as a percentage of the total sales or purchase price, so that it might cost $60 or so to buy or sell 100 shares of a $30 stock (2%) and progressively less for larger transactions. The rates for very large orders, such as those usually placed by institutional investors, are negotiated between the customer and the brokerage firm; in some cases, this has resulted in reductions of more than one-half of the commission previously charged.

Some brokers offer multi-rate plans for small investors. These might provide reductions of up to 50% on sales of securities that had previously been purchased within a specified time of perhaps 30 to 60 days, or offer less expensive rates if the amount to be invested is prepaid. Also, some firms might offer lower rates for executing orders, but charge for research reports or other services such as computer analysis of stock holdings, or overnight notification of new recommendations.

If no-frills execution of orders is all a customer wants, a few barebones discount firms will provide it at rates one-third or more below those of the established brokerage houses. Some of the discounters are: Source Securities, New York; W. T. Cabe & Co, New York; Columbine Securities, Denver; C. Clayton & Co, Boston; Letterman Transaction Services, Newport Beach; and Rose & Co,

Chicago. A few might limit discounts to transactions of a few thousand dollars or more, or require sufficient business to generate some minimum amount, perhaps $250, in commissions per year.

In early 1979, the first of the big-time firms (Fidelity Management and Research, which manages over $6 billion in mutual fund and pension plan assets) moved into the retail discounting brokerage business. In time, it plans to offer cut-rate services throughout the country by means of toll-free WATS lines to its Boston headquarters. In addition, it will provide custodial services for its customers' securities, and pay short-term money market rates on credit balances left with it. If Fidelity's venture succeeds, it could have a significant impact on how the retail brokerage business is conducted by the large firms that are established in that field.

Experienced investors who do their own research and invest primarily in major stocks can save money in commissions by dispensing with the hand-holding that is provided by most salesmen for the larger firms. However, the discounters are not for everyone, and most people find the additional sums paid regular brokers worth the services and advice they receive.

Margin Accounts. Securities may be bought on credit, as may most other things. Since 1934, however, the government, through the Federal Reserve Board, has controlled the use of credit for this purpose by limiting the amount a broker may lend a customer to buy listed securities. Before then, brokerage houses fixed their own requirements, and in the late 1920s some reputable firms asked customers for only 10%. This condition undoubtedly aggravated the severe 1929–1933 market slump.

Under FRB control, the margin which purchasers have been required to put up has ranged from 40% to 100%. Currently, the rate is 50%, which means that a purchaser may borrow up to one-half of the cost from his broker, for which an interest charge (perhaps 1% to 2% above the prime rate) is made. At the present time, a customer must have at least $2,000 to open a margin account. Most over-the-counter stocks are not marginable, and brokerage firms generally will not margin any security that sells for less than $5 or $10 a share. If the FRB believes there is too much speculation in the market, it will increase the initial margin requirements. Conversely, the rate will be lowered to offset a falling market. Often, though, the desired outcome of a margin requirement change is not realized for several months.

Although the FRB establishes the initial margins, the exchanges fix the minimum requirements for the maintenance of accounts. Usually, a customer's equity may never be less than 25% of the market value of the securities in the account. Moreover, many brokerage houses independently establish higher minimums. If a customer's equity falls below the prescribed amount, he will be called upon to deposit more funds. If he fails to do so, his margined securities may be sold to satisfy his debt.

The use of margin obviously enables a buyer to exercise more leverage than he could with cash alone. For example, if a stock were selling at 40, $4,000 plus commission would be required to buy 100 shares. If the margin requirement were 50%, the same purchase on margin would cost 0.5 ($4,000), or $2,000 plus commission. If the stock were to move up to 60, the cash buyer would have a profit (excluding costs) of $2,000, or 50% of the sum he invested. The margin buyer, though, would have a gross gain of $4,000 or 200%. This, of course, is only one side of the coin. If the stock were to decline to 20, the cash buyer would be out 50% plus costs if he sold, while the margin buyer would have lost his entire investment.

The moral should be apparent: an inexperienced investor should never buy securities on margin. For adept traders, margin increases the potential for profits. But unless or until you acquire the skill and experience to use it sensibly, stick to cash, no matter how tempting the prospects for a particular security may appear to be at the moment.

Short Sales. The opposite of buying a security (going long) is selling short. This technique permits a person who believes the price of a particular stock will decline to borrow shares through his broker, sell the shares lent to him, and if his judgment was correct, later replace them at a lower price. Until the borrowed shares are replaced, the short seller must pay all dividends the company may declare. Eventually, of course, he will have to buy an equal number of shares on the open market, and sometimes a stock which seemed so vulnerable to a sharp decline continues to go up. While there is nothing complicated about selling short, it is an operation that is not well-suited for an amateur.

Periodic Investment of Small Sums

Very few young people are able to invest large sums of money; yet if they manage their personal finances sensibly, they should be able to save from $25 to $100 or more a month. This in time would enable them to build a comfortable estate by periodic small investments.

There are several ways to accumulate stocks with relatively small sums. But before venturing into the securities markets, a reasonable amount (perhaps equal to 4 to 6 months' pay) to provide for unforeseeable emergencies should be set aside in some convenient and readily accessible form, such as a savings account, Series E bonds, or a money market fund. Thereafter, surplus funds might be saved monthly and used to buy securities once or twice a year. Alternately, in the early stages of building an estate, consideration might be given to a mutual fund accumulation plan or some similar arrangement, such as an automatic stock investment plan. The latter, under which amounts as small as $20 a month will be deducted from a checking account to purchase fractional shares in any of two dozen or so listed stocks a depositor selects, is available from some of the larger metropolitan banks. A periodic investment plan of some sort could have advantages, the most apparent of which is that once a regular program is commenced, there is a greater likelihood that the funds intended for investment will be used for such purpose rather than spent for something else.

Another advantage of periodic investment is *dollar-cost* averaging, which simply involves investing the same sum of money in the same security at different times, as contrasted to buying a particular number of shares of the same security at the corresponding times. When the price of the shares is low, more can be purchased with the same number of dollars than when the price is high. The net result is that *the average price paid per share is less than the average price of the shares at the times of purchase.*

To illustrate, assume that on five different dates, the common stock of Baldachi Enterprises sold at 12, 16, 11, 9, and 12 (see Figure 7.4). The average price per share paid by anyone purchasing the same number of shares at each of the times would have been 60 divided by 5, or 12. However, if instead of buying the same number of *shares* each time, the same number of dollars—say $100—were invested, the number of shares and fractional shares acquired, exclusive of commissions, would have been 8.333, 6.250, 9.090, 11.111, and 8.333, or a total of 43.117, and the average price per share would have been $500 divided by 43.117, or about $11.60, as shown in Table 7.5. Although Baldachi sold at the same price on the dates that the first and last purchases were made, the same result—

FIGURE 7.4. Dollar Cost Averaging.

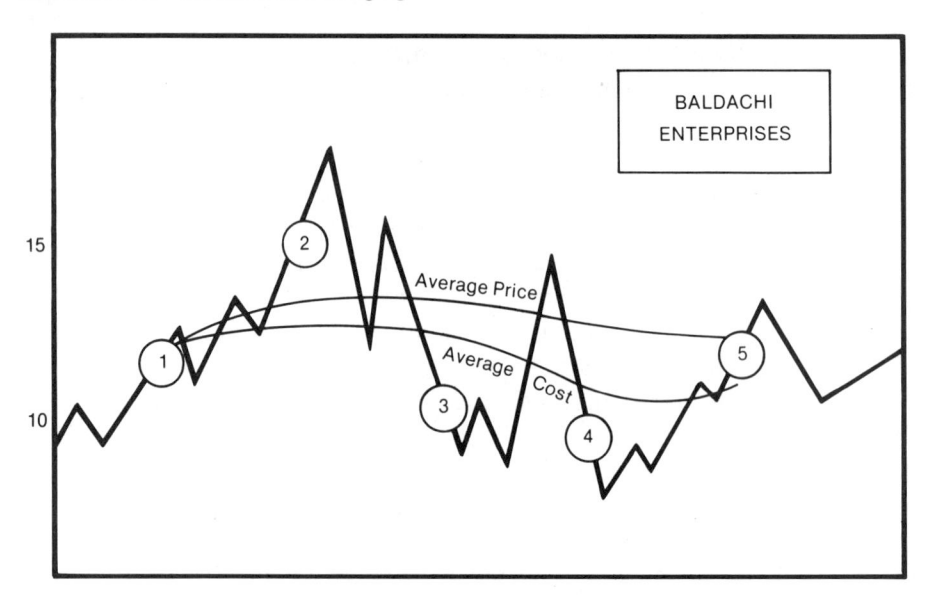

TABLE 7.5. Dollar Cost Averaging.

	Sum Invested	Market Price	No. Shares Bought	Total Shares	Average Market Price	Average Cost of Shares
1.	$100	12	8.333	8.333	$12	$12.00
2.	100	16	6.250	14.583	14	13.72
3.	100	11	9.090	23.673	13	12.67
4.	100	9	11.111	34.783	12	11.50
5.	100	12	8.333	43.116	12	11.60

a cost lower than the average cost per share—would be true regardless of whether the price had been higher or lower at the end of the period than it was at the beginning. Of course, if the shares progressively decline over a prolonged period of time (as most mutual funds, which had pushed the dollar-cost-averaging concept, did from the late-1960s until the mid-1970s), all the system ensures is that the buyer will have paid a higher average price than the shares are later worth.

Management Investment Companies

A management investment company provides continuous management and supervision of a portfolio. There are two basic types of such companies: the *closed-end* and the *open-end*; the latter are commonly called mutual funds.

Closed-End Companies. The closed-end companies are similar to most corporations in that their capital structures are fixed (closed). Capitalization usually consists of common stock only, but it might also include preferred stock, bonds, and other securities. Unlike a mutual fund, the number of shares outstanding does not fluctuate daily, for a closed-end company is not in the business of selling or redeeming its shares. Instead, the company's stock, similar to that of AT&T, IBM, and other publicly owned corporations, is traded either on an exchange or over-the-counter, so those who wish to purchase shares must do so from those who own and wish to sell them. Consequently, the price depends upon supply and demand, and may be more or less than the net asset value per share (total assets minus liabilities divided by the number of shares outstanding).

Customarily, and particularly in depressed markets, the shares of many closed-ends sell for less than their proportionate share of the company's assets. At times, this discount might be 25% to 50% or more, which can create a favorable buying opportunity. In a bullish market climate, shares of some companies may sell for more than the assets they represent. Whether the shares of a particular company are available at a discount or selling for a premium can be determined by checking the tables published weekly in Barron's or on Mondays in *The Wall Street Journal.*

The portfolios of the principal closed-end companies consist primarily of diversified common stocks. Some, however, concentrate in particular industries or in certain types of securities such as gold mining (ASA) or Japanese stocks (Japan Fund). The larger closed-ends include Tri-Continental, Madison, Lehman, and ASA, all of which are listed on the New York Stock Exchange.

You may obtain more information about this form of investment by writing the Association of Closed-End Investment Companies, 330 Madison Avenue, New York, N.Y. 10013.

Mutual Funds

The basic idea behind an open-end company is to pool relatively small sums of money from many investors to create a large investment fund through which shareholders might obtain some of the advantages normally available only to the biggest investors. These include continuous management of assets, reduction of risks through wide diversification, and the buying power inherent in size. Many people, including those who are inexperienced or who lack the time, interest, or resources to manage their own portfolios or to pay for such services, regard mutual funds as the best way for them to invest in equities. Their biggest disadvantage is that all but the smallest are so large that they must invest in a very broad spectrum of stocks; this usually limits performance to about that of the popular market averages.

Mutual fund shares are sold either by salesmen or by the fund itself. If you buy shares from a salesman, you will be purchasing what is called a "load" fund and in most cases paying a commission (load) of 8.5% more than the net asset value per share. This charge is deducted from the sum invested, so that an investor actually receives only $91.50 in asset value for each $100. Thus, the typical commission works out to about 9.3%. All of this goes to pay the distributor and the salesman, none to the fund.

For those who object to this rather sizeable bite, there are several funds that do not charge any commission. These "no-load" funds are sold at net asset value per share directly to investors by mail, thereby eliminating the middleman's costs. Whether a particular fund is a load or no-load type can be determined from the mutual fund columns of newspapers. If the "bid" price (the net asset value per share) is the same as the "asked" price (the cost of a share), or if the notation "NL" is used, the fund is a no-load. Figure 7.5 is an extract from such a table, showing the bid and asked prices of several funds; changes in net asset values occur daily, of course. Shares of both types of mutual funds may be redeemed at net asset value, usually without cost.

Both the load and no-load funds pay fees to their investment advisors. The amount may vary from fund to fund, but about ½% to 1% of total assets a year is usual. This cost, in addition to other expenses (e.g., salaries and overhead), is what, in effect, the investor pays for management services. The expenses of smaller funds often are greater than those of larger funds, but the average is around 1%; moreover, the difference between load and no-load funds is insignificant (e.g., less than 10 cents per $100 a year, on average). However, there can be decisive differences between particular funds of either type, so a prospective buyer should consider costs before investing.

The open-end companies have developed a broad variety of

FIGURE 7.5 *Mutual Fund Table.*

ChartFd	14.82	16.20	MMM	1.00	NL	Hor Man	14.85	16.05
Chase Gr Bos:			Optn	13.43	14.36	INAFd	11.43	12.26
Fund	6.49	7.09	TxFre	12.12	NL	ISI Group:		
Front	4.80	5.25	US Gvt	8.98	NL	Grwth	5.69	6.22
Share	7.20	7.87	Fidelity Group:			Incom	3.86	4.22
Specl	6.71	7.33	Agres	9.63	NL	Trst sh	11.85	12.95
CheapD	12.54	NL	Bond	8.03	NL	TrPaSh	3.20	...
ChemFd	7.40	8.09	Capit	8.42	9.20	Industry	4.20	...
Colonial Funds:			Contfd	10.54	NL	Intcap	1.00	NL
Sen Sec	8.78	9.60	Daily I	1.00	NL	Int Invst	15.01	16.40
Fund	9.23	10.09	Dstny	10.83	.....	Inv Guid	9.88	NL
Grwth	4.94	5.40	Eq Inc	18.17	NL	Inv Indic	1.22	NL
Incom	8.12	8.87	Magel	38.20	NL	Inv Bos	9.24	9.96
Optn	10.40	11.37	Mun Bd	9.52	NL	Investors Group:		
Tax Mg	13.74	15.02	Fidel	15.45	16.89	IDS Bd	5.42	5.62
Colu Gth	17.39	NL	Hi Yld	14.39	NL	IDS Csh	5.00	NL
Cwlth AB	.95	1.03	LtMun	9.26	NL	IDS Grt	7.04	7.66
Cwlth C	1.39	1.50	Puritn	10.36	11.32	IDS ndi	5.70	6.20
Comp Bd	8.49	9.13	Salem	5.39	5.89	Mutl	8.83	9.60
Comp Fd	7.72	8.30	Thrift	9.79	NL	Prog	3.44	3.74
Concord	14.61	NL	Trend	24.31	26.57	TaxEx	4.68	4.87
Cons Inv	9.62	10.00	Financial Prog:			Stock	18.26	19.85
Constel G	8.40	NL	Dyna	5.80	NL	Select	8.71	9.37
Cont Mut	6.19	NL	Indust	4.51	NL	Var Py	7.10	7.72
CvYld Se	11.53	12.33	Incom	7.23	NL	Inv Resh	5.90	6.45
Ctry Cap	11.27	12.18	Fst Investors:			Istel	24.80	25.57
Dly Cash	1.00	NL	Bnd Ap	14.70	15.85	Ivy	6.71	NL
DlyIncm	1.00	NL	Disco	7.60	8.31	JP Grth	10.38	11.28
Delaware Group:			Grwth	7.78	8.50	Janus F	18.90	NL
Decat	12.13	13.26	Incom	8.04	8.79	John Hancock:		
Delaw	11.28	12.33	Stock	7.87	8.60	Bond	17.30	18.80
Delch	8.71	9.52	FstMlt A	8.69	NL	Grwth	6.36	6.91
TxFre	9.21	9.64	FtMltDI	.93	NL	Balan	8.31	9.03
Delta	5.84	6.38	Fst Var	10.00	NL	TxEx	13.84	15.04
CshRsv	10.00	NL	44 Wall	unavail		Johnstn	21.69	NL
Dir Cap	3.06	3.34	Fnd Gth	4.02	4.39	Kemper Funds:		
DodCxB	21.76	NL	Franklin Group:			Incm	9.98	10.6?
DodCxSt	16.38	NL	Brown	3.56	3.8/	row	8.76	9
Drex Bur	10.63	NL	DNTC	8.63	9.	'd	11.30	'
Dreyfus Grp:			Grwth	6.20	/		1.0r	
Dreyf	12.07	13.1r	'tils	4.52				
evge	17.75	19	?m	1.9'				
As	1.00		`ov	8	'			

Courtesy of Associated Press Newsfeatures

portfolios to suit almost any investment objective. In addition to the previously mentioned bond funds and money market funds, these include balanced funds (which invest in both stocks and bonds), diversified common stock funds, and numerous specialized types such as those emphasizing growth, technology, or stocks in particular industries. At least one fund specializes in out-of-favor stocks on the sometimes valid theory that acting contrary to the majority offers the best assurance of success, and there are some funds that invest exclusively in the shares of other funds.

While the gains of most mutual funds exceeded those of "unmanaged" popular indices such as the Dow Jones Industrial Average in the 1962–1968 bull market, their losses were greater than those of most market indices during the 1968–1974 bear market.

Obviously, though, there has been a wide variance in the performances of different open-end companies. On balance, those emphasizing growth—which usually involves a higher risk factor— have shown excellent long-term results over the post-World War II period. Although they suffered the sharpest reversals during the

147

1973–1974 stock market debacle, they were the only category to outpace the popular averages during the strong markets of the first half of 1975. Don't expect more of the average fund, though, than to match the market averages. Professor Jensen of the University of Rochester Graduate Business School concluded in his definitive research paper:

> The evidence ... indicates not only that ... mutual funds were *on average* not able to outperform a buy-the-market-and-hold-policy (from 1945 to 1964), but also that there is very little evidence that any *individual* fund was able to do significantly better than that which we expected from mere random chance. [Jensen, *The Performance of Mutual Funds in the Period 1945–1964*, 23 Journal of Finance 389 (1968); see also Springer, *The Mutual Fund Trap* (1973)]

Load or No-Load? Although fewer than 25% of the more than 400 principal mutual funds are no-loads, they have been growing faster than the load funds in recent years as more and more small investors have become aware of their existence and have concluded that it does not make much sense to pay one-twelfth of their investment dollars to a salesman and distributor when no-load shares are available without any sales charge. For transparent reasons, many mutual fund salesmen deprecate the no-loads. In a word, humbug. The ultimate test is results, and in this respect:

> Numerous studies have made it clear that the performance of no loads is as good as that of load funds, and there is really no reason for an investor to pay the standard 9.3 percent sales charge. (Ehrbar, *Some Kinds of Mutual Funds Make Sense*, Fortune, July, 1975, p. 57).

Past performance is based on *average* results, of course, and averages cannot be purchased. Also, most no-loads have growth as their primary purpose, while many of the load funds concentrate on other objectives; and as previously mentioned, over the years growth type securities have outpaced the market as a whole. Salesmen are rapid to represent that the particular fund they are trying to sell has done better than the averages or no-loads in general. Often, this is true, but usually it is due to a higher risk factor. If there were any assurance that a load fund would outpace a no-load sufficiently to compensate for the acquisition costs, it might be the better buy. But no such guaranty can be given. Consequently, it makes little sense to pay a stiff fee to have something sold to you when you could buy at least the equivalent without any cost. And the widely touted services provided by salesmen, such as helping you select the fund best suited to your investment objectives, are more illusory than real unless you are an utter novice.

If mutual funds appeal to you as a means of commencing an investment program, a reasonable approach would be to carefully consider several of the no-loads and select the one or more you believe best suited to your objectives. A few of the principal equity no-loads are listed below. A complete roster is available from No-Load Mutual Fund Directory, Valley Forge, Pa. 19481, and for $4, NoLOAD FUND*X, 57 Post Street, San Francisco, Calif. 94104, will send you its current analysis of performances. Write several of the funds for a prospectus and a recent report, to provide you with a basis for making a comparison and an informed choice.

T. Rowe Price
100 E. Pratt Street
Baltimore, Md. 21201

Energy Fund
Neuberger & Berman Mgt.
522 Fifth Avenue
New York, N.Y. 10036

One William Street Fund
1 William Street
New York, N.Y. 10004

Johnston Mutual Fund
460 Park Avenue
New York, N.Y. 10022

USAA Capital Growth
9800 Fredericksburg Rd.
San Antonio, Tx. 78288

The Acorn Fund
120 S. LaSalle Street
Chicago, Il. 60603

Penn Square Mutual Fund
P. O. Box 1419
Reading, Pa. 19603

Detailed information about management investment companies is outlined in the current editions of Wiesenberger's *Investment Companies* or Johnson's *Investment Company Charts*; one or the other should be available in any moderately sized library. As a prospective purchaser, you should carefully investigate all facets of a company, including its past performance, objectives, relative prospects, and expenses before committing your savings. In other words, obtain sufficient information to be a buyer, not merely a sellee. In this connection, the advice of Professor Malkiel of Princeton might help:

1. Never buy a load fund. No-loads perform as well as and are particularly advantageous for dollar-cost averaging.
2. Pick a mutual fund on the basis of your willingness to take risks.
3. Buy closed-end funds whenever they are selling below their average historical discounts. [Malkiel, *A Random Walk Down Wall Street*, p. 213 (1973)]

Mutual Fund Accumulation Plans. With the small investor in mind, most funds have plans that enable purchasers to accumulate shares by periodic investments. Under most of these, dividends and capital gain distributions may be reinvested automatically. An important detail of any plan is how much it costs in commissions. As previously mentioned, the no-load funds sell directly to investors and do not charge any fee.

The load funds collect commissions on their plans in one of two ways. They either charge it at the time of each purchase (known as a "voluntary plan"), or they use a *front-end load,* which simply means they collect most of the total commissions payable over the entire period of the plan at the beginning, or front-end. If an investor carries an accumulation plan through to completion, which may take 10 to 15 years, the total commissions are about the same as those that would have paid with a level charge. But if the plan is dropped, commissions are paid on purchases that are never made.

The obvious drawbacks of a front-end load are that the buyer loses the use of a disproportionately large share of his early payments, and if he fails to complete his plan for any reason, he will have paid commissions which are never earned. One of the few advantages from an investor's viewpoint is that a front-end load furnishes some form of compulsion to complete his plan. To protect inexperienced buyers, though, some states such as California prohibit sales involving prepaid commissions. As a general rule, since there is little reason to buy a load fund rather than a no-load, there is even less reason to ever become ensnared in a front-end load.

Mutual Fund Withdrawal Plans. The idea here is not complicated: a participant simply purchases shares in a fund and requests that his regular dividends be supplemented with small withdrawals from principal, to enable him to receive a monthly check in some specified amount. The investment usually must be of some minimum amount, perhaps $5,000 or $10,000, and the annual withdrawal is generally limited to 10% or so of the sum invested.

Prior to the 1968–1974 decline, market values as a whole had appreciated to such an extent that under most plans a shareholder might have withdrawn 8% or more annually, and at the end of the period his principal sum would have had a market value greater than his initial cost.

Understandably, results like this are quite appealing to those who require a high income from their investments. Nevertheless, they are all based on past experience and do not, of course, justify expectations that comparable results will be achieved in the future. Hence, anyone considering a withdrawal plan as a means of supplementing his retirement income or his survivors' benefits should clearly recognize that he cannot reasonably anticipate that continuous increases in the value of his shares will always make up for any sums withdrawn from principal.

While the convenience of a mutual fund withdrawal plan is indisputable, a prospective buyer should consider whether he might not realize even better results by buying shares of one or more high quality, growth type stocks which, to the extent that cash dividends do not equal the income he desires, could be slowly liquidated.

Investment Counseling Firms

Another method of accumulating an estate in securities is available for those who, for one reason or another, would prefer not to make their own common stock selections but who do not find either mutual or closed-end funds an entirely satisfactory solution. This is to have an investment counseling firm manage your portfolio.

Until a few years ago, most portfolio managers, whether independent or affiliated with brokerage firms, were unwilling to work with small accounts. One hundred thousand dollars was a common minimum, and in some cases $1 million was needed for openers. Today, however, many brokerage firms as well as trust departments of larger banks offer portfolio management services for accounts ranging from $10,000 to $50,000, and several independent counseling firms provide such services for accounts valued at as little as $5,000. Due to the widespread disappointment of many investors with the performances of their common stocks or mutual funds during the 1969–1970 and 1973–1974 market declines, it is reasonably foreseeable that the number of firms offering portfolio management for small investors will expand within the next few years. They can make a great deal of sense for a great many people.

Essentially, all that is involved, once an investor has acquired the minimum sum required in cash or securities, is to open an account with one of the firms or trust departments and turn his cash or securities over to it, with an indication of what his investment goals are (e.g., long-term capital appreciation, high current income, safety of principal). From then on, the firm will make all the investment decisions, consistent with the investor's aims. Normally, with a minimum-sized account, it is not likely that more than 5 to 10 different securities will be purchased. Occasionally some will be sold and replaced by something else the firm then regards as more appropriate for the particular account, but "churning," or rapidly turning over a portfolio, would be unusual, for most firms do not make anything from the transactions. Instead, their income is derived from a small fee (1% to 2% a year on the value of a minimum portfolio, and less for larger accounts), which is payable annually or quarterly.

Upon entering into a management agreement with an investor, a counseling firm will open an account in his name with a brokerage firm it selects. Because orders on behalf of many investors may be lumped together, some savings on commissions is possible. Securities are held in the names of the individual portfolio owners, not of the counseling firm, and a portfolio owner may withdraw securities or cash from the account. The owner may close his account at any time, of course.

Whether a particular investor would fare better by having a counseling firm or a trust department manage his investments rather than by making his own decisions (aided, perhaps, by suggestions from his customer's man or an advisory service), or by turning the responsibility over to a mutual or closed-end fund, obviously depends upon the results achieved. Barring prescience, there is no assurance that stocks selected by others for an investor will outpace those he might have selected himself. However, once an investor who desires to have others make his investment decisions has accumulated several thousand dollars, he might consider placing a portion of his assets with a counseling firm or trust department. If the results are satisfactory, he might elect to switch more of his savings to his managed account. If not, he is at liberty to withdraw, perhaps poorer but wiser.

If you believe a managed account might be for you, ask some full service banks about arrangements they offer, or write to firms in the business such as Danforth Associates, Wellesley Hills, MA 02181 for information. Alternately, if you prefer to control your own portfolio but desire specific, individual investment advice, there are companies that for a fixed fee, regardless of the size or value of your holdings, provide counsel tailored to your particular objectives. The Investment Management Division of Babson's Reports, Wellesley Hills, Mass. 02181, is one of these.

Off-Beat and Other Investments

During the 1970s, the spurt in the rate of inflation and a declining stock market led many investors to seek some means other than stocks to protect and increase their capital. In addition to massive shifts into fixed-dollar securities offering unprecedented, high yields, these included raw or developed real estate; real estate syndicates; stock options; commodities futures; limited partnership interests in livestock feeding, citrus growing, or oil and gas drilling (where the primary purpose usually is income tax savings); silver bullion; art, stamp, and coin collecting; and even a short-lived spree in commodities futures options (which collapsed when the leading firm was forced into receivership, leaving countless get-rich-quick aspirants with dashed dreams and empty pockets).

These and similar uses for surplus funds have enriched countless persons, mostly the promoters or those engaged in the trade or business. Too often, individual investors have either suffered crippling losses or ended up with their capital locked in for years. There is nothing inherently wrong with such investments, of course, but if you are tempted, first make sure you do not jeopardize your estate, you can afford a wipe-out if expectations go awry, and—most importantly—*you know what you are doing*. The last caveat is meant to imply a degree of experience and expertise not found in most people, who necessarily must devote the bulk of their time and effort to their jobs.

chapter 8
How to Allocate Your Resources

The problem common to everyone in the process of building an estate is to make intelligent decisions about the allocation of his resources. Having surveyed the principles of life insurance and the fundamentals of investments, we will now proceed to some elementary observations that might help you decide how to use both to maximum advantage. How you actually go about accumulating a present estate, while at the same time providing financial security for your family in the event of your premature death, must be your personal decision, of course. But the more information you obtain and the more insight you acquire, the greater will be your chances of avoiding costly mistakes.

Aside from the problem of protecting dependents financially in the event death is premature, any responsible person also is concerned with acquiring sufficient means to meet various future needs, such as college expenses for children or supplemental retirement income. Simply accumulating cash or its equivalent is not a practical solution, of course, because dependents would be insufficiently protected early in a person's career, when the need for protection usually is the greatest. Consequently, the initial question is how dependents might be most effectively protected while an estate is being built.

LIFE INSURANCE

For the young person who has yet to acquire substantial assets, as well as for almost everyone else, the obvious answer to the protection problem is life insurance. Yet, as we have seen in Chapter 6, life insurance comes in so many forms that even a normally discerning person may have difficulty deciding which is the most advantageous for his needs. The decision is simplified, however, once the buyer decides whether to use life insurance solely to provide his dependents with financial protection, or for both this purpose and also as a means of accumulating savings. And in this connection, a prospective buyer should recognize that despite the baffling variety of policies available, there actually are but two basic types. The first affords protection only (term insurance), while the second combines protection and savings (whole life, limited-payment life, and endowment). A brief review of the differences is appropriate.

Term vs. Cash Value Life Insurance

Just as fire or casualty insurance furnishes nothing more than indemnity in the event of certain losses, term insurance offers no more than financial protection for survivors. The charge for such protection depends upon the insurer's mortality costs and overhead, and because mortality costs advance with age, so does the premium.

Keep in mind that because term policies normally are either not available or inordinately expensive above age 65 or 70, anyone who relies entirely on such form of insurance must anticipate not having any coverage if he or she lives to such an age, which means that in later life the survivors' needs would have to be met by government benefits plus whatever estate has been accumulated.

Whole life or limited-payment life insurance is referred to as "permanent" protection; the coverage remains in effect for life, and the premiums remain the same. At any age at which a policy is purchased, this level premium is substantially larger than that charged for the same amount of term insurance, for in addition to paying for mortality expenses and overhead, it includes a third element for the purpose of accumulating a cash value (the "savings" component). For instance, the cost per $1,000 for a non-participating whole life policy might be about two or three times greater, and a 20-pay policy about five times as much as the same company would charge a particular insured for 5-year renewable and convertible term purchased at the same age.

Once a "permanent" policy is issued, the insurer is able to provide the same dollar amount of coverage (the face value) in later years without increasing the premium even though the mortality risk has increased, because the policyholder's "savings" and the earnings from them reduce the insurer's risk. In other words, although the death benefit remains "level," the actual amount of pure insurance progressively declines. Thus, *the actual insurance portion of every permanent policy is decreasing term, the precise amount of which at any particular time is the difference between the face value of the policy and the policy's reserve.* In a sense, then, the policyholder insures his own life to the extent of his savings.

The Savings Element of Permanent Insurance

Remembering that there are but two essential charges for life insurance—the mortality costs and the company's overhead—a prospective buyer must choose whether to pay an additional amount to create what might be regarded as a restricted type of savings account. The main rationale for buying cash value life policies is that without the compulsion to save, which the periodic payment of insurance premiums supposedly furnishes, most people would not otherwise conserve their surplus money for needs which will arise later in their lives. Unquestionably, this view has considerable validity in many cases. Nevertheless, it is rather specious as applied to anyone who is capable of managing his income sensibly and who does so.

A prospective buyer should also realize that not all the difference in premiums between cash value and term insurance represents "savings" that are credited to the cash value of the permanent policy. If, for example, a 25-year-old prospective buyer who is considering a $10,000 whole life policy at a cost of $133 a year, or the same amount of 5-year term for $56, cannot correctly assume that the $77 difference would become part of the "savings" portion of the whole life policy.

For one thing, commissions are based not only on the *amount* of insurance sold but also on the *type* of policy. Under a representative schedule, the salesman would receive 20% of the entire first year's premium on term policies of short duration, 30% on term policies of longer duration, 55% on whole life, and 40% on 20-year endowments. Thus, in the first year alone, if the $10,000 whole life policy were purchased, the company would have to pay $73 of the $133 premium to the salesman; the balance of his commission, probably another $60, would be derived from premium payments made over the next several years. Mention of commission schedules is not meant to imply that life insurance salesmen are overpaid, but it would be naive to believe that everyone who sells insurance, or for that matter anything else on commission, is so altruistic as not to be influenced by this factor. In the preceding example, the salesman might earn about $17 if the prospect purchased the $10,000 term policy, but $133 if the $10,000 whole life coverage were bought.

Exclusive of commissions, which industry-wide consume over 7% of all premium and investment income, most companies spend about 10% of their total revenues for other expenses, which further limits the amount that goes into the cash values of policies. On the average, in the last few years insurers have earned over 6% on their investments. Most cash surrender value tables are constructed to guarantee a 2.5% to 3% return on the cash value of the policy. Part of the difference between the guaranteed return and the company's net earnings might be paid as a "dividend" (i.e., rebate) if the policy is a participating type, but some usually ends up in the company's special reserves or surplus. If the insurer is a stock company and the policy is non-participating, the premiums will be significantly less (perhaps only two-thirds those charged by a mutual company), but earnings above the guaranteed return belong to the company.

Life Insurance and Taxes

For some reason, many people think that life insurance paid to a named beneficiary, such as an insured's wife, is not subject to estate taxation. Not so. Although several states do not impose inheritance taxes unless the proceeds are paid to the insured's estate, and a few exempt amounts below a specified sum, about one-half of the states as well as the federal government treat all life insurance owned by a decedent as just as much a taxable part of his estate as his real property, personal effects, securities, and other assets.

There is a way, though, to avoid death taxes on life insurance proceeds (assuming the estate is large enough to be taxed): the insured can simply give up all "incidents of ownership" (such as the right to change beneficiaries, borrow on his policy, or surrender it). This is usually done by having a wife apply for, purchase, and pay the premiums for a policy on her husband's life, or by having a husband assign the ownership of existing policies to his wife. However, doing so could be a costly mistake.

Because of the 1976 changes in the federal gift and estate tax laws, the once-popular technique of transferring ownership of life insurance has become a tax trap for many. Previously, the marital deduction was only one-half of the adjusted gross estate, and a mere $60,000 above that amount was exempt. Since anything more than $120,000 was vulnerable, a strong inducement existed to remove as much as possible from an estate. Under the new laws, the marital deduction is the larger of $250,000 or one-half of the estate, and tax credits protect another $175,000 if death occurs after 1980 (and somewhat lesser amounts before then). Consequently, a husband may leave his wife up to $425,000 free of federal estate taxes. Another part of the equation, however, is the future tax on the widow's estate. Because no marital deduction would then be available, anything above $175,000 would be levied upon at rates commencing at 32%.

In brief, then, if total assets, including the face value of life insurance, are not likely to exceed the $175,000 break-point, there is no estate tax advantage in giving up control of a life insurance policy. And if an estate is much larger than that sum, an insured probably would do better to retain ownership of his policies and use the proceeds to fund a trust providing lifetime benefits for his widow, with the remainder to go to their children (see Chapter 9). Such an arrangement would avoid all taxes on the insurance proceeds when she dies.

Another consideration is what happens if the insured lives longer than the new owner. Briefly, if this were to occur, additional probate costs and death taxes might be incurred. Also, a transfer of the policy back to the insured or even to someone else, such as a child, could create other problems. Still another factor to weigh is the possibility, remote as it might seem at the time, of serious marital discord resulting in a divorce. Once a transfer is made, the policy is the separate property of the new owner—usually the insured's wife. If the insured still needs insurance after a divorce, additional complications would arise if, for example, he is no longer insurable.

160   *Estate Accumulation*

In the area of *income taxation*, some salesmen stress the point that a beneficiary of life insurance does not have to pay any income taxes on the proceeds from a policy. This is on a par with saying that if someone buys his house, he won't have to pay rent. The claim is quite true but quite misleading, for neither is anything else in a decedent's estate (e.g., cash, securities, or real estate) taxed as *income* to a legatee or devisee. Apparently, though, this illusory "advantage" impresses many financially uninformed prospects.

Can You Afford What You Need?

For most people, the single most important factor is how much they can afford to pay for the amount of life insurance they need. And in this connection, a typical young husband usually does not have sufficient income to be concerned initially with much more than providing adequately for his survivors in the event he dies prematurely. Accumulating savings for distant years, when his children will no longer be dependent upon him and his needs will be far less, is important but secondary. However, *most people are badly underinsured not because they cannot afford a sufficient amount, but because they have been sold the wrong types of coverage for their circumstances*. And for those whose deaths occur at an early age, surviving dependents are severely penalized. Hence, you should know just what your premium money will buy. Table 8.1 shows the approximate amounts of insurance a net premium of

TABLE 8.1. *What $240 a Year in Premiums Might Buy.*

Type Policy	Purchased at Age			
	25	35	45	55
Association (Group) Term	$174,000	$113,000	$45,000	$26,000
Five-Year R&C Term[a]	68,000	53,000	27,000	11,000
Whole Life (NP)[b]	19,000	13,000	9,000	5,000
Whole Life (Par)[c]	14,000	11,000	7,000	5,000
20-Pay (NP)	13,000	10,000	7,000	5,000
Endowment-at-65 (Par)	12,000	8,000	5,000	2,000
20-Pay (Par)	9,000	7,000	5,000	4,000

[a] R&C is "renewable and convertible."
[b] "NP" is a "non-participating" policy.
[c] "Par" is a "participating" (dividend-paying) policy.

$240 a year will purchase with different types of policies initially acquired at various ages.

The point is that a person who needs substantial protection might do a grave disservice to his family if, prior to the time he has ample pure life insurance or a sufficiently large estate, he uses his premium dollars to acquire cash values rather than maximum protection. And to purchase in permanent form the amount of insurance he might need would strain the budgets of most young couples (for example, if $50,000 protection were needed at age 25, the premium would be about $50 a month for nonparticipating whole life and $65 to $70 a month for participating whole life; the same amount of five-year renewable and convertible term would cost about $15, and association term would be even less). Once the higher costs can be afforded, cash value insurance might be considered if a couple believes that it should occupy a place in their estate accumulation plans.

What If Death Is Not Premature?

Losing insurance protection at 65 or 70, together with the high cost of term policies in the late 50s and 60s, often are advanced as reasons for buying permanent life policies. These matters certainly deserve consideration, but a discerning buyer should also realize that by age 65 or 70 the need for family protection usually has become much less, and that the benefits available to survivors normally would provide the bulk of the income required by an elderly widow. For example, if the estate programming technique described in Chapter 5 were used to project approximate estate requirements throughout a lifetime, the results in a typical case might be roughly similar to those shown in Figure 8.1.

Because estate requirements (R) can be met with a combination of life insurance (I) and other assets (O), the amount of life insurance needed at any age is simply the estate requirement minus other assets (I = R−O) (Figure 8.2). If an individual accumulates adequate present assets (and the longer he lives after his children become financially independent, the less he would need), in time he will become, in effect, self-insured. Consequently, the frequently raised specter of not having any life insurance in later years should be laid to rest.

FIGURE 8.1

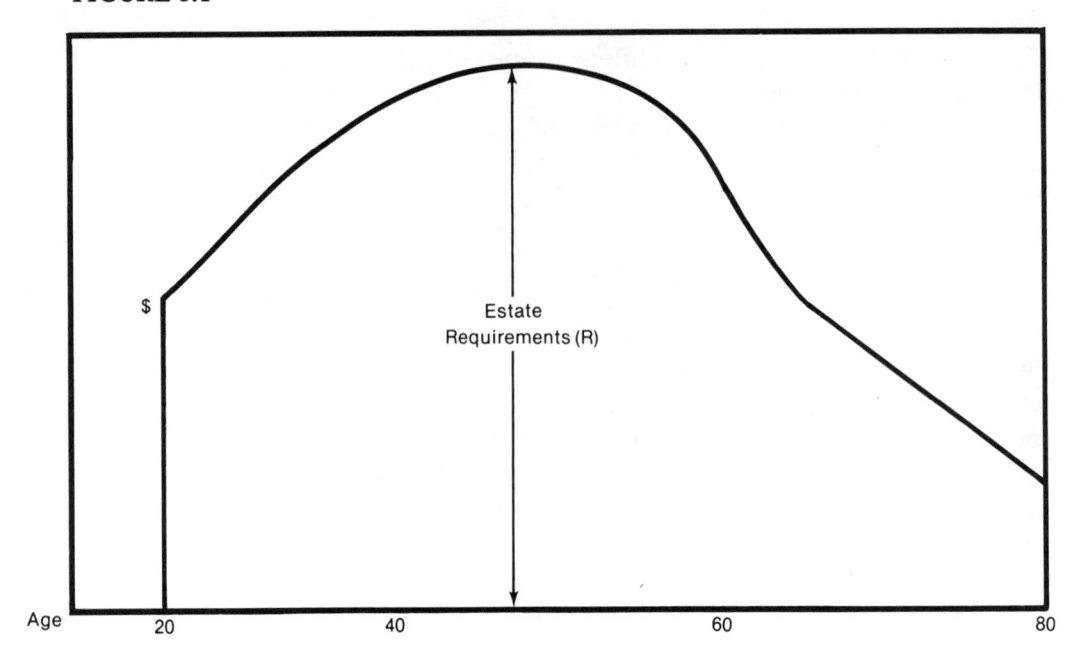

FIGURE 8.2

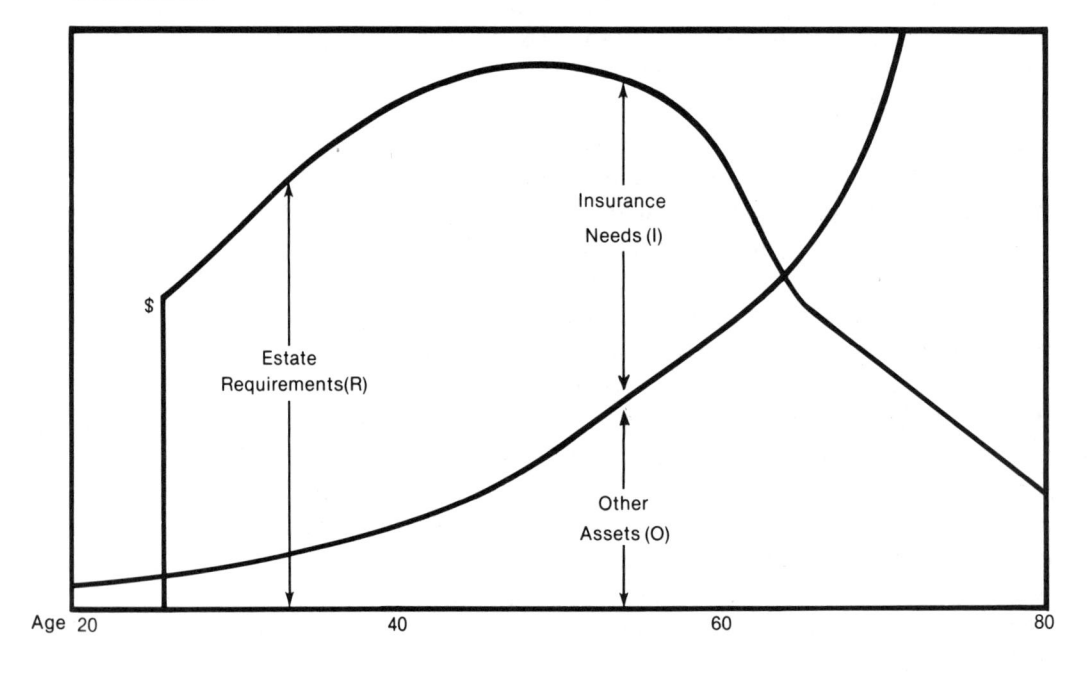

Why Buy Permanent?

Permanent life insurance does have some advantages, of course, over the pure protection available in term coverages. Among these are safety of principal (which in general is surpassed only by federal obligations), and its much-maligned feature: forced savings. The latter might be one of the few ways of accumulating anything for people who are financially inexperienced, incapable of managing their assets productively, or lacking in self-discipline. There are a frightening number of them running around. What is more, garden-variety prudence suggests that most people should have a balanced estate accumulation program. Hence, a reasonable approach might be to place a portion of surplus funds in some types of fixed-dollar assets, such as bonds, savings accounts, or even the cash values of permanent life insurance, and the rest in equity-type investments, such as common stock, mutual funds, and developed or raw land.

Estate liquidity is sometimes mentioned as another need that permanent life insurance fulfills. In other words, if someone has a relatively large estate consisting mainly of illiquid assets, such as land, a business, or equities, her executor might have to sell part of the estate at sacrifice prices or in a depressed market to pay the death taxes. If this is a prospect, the owner should try to ensure that it does not occur. Life insurance is well-suited to this purpose, but so are some other types of assets, such as large savings deposits, short-term Treasury issues, or money market instruments, assuming that the size and nature of the estate enable the owner to devote a sufficient part of it to uses of this sort. At times, though, she cannot do so, simply because almost everything she has is needed for other purposes.

Another factor stressed by those within the life insurance fraternity is that someone who purchases permanent coverage though a salesman acquires not just life insurance, but also the continuing services of the salesman and his company. In addition to advice concerning a customer's insurance needs and how to meet them, these services might include rather comprehensive estate analyses, information or suggestions on such matters as taxation and dispositive arrangements, future contacts to assure that the amounts and types of insurance reflect the insured's changing circumstances, and related assistance such as help in obtaining policy loans when desired. Also, after the insured's death, the salesman or his successor will be at hand to provide financial guidance to the surviving beneficiaries and to assist them in filing insurance claims.

Product service can be a very potent influence and even the key to success, as IBM has convincingly demonstrated. And for many people, the personalization of life insurance might be the controlling factor in deciding what to buy from whom. To a lesser extent, of course, anyone who buys mutual fund shares from a salesman or stockbroker rather than directly from a no-load firm, or a housewife who purchases cosmetics from a saleswoman who comes to her home instead of buying comparable goods at a store, is electing to pay more to obtain the individual services furnished them. And provided they are aware of the alternatives—in other words, if their decisions are informed—their choices can hardly be faulted.

In brief, buying permanent life insurance can unquestionably have some advantages for some people. But in trying to decide whether it would meet your particular needs better than some alternate use of your money, evaluate your situation as objectively as you can, and do not succumb to appeals such as:

> ... Life insurance is the best tangible economic evidence of the love that Christ taught us to bear for one another. [Gaines, *The Question Marks of Property*, 24 (1967)]

Without intending any sacrilege, that type of sales pitch rates at least three guffaws and a couple of knee-slaps. But you can expect to hear it or something similar, somewhere, sometime.

TERM INSURANCE PLUS FIXED-DOLLAR INVESTMENTS

Series E Bonds. The cash values in permanent life insurance are only one of many solutions, of course, for those who desire some balance between fixed-dollar and equity assets, and find compulsory saving easier than voluntary saving. Another convenient risk-free repository for surplus funds, which also provides a form of compulsion, is found in government savings bonds (Series E) acquired through payroll deductions. While these are being accumulated, financial protection against premature death could be obtained with term insurance.

Savings Bonds or Endowment?

Retirement income policies, which emphasize savings but also provide financial protection for survivors if death should occur before the policy "endows," no longer enjoy much popularity; nevertheless, they are a convenient and valid basis for comparison with a term-plus-savings bond approach.

Assume that a 30-year-old man is seeking some virtually risk-free way to build a supplemental retirement fund that will simultaneously furnish some additional financial protection for his family, and assume that he can afford about $600 a year for these purposes. How about a retirement income policy? The average premium charged by the largest stock insurance companies would be $592.75 a year for $20,000 of non-participating income-at-65 coverage. This would pay him a total of $2,400 a year ($10 a month for each $1,000 face value, with 10 years of payments guaranteed) for the rest of his life, commencing at age 65; if death occurs before 65, his beneficiary would receive at least the $20,000 face value of the insurance (and even more, if the insured were past age 56 or 57 when he dies). Sound attractive? Maybe. But consider an alternative.

What if he purchased the same amount ($20,000) of term-to-65 insurance, and bought Series E bonds with the difference between its cost and the $593 a year he otherwise would have paid for an income-at-65 policy? The difference should amount to at least $422 a year. (Among the major companies that sell term-to-65, the average annual premium for a $20,000 policy issued at age 30 is about $171, so let's use that sum, even though term-to-65 is neither a very popular nor especially inexpensive form of term insurance.)

If $422 a year were placed in Series E bonds (or for that matter, savings certificates or other fixed-dollar instruments that have a net yield of 6½%) from age 30 until age 65, the amount saved and earned would total over $50,000—or more than 50% greater than the $31,385 cash value of the average income-at-65 policy. The difference would be narrowed somewhat, however, by the amount of income taxes levied on the interest accrued in the Series E's (minus the taxes assessed upon payments under the income-at-65 policy). But if the E's are exchanged for Series H bonds, the gain could be deferred or spread out beyond age 65. At current rates, the interest from $50,000 of Series H bonds would be $3,250 a year, compared to the $2,400 that the income-at-65 policy would pay. Far more importantly, however, when the bond owner dies, the $50,000 in bonds would be part of his estate to pass on to his survivors, but nothing whatsoever would remain of the income-at-65 policy once $2,400 a year has been paid for 10 years.

What is more, if death were to occur before age 65, the bond buyer's survivors would always be better off financially, because they would have not only $20,000 from the term policy but also whatever savings bonds had been accumulated prior to death. These differences are graphically illustrated in Figure 8.3.

If a term-bond plan is contrasted with a *short term endowment*, the costliness of the latter is immediately apparent. Short term endowments, such as those sold as "college education" policies, are a singularly ill-advised way of saving. Although they have paid college costs for countless children—both the policyholders' and the insurance agents'—they are simply not competitive with a term-bond plan. No reputable salesman would recommend their use when the circumstances indicate that a father should buy less costly

FIGURE 8.3. *Endowment-at-65 vs. Term-to-65 plus Series E's.*

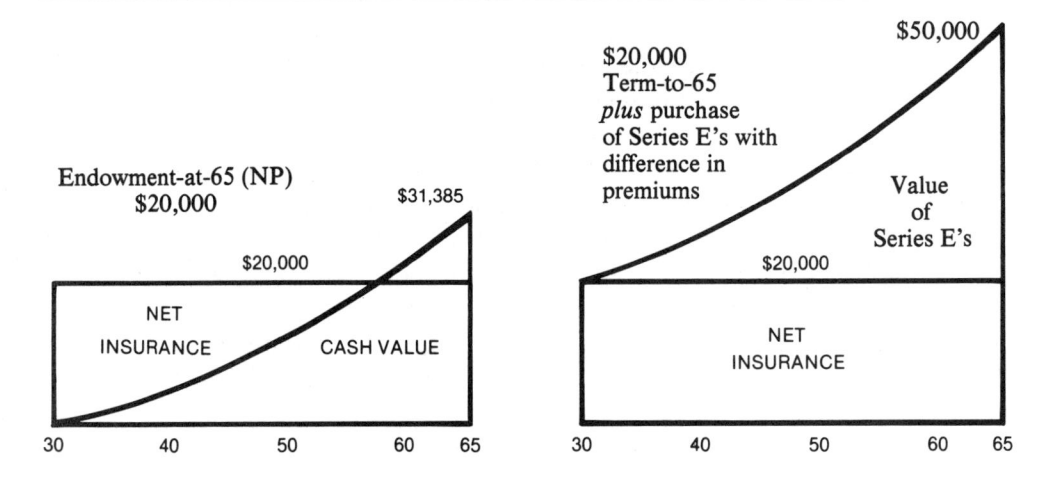

coverage, such as whole life, on himself, and the better companies don't even offer them. Nevertheless, they are still promoted in some advertisements and by a few agents. If anyone tries to sell you such a policy, you might justifiably consider biting his good hands or throwing a piece of the rock at him.

Savings Bonds or Whole Life?

"Very well," you snort, "but my mother didn't raise any endowment-buying children." So how does whole life stack up against savings bonds? In brief, much better than a life-income-at-65 policy, but nothing to get excited about.

For an annual premium of about $660 (the average amount charged by five of the largest stock companies), a 30-year old man could purchase a $50,000 non-participating whole life policy. The same amount of 5-year renewable and convertible (R&C) term insurance (a more realistic alternative than term-to-65) would cost $153 for each of the first five years; thereafter, the premium would increase in five-year increments to $197, $266, $383, $574, $877 and, finally, to $1,404 a year from ages 60 to 65. The annual differences between the amounts charged for the whole life and the successive 5-year R&C term coverages would be $507 from ages 30 to 35, $463 from 35 to 40, $394 from 40 to 45, $277 from 45 to 50, and $86 from 50 to 55; after age 55, the premiums for the whole life would be less than those for the term by $217 a year to age 60, and by $744 a year to age 65.

If the term coverage were used instead of the whole life approach, and if the buyer placed the difference in premiums in savings bonds (at the rate of $507 a year for the first five years, $463 a year for the next five years, and so on), he would accumulate bonds worth about $38,780—if and when he reached age 65. In comparison, at the same age the cash surrender value of the whole life policy would be $26,740.

Figure 8.4 shows what sums would be available to the insured at various times under both the whole life and the term-plus-savings bonds approaches, and how his beneficiaries would fare when death occurs. A cursory examination of the chart and the tables beneath it will disclose:

FIGURE 8.4

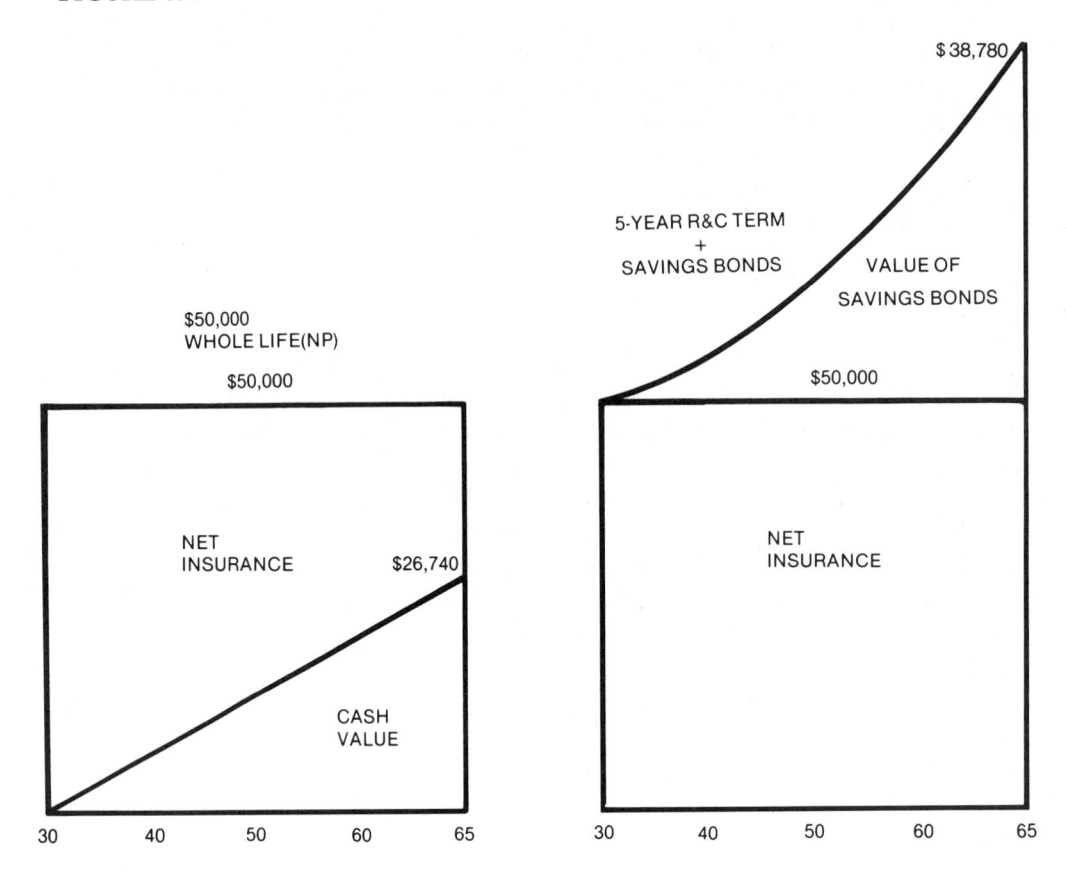

Amount Available for Survivors if Insured Dies at Age

	40	50	60	71[a]	78[b]
Whole Life	$50,000	$50,000	$50,000	$50,000	$50,000
Term + E's	$56,520	$66,980	$81,420	$60,920	$99,980

[a] Life expectancy at age 30.
[b] Life expectancy at age 65.

Amount Available to Insured if He Survives to Age

	40	50	60	65
Whole Life	$5,530	$14,140	$22,520	$26,740
Term + E's	$6,520	$16,980	$31,420	$38,780

If death occurs before age 65, the term-plus-savings bonds would always be superior to whole life insurance. (And about three out of ten 30-year olds will never reach 65.)

If the whole life insurance is surrendered, its cash value would always be less than the value of the savings bonds.

If death occurs after age 65 and before age 69 or 70, the $50,000 proceeds from the whole life policy would exceed the value of the bonds.

Obviously, though, these dollar amounts alone do not tell the entire story. Other significant factors to consider include:

Will the term buyer really use the premiums he saves to buy savings bonds? (If he instead spends these sums, he probably would be better off with the whole life.)

What if the insured lives beyond 65 and still needs or wants insurance? (The whole life policy would continue to provide $50,000, regardless of how long the insured lives, but the term would expire at age 65. If the bonds are retained, however, their value would continue to increase, so the financial protection that would be available for survivors depends upon when death occurs; actuarially, a 65-year old man should live about 13 more years; by then, the bonds would be worth almost $100,000 if he continued to buy them at the rate of $660 a year (the amount he otherwise would still be paying for the whole life policy), or over $75,000 even if no further purchases were made.)

What if the differences between the whole life and the 5-year R&C term policies were more or less than those indicated? (Any change in costs would alter the results one way or another, of course. The cost of the non-participating, whole life policy used in the illustration is an average of the premiums charged by some of the prominent stock companies. Most participating policies would be more expensive until around the 15th to 20th year, when because of increases in "dividends," they usually become cheaper than non-participating coverage. Conversely, less costly term insurance, such as association term or one-year R&C policies, is available. The point, though, is simply that you should carefully compare insurers, policies, and prices. Detailed price information can be found in Best's *Flitcraft Compend*, and Best's *Life Insurance Reports* rates the companies; also, Dr. Belth's book and the Consumers' Union Report referred to in Chapter 6 contain much valuable information that should help you make the decision that is the soundest for you.)

One final caveat: *anyone choosing to separate his life insurance from his savings should be confident that he will be able to continue an independent savings program, because the success of such a plan depends upon systematically and diligently adhering to it.*

Fixed-Dollar Investments Other Than Savings Bonds.

So far, cash value insurance has been compared with a combination of term insurance and government savings bonds. If a higher net yield can be obtained elsewhere without unduly sacrificing safety, it also should be considered. In recent years, yields of 8% to 10% have been available on many low-risk, fixed-dollar investments, such as highly rated corporate bonds or income mutual funds, and nontaxable returns of 5% to 7% have been offered by municipal bonds or munifunds. Any of these or a combination of them could be substituted for Series E's, if the buyer so chooses. But another factor, since we are considering long-range savings programs, is what today's dollar and the nominal interest it earns in savings bonds or elsewhere will be worth when the time comes to spend it.

INFLATION AND FIXED-DOLLAR ASSETS

If you were to put aside $1 at 5% interest compounded annually, in about 14 years your $1 would double. Dandy. But what if more than $2 were then needed to buy what $1 would buy today? Essentially, that is what has been happening to the purchasing power of the dollar over the last several years. Whether its value will continue to erode, and at what rate, are crucial considerations for anyone trying to decide how he can most effectively use his surplus funds to build an estate.

The first thing to recognize is that neither the dollar nor any other currency is inviolate. Just how much particular goods and services might cost in the future depends upon numerous factors, of course, but as Figure 8.5 shows, over the long term, the trend of the dollar has been inexorably downward.

In more recent times, prices as measured by the Consumers'

FIGURE 8.5. *Relative Value of the Dollar (1820–1978).*

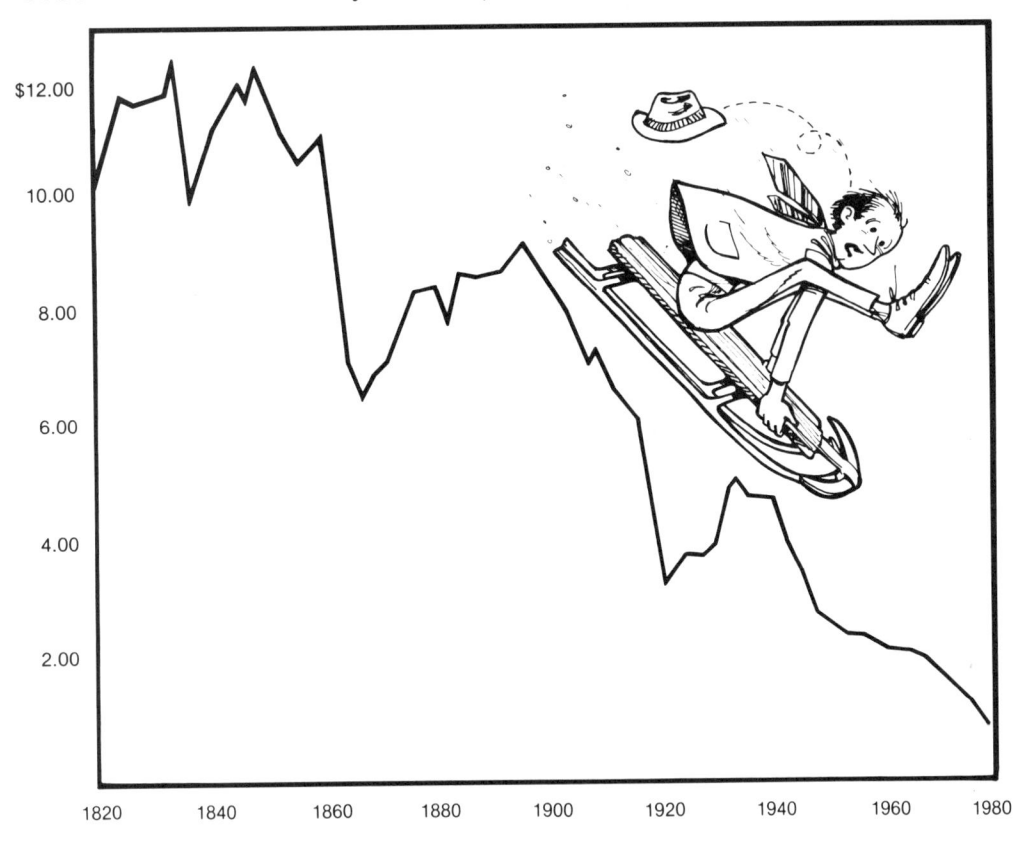

Price Index (CPI) have been increasing at an accelerated rate. For example, it took from 1820 until World War I for the cost of living to double, but since the beginning of the Second World War, it has quadrupled. So in effect, the good 5-cent cigar of 1940—if there ever were such a thing—is now a 20-cent item, and the $15 weekly grocery bill for a family of four is at least $60 today. Even more alarming, the value of the dollar has plummeted since the late 1960s, climaxed by a 12.2% surge in the CPI in 1974 alone (see Figure 8.6).

With our economic, political, and social structures potentially jeopardized by what could have turned into rampant inflation, moderately restrictive monetary and fiscal policies finally were imposed by the Federal Reserve Board and the Administration. These appear, at least temporarily, to be serving their intended purpose. Whether further significant progress can be achieved,

FIGURE 8.6. *Consumer Prices Since World War II (1967=100).*

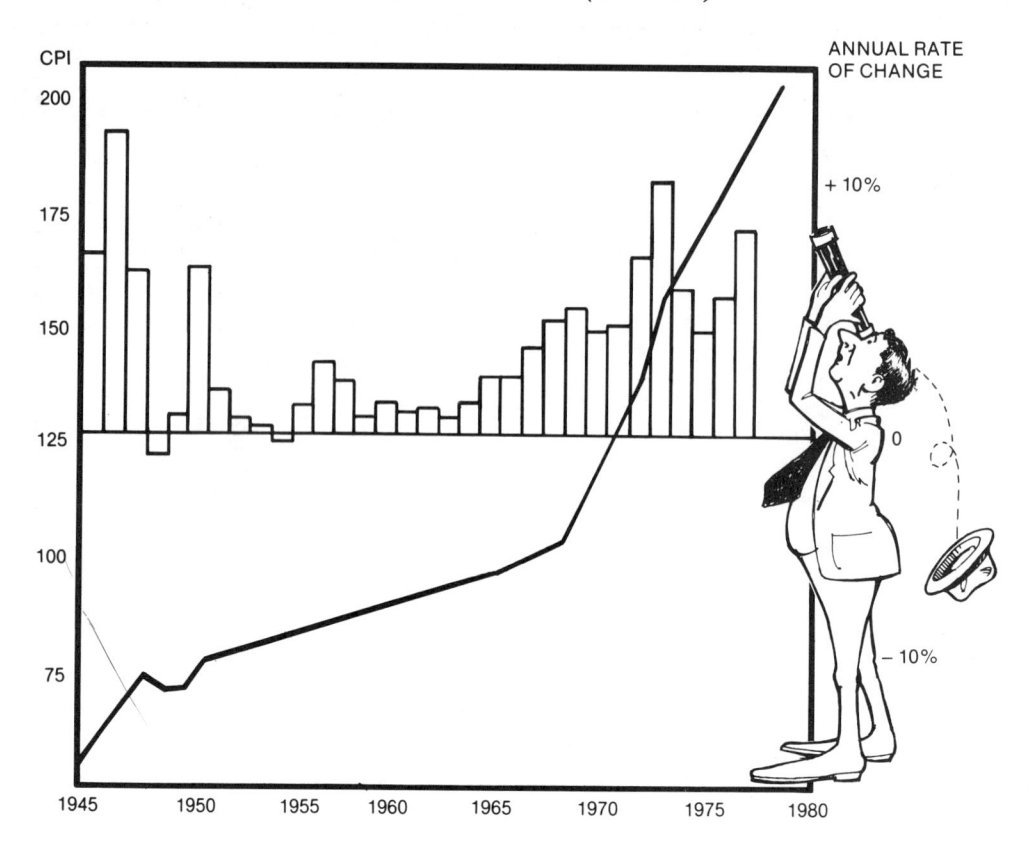

given present day political pressures and realities, is problematical at best.

To better judge what the long-range future of the dollar might be, you should understand how we got where we are. The present escalation of living costs was not a sudden nor unexpected aberration; rather, it was rooted in developments occurring years earlier. First, the seeds of inflation were sown in the early 1960s by the proliferation of welfare programs and their later explosion in coverages, benefits, and costs (for example, the federal budget now calls for "human resources" expenditures in excess of one-quarter *trillion* dollars, which is more than twice the amount spent for defense). Next, germination was assured by the decision in the mid-1960s to simultaneously wage an ambitious "war on poverty" and a war in Southeast Asia. Cultivation was by such "random shocks" as the dollar devaluation of 1972, the expansionary monetary policies of the same year, the wheat deal with the USSR, the quadrupling of oil prices by the OPEC cartel in the fall of 1973, and the "energy crisis" that, after simmering for a quarter of a century, erupted in 1977.

Fundamentally, of course, *the cause of inflation is an expanded money base without a commensurate increase in production.* And with only minor respites, a policy of monetary inflation has been followed in this country since the early 1930s. You don't have to be an economist to realize that prolonged, excessive growth in the supply of money results in higher prices. But what is excessive? Reduced to basics, the gross national product (the total value of goods and services produced in a year) has demonstrated an ability to expand at an average annual rate of about 4%, adjusted for price changes. Thus, if money were increased at roughly the same long-term rate, relative price stability should result. But if money continually grows more rapidly than the economy (as it has in most years), price increases ensue as a simple matter of supply and demand.

The prevailing view seems to be that perpetual prosperity, "full" employment, the welfare of the individual, and the redress of all social and economic inequalities are government responsibilities. What is more, the programs and commitments of the 1960s have created a "rights syndrome" in millions of people who seem to feel that, regardless of their own productivity or contribution, they are entitled to countless benefits. If these increasing wants continue to be satisfied, chronic inflation is almost inevitable because of the enormous costs involved.

At the risk of over-simplification, if spending exceeds revenues, the Treasury must borrow the difference in the money markets, where it competes with the private sector for funds it must have to function. To meet these needs, the Federal Reserve Board is compelled to increase the money supply faster than the economy is capable of growing; otherwise, a crowding-out effect would result in economic stagnation or worse, with attendant unemployment that in turn would require even larger federal expenditures and cause declines in corporate and individual income taxes. And as one observer noted:

> ... If governments have a choice between attempting full employment and defending their currencies, they will nearly always pick jobs over the worth of the currency. Currencies do not vote. ... Long range inflation is the policy, articulated or not, of every country in the world. (Smith, *The Money Game*, p. 282 (1968)).

The implication should be clear: *nothing guarantees that fixed-dollar savings will have the same purchasing power in the future that they do today.* In fact, the question is not so much whether it will require more dollars to acquire goods and services years hence, but how many more. In that connection, a definitive study indicates that between 1975 and 2000, the mean expected inflation rate will be 6.7% a year (see Ehrbar, *The Long-Term Case For Common Stocks*, Fortune, Dec. 1974, p. 97). If this proves accurate, any long-term, fixed-dollar use of savings that does not yield an equivalent nominal rate after taxes would be a losing proposition.

A growing awareness of what has happened, is happening, and might happen to the value of the dollar has had an impact on popular savings media of the past, such as cash value life insurance, about which one writer commented:

> Significant changes have occurred in recent years which have affected the life insurance industry. Among them are inflation, affluence, education, the population explosion, growth in financial services, and the public's increased financial sophistication. (Bowles, *Where the Life Insurance Industry is Headed*, Best's Review, Dec. 1969, p. 12).

And the former Insurance Commissioner of Pennsylvania put it even more bluntly when he wrote:

> Inflation is making cash value life insurance more obsolete every day ... The only thing "guaranteed" by cash-value life insurance is continual erosion of its investment component. (Denenberg, *Insurance in the Age of the Consumer*, Best's Review, April 1970, p. 34).

Yet, if today's $60,000 house, $30,000 college education or $6,000 car do triple or quadruple in cost by the end of the century, what can you do in the meantime if you hope to be able to afford them then?

PROTECTING PURCHASING POWER

The final quarter of the 20th century could be a difficult period for anyone trying to build an estate, for in addition to inflationary prospects, the social, economic, political, and technological upheavals already under way portend a greater degree of investment uncertainty than ever before. Consequently, without some financial wizard to guide the way, there is no sure and simple solution for using savings most productively, and over the years some flexibility might be required to accommodate to changing conditions. Nevertheless, it is possible to develop some general guidelines that might help you reach your goal.

First, the most unlikely scenario of all involves a complete reversal of economic growth accompanied by chronic deflation. If these conditions were to develop, the soundest use for estate assets would be in a very long-term, fixed-dollar securities of the highest quality, such as Treasury bonds or top-rated corporates. Otherwise, though, bonds are likely to be a bummer for long-range holding by the average investor; so, too, committing a significant portion of lifelong holdings to other forms of fixed-dollar assets has little appeal.

Next, present probabilities do not suggest that the United States will succumb fully to the near-total welfare state concept that brought economic deterioration and a swift rise in living costs (25% in 1974) to the once-mighty British. If a similar course were pursued in this country, there would be little refuge anywhere for savings, but the safest approach probably would be to own gold or other high value tangibles that have some prospect of retaining their relative worth.

Investment alternatives might be narrowed considerably, however, provided economic and political extremes are avoided in this country, interest rates remain relatively conducive to economic growth, and cost of living increases moderate. None of these is certain, but all appear reasonably attainable. Under such circumstances, the most promising long-term holdings for the average investor probably would be equity interests in which the total return (current yield plus capital appreciation) has the potential of outpacing inflation and producing substantial gains over an extended period of time. Real estate might be in this category and so are common stocks. These carry a risk of loss of principal, of course, but the risk of loss of purchasing power could be greater in even the most gilt-edged of fixed-dollar assets. Essentially, to succeed financially you should measure results in terms of *real* rates of return, not just *nominal* yields.

176   *Estate Accumulation*

On a short-term basis, there is no intrinsic relationship between common stocks and protection against inflation, as many investors learned to their dismay over the last few years. In fact, while stocks tend to rise during the initial phase of an inflationary spiral, the opposite occurs as purchasing power continues to erode. This negative correlation results from several factors, including the adverse impact of inflation on doing business profitably, economic uncertainties, and the competition for investors' dollars from the high nominal yields available then in fixed-dollar instruments.

Predicting rates of return on stocks is hazardous. Nevertheless, a number of studies of past performance and future probabilities provide a basis for optimism. Most stocks performed dismally

FIGURE 8.7. *Dow Jones Industrial Average (1945–1978).*

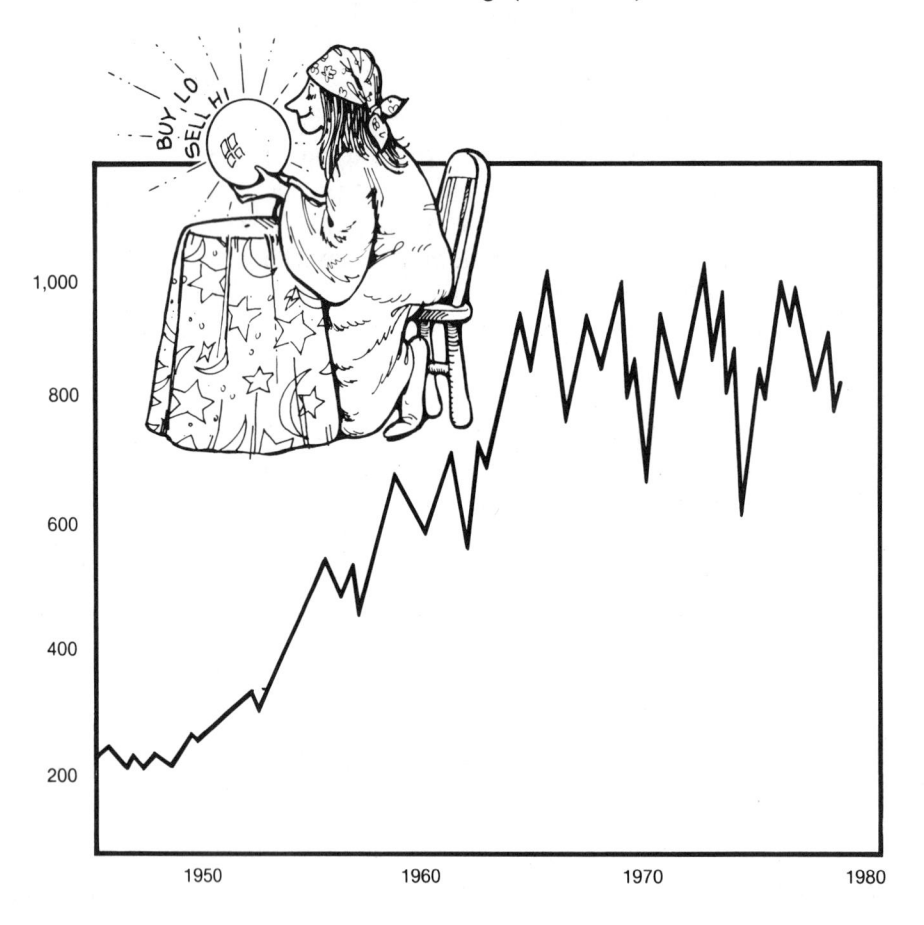

over the 1968–1974 period, which included a severe inflationary spurt and exceptionally high interest rates. Going further back, though, stock prices have ended higher at the end than at the beginning of seven of the last nine decades, including the extraordinary gains registered between the early 1950s and late-1960s (see Figure 8.7). Moreover, over the entire 50-year span commencing in 1926, which contained more than its fair share of disruptions, the total annual compound rate of return on stocks compared to fixed-dollar uses of savings has been impressive.

Total Rates of Return (1926–1975)

	Nominal	Real
Stocks	9.0%	6.7%
Bonds	3.8	1.5
Treasury Bills	2.3	0
Inflation	2.3	—

[See Massey, "For the Long Haul," Barron's, Jan. 31, 1977, p. 5; see also Fisher and Lori, *Rates of Return on Investments in Common Stocks,* 37 Jour. Bus. 1(1963), and the same authors' article in 41 Jour. Bus. 291 (1968).]

As for the future, authoritative studies, particularly those of Ibbotsen and Sinquefield, project even higher *real* (constant dollar) returns from common stocks between now and the end of the century.

Projected Total Rates of Return (1975–2000)

	Nominal	Real
Stocks	13.6%	7.7%
Bonds	8.4	2.5
Treasury Bills	7.1	1.2
Inflation	5.9	—

[See Ehrbar, *The Long-Term Case for Common Stocks*, supra, and Massey, *For the Long Haul*, supra.]

Obviously, no one can foresee with precision what events or developments might alter the most scholarly forecasts. But barring a worldwide nuclear holocaust or the emergence of a near-total socialistic society in this nation, these projections appear reasonable. Keep in mind, though, that they relate to stocks in general, not specific issues, and that for estate building purposes, equities are not a short-term proposition. Interruptions are bound to occur, and at times might be severe. Thus, don't look for a steady, year by year return of 14% or so in an inflationary climate of 6%; instead, expect some years to show losses and others gains. The risk factor, of course, is why over the long term the total rate of return on stocks has been greater than that from fixed-dollar uses of money. But stocks do not provide guaranteed yields or assurance that a saver will get back all his funds, so timorous investors might feel more at ease with bonds or savings accounts. And even the venturesome should not commit themselves to the extent that they might be forced to sell at a time when crippling losses would result.

IS TWISTING SINFUL?

A twister means one thing to a Kansan and something else to a Greenwich Village disco patron. But among those in the life insurance business, mention "twister" and you are likely to set off a conditioned reflex that starts with eye-rolling and ends up with cussin', spittin' and stompin', for in the lexicon of the trade, "twister" is an epithet for someone who tries to convince an insured that he should drop an existing life insurance policy and replace it with something else.

But is twisting really so abominable, and are twistees always the victims of unprincipled villains who slink around in the dark, sinisterly smirking and twisting the ends of their waxed moustaches? The answer is yes, no, and maybe.

Replacing coverage that has been in effect for many years with a similar type of policy often can be a serious mistake, for the insured has already paid for the high, early-year costs of his present policy, and it might require five to ten years to reach an equivalent position with the substitute coverage. Yet to assert that *any* switch is evil presumes both infallibility and unchanging circumstances, neither of which exists. For example, because of the vast differences between insurance companies and policies, a careful evaluation of all factors—including a comparison of interest-adjusted costs (see Chapter 6)—might show that in an inflationary economy, surrendering an old policy and buying a new one of the same type elsewhere could be cost-effective.

More often, though, denunciations of "twisting" are directed at those salesmen whose success largely depends on having their customers replace cash value policies with a combination of term insurance and some mutual fund accumulation plan. This practice deserves scorn in those cases in which an unsophisticated customer might be sold something wholly unsuited to his particular needs. Nevertheless, others might benefit from such an approach. Even so, if they knew more about what they were doing, they probably would by-pass all salesmen and seek out an appropriate no-load mutual fund (saving 8.5¢ of every investment dollar in the process), or some other estate building method; also, less costly term insurance than that sold as part of such packages usually is available.

Twisting, then, is not necessarily all bad or all good. In different situations, it could be either—or some of both. But if you are ever tempted to bail out of a policy you already own, thinking that you made a mistake when you bought it or that you would be far better off with something else, be sure that your decision is an informed one, not just an impetuous response to a pitchman's slick presentation. Obtain all the hard data that he will provide, then write your insurance company to tell them what you plan to do. In most cases, you will receive either a written reply or a visit from a local representative. (If neither is forthcoming, it's a good indication that you might improve your situation by switching.) The insurer usually will try to dissuade you. Listen to the reasons, and study the numbers (especially the interest-adjusted costs) presented. (If there is a reluctance or refusal to talk about interest-adjusted costs, don't listen too intensely.) Finally, take sufficient time to critically compare and evaluate your alternatives. Impartial advice from a competent source, perhaps your lawyer or financial counsellor, might help also.

If you ultimately decide that a switch from what you have to something else would be in the best interests of you and your family, have at it. But do be cautious about one thing: *don't surrender any existing policy until your new insurance has been issued.*

WHAT SHOULD YOU DO?

As the preface to this book indicates, it is merely a primer that endeavors to provide you with some elementary, disinterested information that might serve as a basis for more intelligent decisions relating to estate accumulation and distribution. The purpose has not been to provide estate planning or investment counsel, but instead simply to acquaint you with certain fundamentals that elude too many people throughout their lives. Nothing is advocated, other than that you *carefully consider all pertinent facts and alternatives before making any major estate planning decision, then do what is best suited to your particular needs.*

A primary concern should be adequate financial protection for dependent survivors. For most people during their working years, this means life insurance. The basic questions, though, are whether you need, want, and can afford something other than pure insurance, and whether you might use to better advantage elsewhere the additional premium dollars that cash values would cost you. Of course, if you are unmarried and no one, such as a parent, is presently or prospectively dependent upon you for financial support or help, there seldom is any sound reason to have much, if any, life insurance. The risk of later becoming uninsurable exists but is slight, and the usual platitude that "the younger you are, the less permanent coverage will cost you throughout your life," is pure sophistry.

A priority for everyone, though, should be a readily available emergency fund for unforeseeable needs. The amount needed varies with the individual, but until you have set it aside, investment actions generally should be deferred.

Another consideration might be home ownership, at least if you expect to be in the same community for a few years. But if your job requires relatively frequent moves, realtors' commissions and other costs usually would more than offset any appreciation, equity interest, or income tax savings you might realize.

Once the life insurance—emergency fund—home ownership issues are taken care of, you will be in a position to invest. Initially, you should decide whether or how to allocate your savings between fixed-dollar assets and assets that might appreciate in value. Here, a realistic appraisal of your ability and willingness to save is critical. While not outright wastrels, many people lack financial self-discipline and need some mild form of compulsion, such as buying Series E bonds through payroll deductions. Others do not.

If you decide that common stocks should have a place in your plans, the question is where to commence. For many people, a no-load mutual fund is the answer, at least until they have accumulated several thousand dollars, at which time something else (e.g., direct investments in stocks or some type of managed account) might be indicated. Others might choose to start with one or more good quality growth stocks to buy as their savings permit. Generally, if they have selected the right stocks for their purposes, there seldom should be any reason to disturb their holdings until future needs arise. However, they should realize that declines will occur from time to time.

If you elect the direct investment approach, try to avoid assuming more risk than is appropriate for you at any particular time; buying and selling in the hope of fast gains; taking profits just because your stock has had a phenomenal rise; permitting a broker to churn your account; or becoming overly diversified. Don't hesitate, however, to take an occasional loss if your selection falls short of expectations—no one is infallible.

Eventually, you might develop sufficient knowledge and experience to want to try trading securities, options, or even commodities futures. If you are so inclined and have both the means and the stomach for it, fine, but the cardinal principle should be never to risk more than you can afford to lose. Most investors, large or small, lack the expertise to go much beyond mutual funds or quality growth stocks purchased for the long pull.

Of course, no one who relies primarily on equities for estate accumulation purposes is likely to always have all his assets committed to them. In fact, in addition to keeping a reserve to take advantage of market declines, some flexibility usually is prudent, particularly as an estate grows. Most endowment funds, large trust accounts and institutional investors will vary the proportions of their holdings as conditions and prospects change, in an effort to achieve the largest real return commensurate with the degree of risk assumed. Not infrequently they misjudge, but they get paid for it. And there are times when something such as high-yield, short-term fixed-dollar instruments offers better immediate prospects than most equities, just as there are other times when a fully or nearly fully invested equity position is indicated. So perhaps aside from the few very long-term, core stocks in your portfolio, be prepared to alter the composition of your holdings on occasion as the situation might indicate.

In the final analysis, of course, it's your money, your estate, your family, and your financial future you are trying to assure. How you go about it is up to you, but try to make the most of what you have.

part II
Estate Distribution

chapter 9

Trusts and Sundry Non-Probate Transfers

In the preceding chapters, the emphasis was on accumulating an estate and providing financial protection for your family while you were doing so. Now, we'll shift our attention to considering some ways to preserve and dispose of an estate once it is accumulated. In this chapter we will look at trusts and a few other methods of transferring property interests. Then, in Chapter 10 the nature and consequences of some popular co-ownership arrangements between husbands and wives will be discussed. And finally, Chapter 11 will focus on the ultimate dispositive device—a will.

TRUSTS

One of the most useful of all estate planning tools is the trust, yet few people take advantage of it. In part, this reluctance probably stems from a lack of information or misconceptions about the nature and purpose of this form of property arrangement. Most people think a trust is a complicated device involving a dour-looking trustee in a black frock coat (vaguely resembling a character from Dickens), or a scheme used by the affluent to avoid taxes, or a financial straightjacket used to deprive beneficiaries of the full enjoyment of property. It's not.

Trusts—and there are many variations to serve different objectives—are designed primarily to protect beneficiaries by providing more effective property management than is otherwise available. And in some situations, tax savings can be realized even by persons with only moderate estates, although taxes usually are a collateral factor.

Essentially, a trust is simply a three-party relationship that separates ownership of the same property into two parts: the legal and the equitable. The person who establishes the trust might be called the trustor, grantor, settlor, maker, or donor (for consistency, we'll use *"trustor"*). The person (which could be a corporation) to whom the property, known as the trust corpus or principal, is transferred and who has legal title to it is the *trustee*. Those who have equitable ownership are referred to as the *beneficiaries* (historically known as "cestue que trustent"). Beneficiaries are divided into two categories: the *income beneficiaries*, who have the benefit of the property for a certain period, such as the income for life, and the *remaindermen*, who receive the property when the income beneficiaries' interests end.

The trust arrangement was first adopted by the early English ecclesiastical courts to avoid the legal prohibition on dedicating property for religious purposes. Today, of course, most trusts are designed to protect and benefit individuals, although philanthropists sometimes use them for educational or eleemosynary purposes. For the most part, the trust device is unknown outside the English speaking nations, but a somewhat similar system is recognized by Moslem law. Their form differs, however, in that there are two parties in addition to the trustor: the trustee, who is God, and His worldly agent, who manages the property for Him.

The two basic types of trusts used in estate planning are the living (or inter vivos) trust, which might be either revocable or irrevocable, and the testamentary trust. Another type of trust (which has advantages in some situations) is the unfunded life insurance trust; it has gained increased acceptance in recent years.

Although the testamentary trust is the most widely used, each type has its individual characteristics and uses, and all offer a combination of advantages not found elsewhere. These include separation of the burden from the benefit of property ownership; experienced and efficient management (if the trustee is competent); strong legal safeguards; economy (a corporate trustee's fees usually are based on the value of the trust principal; from ¼% to 1% a year is customary); protection for beneficiaries (an especially important factor if the beneficiary is a minor or a financially inexperienced spouse); assurance that the property will be used as the trustor desires; and continuity of assets and family income. Additionally, in some cases significant savings in taxes and in the costs of estate administration might be realized.

Trusts and trust law are complex, so if you are wondering whether some arrangement of this sort might be advisable, you should consult with a lawyer experienced in this specialized field and also confer with a trust officer at your bank. For the present purpose, which is to do no more than broadly acquaint you with these devices, we shall merely highlight some of the characteristics, possible uses, and principal consequences of the more common arrangements, and point out a few of the main provisions in trusts that any prospective trustor should consider and resolve.

Revocable Living Trusts

As its name implies, a living trust is created and operates during the trustor's life. If the trustor has the right to cancel or modify, the agreement is called a "revocable trust."

Such an arrangement could be advantageous in several situations. For example, an elderly person might be concerned that in time, physical or mental deterioration could impair his or her ability to handle financial affairs. Or the desire might simply be to obtain relief from the responsibilities of managing investments so that more time and energy can be devoted to other interests. A revocable trust, containing provisions to pay the income to the trustor or for his or her benefit, and permitting withdrawal of any or all of the principal if desired, might be indicated. If the trustor, for whatever reason, wanted to keep control over investment decisions, the agreement could provide that any sale or purchase would require approval of the trustor, or alternately, authority might be retained to disapprove any proposed transaction.

The primary objective of an arrangement of this nature is, of course, property management during the trustor's life, or during the lives of a husband and wife. But another important advantage is that the property could be transferred to the trustor's children or other survivors without the normal delays (at least several months) and costs (such as attorney's fees and executor's commissions) involved in the probate process. For instance, the agreement might provide that after both spouses die, the trustee will divide the remaining trust estate and distribute it to their children, either all at once or at stated ages. However, if their children already have adequate financial resources, it might direct that the trust continue, with the income to be paid to them during their lives, and with discretion in the trustee to use the principal for them if needed; when the children die, the principal could then go to grandchildren. A generation-skipping arrangement of this type would avoid having the trust corpus taxed in the children's estates, up to a value of $250,000 for each child.

Because a revocable living trust does not involve a permanent surrender of ownership or control over property, the income is taxable to the trustor (regardless of who the income beneficiary is), just as it would have been without the trust. For the same reason, the property placed in trust is not subject to gift taxes; however, to the extent that income payable to a beneficiary other than the trustor exceeds the annual exclusion of $3,000 for each donee, it would be taxable as a gift. Additionally, the value of the principal at the time of the trustor's death would be included in the estate for death tax purposes. Hence, no tax savings to the trustor's estate result from this device; ultimately, though, taxes on the estate of a succeeding income beneficiary might be reduced.

Irrevocable Living Trusts

An irrevocable living trust is just what its name suggests: a trust arrangement under which a trustor transfers property to a trustee without reserving any right to cancel or modify the agreement. It has most of the advantages of a revocable trust, including avoidance of probate, and it also permits some tax savings. The income is not taxed to the trustor if all right and control over it has been relinquished, and if the trust corpus has been irrevocably transferred to the trustee for a period of not less than ten years or for the life or lives of one or more of the income beneficiaries. These savings could be substantial if the trustor is in a high tax bracket and the income beneficiary is in a low bracket. Also, because the trustor has given up ownership of the property, its value would not be subject to death taxes; however, except to the extent that the property might have appreciated in value between the time the trust is established and the time of death, gift taxes could effectively cancel out any reduction in estate taxes (see Appendix D).

Prior to 1977, there was a difference in gift tax and estate tax rates, as well as a lifetime exemption of $30,000 in gifts for each donor. These have disappeared under the present tax laws, which introduced a unified rate schedule for both gifts and estates, and a tax credit that applies against combined gift and estate taxes. Consequently, because much of the tax incentive behind irrevocable trusts (other than those of a short-term variety) no longer exists, their use is likely to decline. Moreover, an irrevocable, non-reversionary agreement almost presupposes considerable wealth, and even then most people are reluctant to surrender permanent control over their property. There are a few situations, though, in which such an arrangement might be useful. For example, a rich parent with a prodigal son might use an irrevocable trust to provide for his needs without indulging his excesses. But a short-term trust can be used to advantage by far more people, so we'll turn to it.

The Clifford Trust. This particular arrangement, which is also called a ten-year trust or a short-term trust, could help people of even moderate means who are helping support another person. For example, assume that you are in the 32% income tax bracket (taxable income of $24,600 to $29,900, if married), and that you give your widowed mother $3,000 a year to supplement her other income. To provide this amount, you have to earn, before taxes, $4,412. If you have other assets (such as stocks, bonds, or savings accounts) that yield $3,000 a year (but net only $2,040 after taxes), you could transfer these to a short-term, irrevocable trust that would pay the income to your mother for the rest of her life, and upon her death, the principal would be returned to you. The savings would be $1,412 a year ($4,412 minus $3,000), less any taxes your mother might have to pay.

Similar arrangements have been used to accumulate funds for a child's college education. However, income used to discharge a parent's duty to support a child is taxable to the parent, so to the extent that college expenses are a parental responsibility, a Clifford Trust is not advised for such purposes.

Testamentary Trusts

While a living trust can be quite useful in certain situations, particularly for an older person, a testamentary trust, which is created by will and does not operate until the testator's death, deserves consideration by a broader range of people. Although no immediate income or estate tax savings are available, the other trust advantages should not be dismissed lightly.

When a significant amount of property is left outright to a widow, there is often the danger that her lack of investment experience or the influence of well-meaning but financially inexpert relatives or friends could lead to the innocent loss of much of it or, far more likely, of its purchasing power. For a small annual fee, this risk can be avoided and the widow can be relieved of the burden of managing the property. Of course, many wives are capable of handling large sums of money, and in some cases of doing so far more competently than their husbands; and, with or without reason, a wife might interpret a trust arrangement as evidence of a lack of confidence in her, instead of something designed to protect her and to relieve her of some weighty responsibilities.

Although a testamentary trust is not for everyone, anyone who has much more than a moderate estate should decide whether, in his or her circumstances, it might be more effective than other arrangements. However, if the estate consists mostly of non-probate assets (such as jointly owned property or life insurance proceeds payable to a named beneficiary), so that relatively little would pass under the will, some other way of achieving the same result (such as a life insurance trust with a "pour-over" of probate assets) should be explored, if a trust is desired.

In any event, even if a husband decides to leave all his probate property to his wife, a contingent trust should be considered if there are minor children. Usually, such an arrangement is preferable to a contingent bequest to them, which would require a cumbersome and rather expensive guardianship if his wife fails to survive him. A trust could avoid this, as well as the inequities that might result from equal distributions to each child, regardless of their differing needs. To prevent the trust approach from being thwarted in the event the husband dies first, though, his wife should have similar provisions in her will.

For those persons whose estates are sufficiently large to be affected by federal estate taxes (see Appendix D), testamentary trusts provide a ready opportunity for later savings. The usual technique is to divide the residue of the estate into two parts: one for the widow and the other for her benefit while she is alive. The widow might be given her portion either outright or in trust. If a trust (sometimes called the "wife's trust") is used, she could be given authority to withdraw as much of the principal as she chooses or as the testator-trustor specifies, and she must have an unrestricted power of appointment (the right to name who will receive the principal), so that it will qualify for the marital deduction. This permits the larger of $250,000 or 50% of the adjusted gross estate to pass to a surviving spouse without being taxed. (Whether or not the full marital deduction should be taken depends upon several factors, such as the size of the estate, the value of the widow's separate property, and her age and health; at times, less is more insofar as eventual tax savings are concerned.)

That portion of the estate not passing to the widow (or in trust for her) is used to fund a trust (known as the "family trust"). The usual provisions direct the trustee to pay the income to the widow during her life and, at the trustee's discretion, to use whatever amount of the principal is needed for her care and welfare. If the trustor wishes, he could also give her the right to withdraw the greater of $5,000 or 5% of the principal a year. Normally, he would let her specify, in her will, how the principal is to be divided among the children. (This is called a "special" or "limited" power of appointment.) On her death, the trustee will distribute what remains to them, either all at once or in whatever manner the trustor or his widow directed. What a family trust does, essentially, is remove the property from the widow's estate for death tax purposes, yet give her the benefit of it during her life.

An arrangement of the type discussed would not have any federal estate tax advantage, of course, unless the widow's estate exceeds $175,000 (see Appendix D). Also, the approach outlined assumes that the husband owns considerably more property than his wife. If each has separate interests that are roughly equal and of sufficient size to make tax planning advantageous, or if substantially all of the assets are community property, other arrangements (such as each using his or her residuary estate to fund a single trust for the other as income beneficiary, with the children as remaindermen) might be indicated.

To give you an idea, though, of the savings that are possible by using trusts, see Table 9.1.

Unfunded Life Insurance Trusts

A life insurance trust is no more than a revocable trust that uses as its corpus the proceeds of insurance on the trustor's life. Because

TABLE 9.1. *Estate Tax Savings by Using Trusts (for deaths after 1980).*

	Tax on Husband's Estate[a]			Later Tax on Widow's Estate[c]		
Taxable Estate	Without Marital Deduction	With Full Marital Deduction[b]	If ½ to W, ½ in Trust	If All Left to Wife	If ½ Left to Wife	Potential Savings
$ 100,000	0	0	0	0	0	0
200,000	$ 7,800	0	0	$ 5,304	0	$ 5,304
300,000	40,800	0	0	26,928	0	26,927
400,000	74,800	0	$ 7,800	49,368	$ 7,800	41,568
500,000	108,800	$ 23,800	23,800	100,708	23,800	76,908
1,000,000	298,800	108,800	108,800	256,368	108,800	147,568

[a]Assumes that the husband dies first.
[b]The marital deduction is the larger of $250,000 or 50% of the adjusted gross estate passing to the surviving spouse.
[c]Assumes that the widow's taxable estate is the same as the amount left her, minus the estate tax paid on her husband's estate, and that she survives him by 10 or more years; if death were to occur within 10 years, a credit for all (if death were within 2 years) or part of the estate taxes previously paid would be available.

these are not available until death occurs, the trust obviously does not become effective until then, nor does it offer any immediate income or estate tax savings. Nevertheless, this device might meet the needs of some people.

If an estate consists of relatively little other than a large amount of life insurance (a situation common in many young families), the insured could use this to fund a trust for his or her spouse and children. After entering into an agreement with the trustee, arrangements are made with the insurance companies to change beneficiaries to the trustee, and the policies are delivered to him. The trustee will hold the policies until the trustor's death (unless the agreement is revoked sooner), collect the proceeds, and then manage and distribute them according to the terms of the trust.

Although a life insurance trust could be "funded" by providing the trustee with funds to pay the policy premiums, an "unfunded" arrangement, under which the trustor continues paying the premiums personally, is used more frequently. The only expenses prior to the trustor's death are the attorney's fees for drafting the agreement (perhaps a few hundred dollars) and, possibly, the acceptance fee of $100 or so that some corporate trustees charge. The acceptance fee usually would be added to the corpus if the trust comes into being, or forfeited if the trust is later revoked.

Unfunded Life Insurance Trust v. Testamentary Trust. Life insurance could be used to fund a testamentary trust, of course, but an unfunded life insurance trust has several advantages. For one thing, if the proceeds were used for a testamentary trust, the insured's estate would have to be the beneficiary of the policies; this would subject the proceeds to administration, claims against the estate, and, in some states, inheritance taxation. The avoidance of probate, with its costs and extended delays, is itself a sufficient reason not to make an estate the beneficiary of life insurance. Also, a life insurance trust can serve as a convenient receptacle for other estate assets, which can be "poured over" into it by the testator's will.

Unfunded Life Insurance Trust v. Settlement Options Other Than Cash. If a life insurance trust is compared to any periodic payment settlement option offered by insurers, the dismal shortcomings of the latter become immediately apparent. The most important advantage of a trust is its flexibility: if an unforeseen emergency arises, the principal could be drawn upon to meet it. The rigidity of an insurance annuity option, on the other hand, would not permit any deviation from the fixed-dollar income plan selected: the widow or widower would receive no more nor less than the monthly stipend, regardless of the circumstances.

Perhaps equally important, a trust is more likely to protect beneficiaries against erosion in the purchasing power of the dollar. The "prudent man" standard that applies in most states requires trust investments to be geared to both the production of a reasonable income and the preservation of capital; and preservation means not just maintaining the same number of dollars (anyone can do that by merely buying Treasury securities), but also increasing capital to offset inflation. There is no assurance, of course, that the trust corpus will appreciate, nor is there any certain return such as an insurer will guarantee. However, there is the potential for gain, because unless the trustor has directed otherwise, most corporate trustees usually invest the funds they manage in high-grade common stocks as well as in quality bonds and other securities.

Also, even if the trust corpus were not to appreciate at all, in most cases the income should almost equal the income-plus-principal payments of a 20-years-certain life income settlement option. Hence, when the life beneficiary of a trust dies, the trust estate, less any amounts that might have been paid out of principal, would be available for the remaindermen. Conversely, upon the death of the beneficiary of a settlement option or upon the expiration of the years-certain guarantee, whichever is later, nothing whatsoever would remain for the children or others.

Contingent Unfunded Life Insurance Trusts. One variation of the typical unfunded life insurance trust is a *contingent unfunded life insurance trust,* in which the trustee is the contingent or secondary beneficiary. This arrangement might be considered by someone who wants his or her spouse to receive the insurance proceeds, but prefers a trust for the children in the event the spouse does not survive.

Some of the advantages of a trust for minor children were briefly mentioned earlier. These include avoidance of the costs and inconvenience of appointing a guardian for their estates, the bonding expense, and the required periodic accountings by the guardian to the court. Also, there might be a problem of financial competence if the guardian is an individual, as well as the question of a replacement if he or she were to die during the guardianship period. Then, too, each child's share would have to be paid when the child reaches majority (which in many states is now 18 for such purposes), even though his or her experience and ability to manage it might be questionable. In addition, a guardianship is subject to the continued jurisdiction of the probate court, which might be undesirable, particularly if the children reside in a state other than the one in which the will is probated.

Another limitation of naming young children as contingent beneficiaries of life insurance is that the proceeds would be divided equally among them. More equitable results are possible if the estate is treated and managed as a unit for the benefit of all the children, although their needs might be disparate. For example, assume that both parents die, survived by three minor children who, as contingent beneficiaries of life insurance, share $100,000 in proceeds equally. If one of the children requires expensive medical care or special training, the costs would be borne by his or her share. Upon reaching majority, that child might have nothing left to be distributed to him or her, but the other two might receive sizeable sums. If the parents had not died, any costs incident to caring for one child would have been absorbed by the family assets, not by any particular portion of such assets. Most parents probably would desire the same thing if they were to die while their children are young. This can be accomplished by a family trust that permits the trustee to "spray" or "sprinkle" the income and use the principal according to the individual needs of the beneficiaries, and to distribute what remains when the children reach majority or at ages or times that the trustor has directed.

2503(c) Trusts. Within the last several years, every state has enacted a Uniform Gifts to Minors Act (UGMA). Before then, it was difficult to transfer property to a child in a manner that might postpone its use until the child was older, yet still permit the donor to take advantage of his annual $3,000 gift tax exclusion and not have the income from the property taxed to him. Section 2503(c) of the Internal Revenue Code provided a way to do so.

The statutory requirements can be met with a living, irrevocable trust that has provisions making the principal and income *available* to the child, and specifying that the trust will terminate and the assets be distributed to him when he is 21. However, the trust may also give the trustee discretion (but not direct him) to accumulate the income, and it may provide that unless the beneficiary, within a limited time after becoming 21, demands termination, the trust will continue.

Because a UGMA transfer serves essentially the same purpose as a 2503(c) trust, and does so more simply and less expensively, it is generally the better way to go. Nevertheless, under some circumstances, a 2503(c) trust arrangement might have advantages.

Administrative and Distributive Arrangements

Deciding what administrative and distributive provisions in a trust would be most beneficial depends, of course, upon numerous factors, such as the size and nature of the trust estate, the desires of the trustor, and the needs of the beneficiaries. A trust is a personal and complex instrument that requires custom drafting by a knowledgeable lawyer, not something you can do for yourself by filling in spaces on a printed form. To provide your lawyer with a clear understanding of your desires, however, there are a few general matters to which you should give some thought, starting with who you want as trustee.

Selecting a Trustee. Similar to an executor, a trustee is a fiduciary, and so is held to the highest standards of loyalty. But unlike an executor, whose duties are short-term, a trustee's duties require him to manage the trust principal productively over a long period of time.

Selecting a trustee can have an important or even decisive bearing on the effectiveness of a trust. In past years, individuals (often relatives or family lawyers) were the usual choices. One advantage of an individual trustee is that he is more likely to know the beneficiaries' needs and to have a personal interest in their welfare. Also, there is the cost factor: although a corporate trustee's fees (¼% to 1% a year) are not unreasonable, if a qualified relative or friend serves without compensation, that much more income is available for the beneficiaries. Often, however, the financial experience and abilities of individual trustees fall short of the competence needed.

In recent years, corporate trustees have become more popular, and today over one-fifth of all banks have trust departments. They are not equally skilled, of course, but most are better equipped than individuals in general to perform investment duties; they provide continuity of management; and by and large, their long-term records have been satisfactory. Although costs are too great to enable them to accept small (perhaps less than $50,000 or $100,000, depending upon the particular institution) individual trusts, most states permit corporate trustees to combine small trusts into a common trust fund. Also, some banks have different funds for different objectives (such as high income or appreciation potential), which permits a trustor to select among them.

Sometimes, a trustor appoints both a corporate trustee and his or her surviving spouse as co-trustee. This does not result in any saving, for most trust departments charge a full fee anyway, and as a practical matter, such an arrangement tends to be inefficient. As an alternative, the surviving spouse could be given power to direct the trustee in certain matters, or he or she could be appointed in an advisory capacity.

Occasionally, circumstances suggest that an individual serve as trustee. But for most long-term, family-type trust arrangements, the advantages, on balance, usually favor an established institution with a proven record of satisfactory performance.

Investment Powers. Unless the trust provides otherwise, most states require trust funds to be invested in accordance with a "prudent man" standard, and a few states restrict investments to those authorized by state law. "Legal lists" tend to be unduly restrictive, so anyone establishing a trust in such a state should consider granting his trustee broader discretion.

Conversely, a trustor should be cautious about limiting investments or directing his trustee to hold certain securities or types of securities or other property, for today's seemingly sagacious choices could be tomorrow's biggest blunders. For example, early in the century railroad stocks and bonds were widely regarded as both prudent and promising, but over the years, the beneficiaries of trusts limited to such investments were penalized: pity the widow locked into Penn Central! Instead of trying to be prescient, the best results are apt to come from giving liberal investment discretion to a trustee in whom the trustor has confidence. If an inexperienced individual trustee is selected, however, he or she should be given powers to invest in mutual funds or to place the trust assets in a managed account; these are particularly well-suited for small trusts managed by nonprofessional trustees, but they might be improper in some states unless expressly authorized in the trust.

Invasion Powers. Probably the most indispensable provision in any long-term trust is a "power of invasion" that permits the trustee to use the principal if the income alone is inadequate for the beneficiaries' needs. Without an express authorization, a trustee would be powerless to do so, regardless of how dire the situation might be or how large the estate. The experience of the last few decades, during which the dollar has declined in value to about one-fourth of what it had been prior to World War II, and the present acceleration of this trend have shown that over the longer term, it would be naive to plan for future needs in terms of fixed numbers of dollars.

Although some invasion power is critical, a more delicate question is how extensive it should be. Giving the trustee an "absolute" discretion to invade principal could be interpreted as relieving him of even a requirement of "reasonableness," so too broad a standard should be avoided. A better solution might be to provide that all distributions are binding on the remaindermen; this should assure adequate liberality on the part of the trustee, and at the same time reduce potential conflicts between the life beneficiary and the remaindermen.

Clear guidance as to the trustor's desires concerning the life beneficiary's care should also be furnished. A common direction is for the trustee to use the income and, if necessary, to invade the principal for the "support, comfort, health, and welfare" of the life beneficiary. Most trustees and courts would interpret such a provision as meaning more than mere necessities, but it might be even clearer if the trust specifies "an accustomed manner of living," if that is what the trustor has in mind, as well as other categories of needs or uses (such as travel expenses) that are contemplated. However, if the trust is designed to escape later taxation in the life beneficiary's estate, he or she should not have such extensive use or control over it as to be tantamount to ownership. Also, the trust should specify whether or not other income available to the life beneficiary (such as a spouse's earnings, if the beneficiary remarries) are to be considered in making distributions. And if the overriding purpose is to provide for the life beneficiary, regardless of whether doing so depletes the principal, say so.

If the life beneficiaries are minors, the trust should explicitly define "support" to include education, as well as the scope of the education the trustor has in mind. A standard of "the best education commensurate with the abilities and interests" of a child is appropriate in most cases, assuming the trust principal is large enough to afford an Amherst as well as a local community college. Also, the educational provision should indicate whether or not graduate or professional school expenses are included. Something else that might avoid future disputes or the need for judicial interpretation is a provision relating to use of the principal for such purposes of assisting a child to buy a house, enter into a business, or establish a professional practice. Finally, the trustor should decide whether prior unequal benefits are to be considered on final distribution. For example, if one child attends Harvard but another does not go beyond high school, should the costs of the former's education be deducted from his or her share of the remainder? In this area, as in others, forethought and planning can often eliminate problems in later years.

Providing for Guardian's Needs. Another provision that deserves consideration in some cases in which trusts are intended to provide for prospectively orphaned minor children is whether the trustee should use part of the income for their guardian's needs. If a father has provided adequately for his family after his death, but if only his children survive, his estate, supplemented by other survivor benefits, probably would be more than ample for the children alone. At the same time, their personal guardian, perhaps a close relative, might have limited income but large financial responsibilities, so that his or her own children are in a vastly different financial position than that of his wards. Under such circumstances, the welfare of the wards might be enhanced if the trustee were permitted to use some of the trust income to assist the guardian or the guardian's children, for they are the only family the trustor's own children then have.

Miscellaneous Other Provisions. There are many other matters that must be considered and resolved when planning a trust, but it would be beyond the limited purpose of this chapter to go into them. They include such questions as: whether to include a "spendthrift" clause (to prevent a beneficiary from disposing of or encumbering his interest, and to protect the trust from creditors); how liberal the trustee's managerial powers should be; and at what ages distributions should be made to children (21 might not be best for a child, but is 35 too old?). A prospective trustor should discuss these and other concerns with his lawyer and with the trustee.

This chapter will have served its purpose if it has given you a general awareness of trusts and of their advantages in some situations. The cardinal point has been that once anyone acquires much more than a modest estate, he should consider whether a trust arrangement of some sort might enable him to use it for his family's benefit more effectively than would otherwise be possible. The answer isn't always "yes"; but when it is, the results can warrant the effort.

SUNDRY NON-PROBATE TRANSFERS

Before leaving the subject of trusts, a few remotely related methods of transferring interests in property should be mentioned. As you have learned, the primary purpose of most trusts is to protect the beneficiaries by providing responsible management for property of significant value. In some cases, income or estate tax savings also might be realized, and most trusts other than the testamentary type remove assets from the probate process. Many people, not just the rich, could benefit from the trust device, but relatively few take advantage of it.

Most people, however, do resort at one time or another to various non-trust property arrangements that are designed to avoid probate or to shift income from a higher to a lower tax bracket. Although property management is seldom an objective and the sums involved might not be large, the techniques used can serve a worthwhile purpose, not just for the millions of people who have only modest resources, but for the more comfortably situated as well. Some familiarity with the characteristics, possible uses, and principal consequences of the more common arrangements might be helpful. Probably the most familiar is joint tenancy or joint ownership (the "poor man's will") between a husband and wife, which will be considered in the following chapter. Other popular methods include:

Outright Gifts. The most clean-cut way to reduce estate taxes and avoid probate is, obviously, to dispose of property before death, and the simplest manner of doing so is to give it away. Consequently, if anyone has ample assets for his needs, presently and prospectively, and if he would not feel uncomfortable about parting with some of them while he is still alive, he should consider making outright gifts.

A gift not only achieves the income-shifting and probate-avoidance goals mentioned, but in large estates, it reduces estate taxes (unless it is made within three years of the donor's death). To be effective, though, a present interest in the property must pass to the donee: a "when I die it's yours" type of "gift" usually would not qualify.

Also, if a gift is sufficiently large, a tax on the transfer would be incurred (see Appendix D). However, the federal law grants everyone an annual, non-cumulative exclusion of $3,000 per donee ($6,000 if a husband and wife make a gift to a third person). Purely from a cost perspective, a wealthy person would be improvident not to take advantage of the annual exclusion: if an estate would be taxed, every $1 transferred prior to the last three years of life equates to at least $1.47 later (and usually more, if state inheritance taxes and other costs are considered).

Even non-wealthy parents, for whom the savings might be more important, can stretch family dollars by making gifts of cash or securities to their minor children. The difficulty, though, is that outright gifts of titled or registered property (other than government savings bonds or savings accounts) can be complicated. This is where the Uniform Gifts to Minors Act comes to the rescue.

Gifts to Minors. Every state now has a Uniform Gifts to Minors Act (UGMA). These provide a simple procedure for making present gifts of money, securities, and other intangibles to minors, merely by placing them in the name of an adult. For example, a stock certificate could not be issued to a minor, but it could be registered in a manner such as, "Joan Adult, as custodian for Amy Child, under the Colorado UGMA." (There may be only one custodian, and only one beneficiary for each account or certificate.) The custodian manages the property (including selling it and reinvesting the proceeds, if appropriate) until the minor reaches 21, when it is transferred to him or her.

The UGMA technique merits consideration by even those persons who cannot afford more than a few hundred dollars a year to provide some degree of future financial security for their children. For example, assume that parents are able to save $50 a month for their child's later use. If this were deposited in an interest-bearing account in their names, the earnings would be taxable to them; if it were placed in the child's name, he or she could withdraw it without the parents' permission. But if, instead, this sum were deposited in a custodial account or used to buy securities under the UGMA, the income would be taxable to the child (hence, in most cases no tax would be due), and the custodian would control the property until the child is 21. By then, if $600 a year had been given since birth and if the average annual net yield had been 6% (disregarding any capital gains), over $25,000 would be available to provide him or her with a fair start as an adult.

Other matters concerning UGMA transfers that you should know about are: (1) If a parent-donor is custodian, the value of the property would be included in his estate if he dies before the minor becomes 21; to avoid this possibility, the other parent or a third person should be designated. (2) Once made, a gift is not revocable, so even if a once-cuddly bundle-of-joy grows into a pot-smoking, van-driving lout, what's his is his. And (3) this arrangement cannot be used to evade income taxes, of course, which would be the result if a parent-donor used the income to help pay for the child's support.

Totten Trusts and P.O.D.'s. Most states permit shares (deposits) in some thrift institutions, such as savings and loan associations, to be the subject matter of what, in a loose sense, is called a "trust." These are not usually authorized for commercial banks, but the same result is possible if the state recognizes "payable-on-death" (P.O.D.) accounts.

Although these arrangements appear to contradict the established rule of law that property transfers taking effect only at death are testamentary (and as such must comply with the statute of wills), they have been sanctioned by state laws and court decisions as effective ways to pass title to a beneficiary who survives the depositor.

No income or estate tax saving is realized through either of these devices. During the depositor's life, he has full control of the account, including the right to revoke it, in whole or in part, simply by withdrawing the funds. Also, the accounts are subject to claims of the depositor's creditors. Nevertheless, as a method of avoiding probate, a multiple party account has appeal, especially to persons with only modest estates.

"Joint" Bank Accounts. Large numbers of husbands and wives, as well as many parents and children, maintain what are known as "joint" bank accounts. These are not true joint tenancies, because either owner, acting independently, may withdraw any or all of the funds on deposit. The usual registration takes the form of "Robert *or* Jane Doe, as joint tenants with the right of survivorship." There is no gift tax liability when funds of only one joint owner are deposited in such an account, unless or until the non-contributor withdraws money for his or her personal use.

When one joint owner dies, the survivor owns the account, although a release from the state inheritance tax authorities normally would be required before it (or all of it above a specified amount) could be released to him or her. What is more, for purposes of estate taxation, the entire value of the account is included in the estate of the first to die, except to the extent that the survivor can establish that his or her separate property (or community property) was contributed to it, or unless, for federal tax purposes, it has qualified as a gift. Hence, although a joint bank account can be convenient, it generally would not, contrary to popular belief, result in any savings in death taxes.

chapter 10
What's Mine Is Thine

How title to property is held between spouses can have an important bearing on estate conservation, yet few people have more than a cursory acquaintance with the legal consequences of various ownership arrangements. An understanding of these might result in significant savings.

OWNERSHIP OF PROPERTY

To start with basics, unless someone is domiciled in a community property state, concepts rooted in the common law apply. Hence, unless a husband and wife have entered into some form of co-ownership, the property of each (which includes their earnings) will be separate from that of the other. Moreover, subject to whatever support obligations and other restrictions might be imposed by law, each may do what he or she pleases with his or her property, during and after life.

As a matter of historical interest, at one time a wife was not even capable, legally, of holding or managing property, but this doctrine was scrapped throughout the United States by the end of the nineteenth century—even though Gloria Steinem had not yet appeared on the scene. Long before the legislatures capitulated, however, various artifices had been used to evade this man-made disability. In ancient Rome, for example, two kinds of marriages were recognized: in one, the wife and her property belonged to her husband; in the other, ownership remained with her father. The first type was referred to as a marriage "with control" (*cum manu*); it resulted from either a formal ceremony, a purchase, or "use." For a marriage by use to exist, the husband had to exercise uninterrupted control over his wife for at least a year. If he failed to do so, the relationship amounted to no more than a marriage "without control" (*sine manu*), and the wife's father continued to manage her property. If the wife or her family desired to avoid a marriage by use, she could merely leave her husband for three nights each year, which was legally sufficient to disrupt his mastery over her (and to also show that legal "loopholes" are not of recent origin).

Over the centuries, many other methods were used to circumvent the property restrictions placed upon married women. For example, Paul Revere resorted to the common technique of bequeathing money ($4,000 each) to his three daughters in trust, with instructions to pay the income from it to them. (His two sons received their legacies outright.) By using a trust arrangement, the daughters' husbands (or their husbands' creditors) could not obtain the funds. Even though wives are now regarded by law as capable of owning property, complete equality between married (or quasi-married) couples has not yet been fully attained. (Right, "Mrs." Marvin?) Nevertheless, co-ownership arrangements are often used, knowingly or otherwise, to create rights that the law might not otherwise recognize.

Today, most married couples—not just young romantics—seem to look upon husband-wife concurrent ownership much as they might sin, believing there must be something good about it, for otherwise so many people would not indulge in it. To an extent, this is so. Nevertheless, co-ownership is not for everyone, and it is not something that should be entered into casually.

Too often, though, highly technical property relationships result from no more than an innocent nod when a real estate agent or other salesman asks a couple whether they want to take title jointly. If the buyers ask what would be best, the odds are that they will be told, joint tenancy. And if they pursue the matter, the salesman might sniff something about avoiding death taxes and the expenses and delay of probate. Such advice usually is based upon little more than superficial knowledge of law, and it could prove costly.

To avoid creating the wrong impression, though, you should

realize that for many or even most people, husband-wife co-ownership with a survivor feature makes sense. But before commenting on when it might or might not be appropriate, you should be familiar with the ways a husband and wife in most states might concurrently hold title to property: tenancy-in-common, joint tenancy, and tenancy-by-the-entirety. In addition, those who live in community property states should have a general awareness of how community property laws operate.

Tenancy-in-Common

Two or more people may have interests in the same property at the same time in any of three principal ways. Perhaps the easiest to understand is called a *tenancy-in-common*, which in some respects resembles a partnership. Each tenant-in-common owns an undivided part of the whole, whether the whole be land, securities, livestock, an automobile, or whatever. The interest of each co-tenant might or might not be equal to the interest of the other or others. For example, if a farmer, Buster Sod, died, leaving his farm to his two sons, Pitch and Fork, they would each inherit an undivided one-half as tenants-in-common. However, if Pitch had died before Buster and had been survived by a widow and three children, in most states each of the children would acquire an undivided one-sixth of the farm as a co-tenant with their Uncle Fork, who would own one-half.

As between a husband and wife, tenancies-in-common usually contemplate equal interests. This could result in a federal gift tax liability at the time the relationship is created if one spouse contributed more of his or her separate funds than the other. However, the exemption for husband-wife transfers ($100,000, cumulatively) would take care of this in most cases. Unlike joint tenancy, when one spouse dies, the other does not automatically own the property; instead, either co-tenant may dispose of his or her interest by will or otherwise. Even if the other spouse is the beneficiary, probate would be necessary in all but the smallest estates.

Joint Tenancy

The far more usual form of husband-wife co-ownership of property is *joint tenancy*, which first came into widespread use in the United States around the time of World War II. This arrangement is similar in most respects to tenancy-in-common, except that each party owns all the property if he or she survives the other. Hence, it is often thought of as a "poor man's will." Strictly speaking, the term "joint tenancy" applies only to real estate, and "joint ownership" refers to personal property; however, "joint tenancy" is commonly used with respect to both.

The Right of Survivorship. The most distinguishing characteristic of joint ownership is the right of survivorship, which simply means that upon the death of one joint owner, his interest automatically ceases and the survivor owns the property. To ensure that there is no misunderstanding, in some states title is taken "as joint tenants with the right of survivorship, and not as tenants-in-common," which might be redundant but isn't vague.

To obtain a clear, marketable title when one joint owner dies, the survivor must notify the appropriate registrar (e.g., bank or other financial institution, securities transfer agent, or state motor vehicle department) and submit a certified copy of the death certificate together with whatever affidavit and other documents might be required. In most situations, a new title in the survivor's name alone will be issued with reasonable promptness; in others, there might be some minor inconvenience, expense, and delay. For example, if title to real property is involved, a state might require a summary judicial proceeding. Also, before a financial institution may release funds in a joint checking or savings account, or before the contents of a joint safety deposit box (other than certain documents, such as a will) may be removed, a waiver usually is required from the state inheritance tax authorities; in some states, though, a survivor might be permitted to withdraw up to a limited amount from an account without a waiver.

Testamentary Disposition. Occasionally a would-be testator who has definite plans for disposing of his property is surprised to learn that, because substantially all of it is owned jointly with his wife, he has virtually nothing to give away unless she dies first. This follows, of course, from the survivorship nature of the interests. So, if a husband wanted to leave something to his widowed mother or to a destitute sister, or establish trusts for his wife and children to save taxes or provide property management for them, he might not be able to do so. Of course, if he is not financially able to indulge in anything other than direct bequests of everything to his wife, the lack of a testamentary estate might be of no importance. What is more, joint ownership does, as advertised, avoid the probate process.

Joint Ownership and Taxes. Perhaps the most pervasive myth about joint ownership is that the property passing to the survivor is not subject to death taxes. To the contrary, the federal rule is that generally the *entire* value of jointly owned property is included in the estate of the first owner to die, except to the extent that the survivor can prove he or she had used separate assets to acquire it (the "consideration furnished" test). However, the 1976 federal tax law revisions have eased this burden considerably, both by enabling more to pass tax-free to a surviving spouse (the larger of $250,000 or 50% of the estate), and by excluding one-half the value of "qualified joint interest" property. Nevertheless, unless or until the domiciliary state modifies its laws, an inheritance tax might be levied upon the value of the decedent's interest.

To "qualify" personal property acquired after 1976 for the federal exclusion, the survivor's one-half interest must be created by one or both of the spouses and must be a gift for gift tax purposes. This rules out "joint" checking or savings accounts and Series E bonds purchased with one spouse's separate assets, because no gift occurs until the non-contributor withdraws funds. With respect to other personal property (for example, securities), filing a timely gift tax return, even though no tax might be due, should establish the latter requirement. If real property (such as a family home) is involved, the donor must exercise the option he has under the tax laws (by filing a gift tax return) to treat the spouse's interest as a gift. If he fails to do so, the "consideration furnished" test would apply. Whether and how some joint interests created before 1977 might "qualify," assuming they were not treated as gifts at the time, will depend upon regulations and decisions yet to be issued. However, if title to real estate acquired before 1977 is held jointly by a husband and wife (and if a gift tax return had not been filed), a re-conveyance of it and the filing of a return probably would be required.

For those estates of sufficient size to be taxed, the exclusion of the survivor's one-half interest in jointly owned property might be advantageous, provided the spouse who dies first had used his or her separate property to create the interest. However, if the non-contributing spouse predeceases the other, his or her one-half would be taxable when he or she dies, then later taxed again in the estate of the survivor, even though the survivor had originally used his or her separate funds to acquire it. This sequence-of-death risk is present, of course, in other husband-wife property arrangements.

Tenancy-by-the-Entirety

Still another form of husband-wife ownership that is recognized in some states, mainly those in the East and South, is the common law relic known as *tenancy-by-the-entirety*. This ingenious device envisions a husband and a wife each owning all of the same property (historically limited to real estate) at the same time. As in joint tenancy, which it closely resembles, on the death of one tenant, his interest ceases and title vests in the survivor. One difference is that while the survivorship rights of a joint tenant are destroyed if the other joint tenant transfers his interest, the survivorship interest of a tenant-by-the-entirety is "indestructible." In other words, a surviving spouse acquires title to the property, even though the decedent might have conveyed his interest during life or devised it to someone else in his will.

COMMUNITY PROPERTY

Eight states, mainly in the far West and Southwest, follow in one form or another the community property system of the civil law that had become entrenched before they became part of the United States. Unlike the early common law doctrine that viewed marriage as a merger of the wife's legal identity into that of her husband, the civil law theory more nearly approached the current view of marriage as a partnership.

Beyond some basic concepts, there is not much uniformity in the present-day community property laws of the eight states. Hence, our brief consideration will be quite general.

What Is Community Property? Because the community property system recognizes both separate and community ownership of property, the initial and at times most difficult problem is to classify particular property as one type or the other. Basically, community property is everything acquired by either the husband or wife *after* marriage, *except* property that one or the other obtains by gift, devise, or descent. Property owned before marriage, as well as that acquired subsequently by inheritance or gift, retains its character as separate property. With respect to the community assets, each spouse owns an undivided, one-half interest.

The standard definition of community property sounds straightforward enough, but it doesn't solve all problems that might arise.

For example, what about income (e.g. dividends, interest, rents) from separate property? Well, in some states it is separate property, but in others it is community property. Other classification issues might involve personal injury awards, gifts between spouses, acquisitions made partly with separate and partly with community assets, and property acquired when the spouses were domiciled in a common law state that would have been community property if they had been domiciled in the community property state at the time it was acquired (quasi-community property). Without going into details that are beyond the scope of our discussion, the general rule is that in cases of doubt, all property is presumed to be community unless its separateness can be established.

Who "Controls" the Community? Traditionally, the husband manages and controls the community personal property. However, spurred by the women's rights movement, some states (e.g., California and Washington) have enacted laws declaring that a husband and wife have equal control and management of community assets. These have added some complications, especially in such matters as creditors' remedies. In all the states, though, a wife usually must join in any transaction relating to the community real property. What is more, even where the husband controls the community personal property, he may not lawfully defraud her nor dispose of it unilaterally for non-community purposes. For example, if premiums for an insurance policy on the husband's life are paid with community funds without the wife's express or implied consent, she owns one-half of the policy during his life and is entitled to one-half of the proceeds on his death, regardless of whom he might have designated as beneficiary.

Disposition of Community Assets on Death. Either spouse may dispose of his or her one-half interest in the community property by will. But if a husband purports to dispose of the entire community, his wife has the option of either accepting what he gave her in his will, or else what she would be entitled to under the laws of intestate succession (the "widow's election"). If either spouse dies without a will in California, Nevada, Idaho, New Mexico, or Washington, his or her share of the community passes to the survivor; in Texas, Arizona, and Louisiana, all or part of the decedent's interest, usually depending upon whether or not there are children, might go to others.

Community Property and Taxes. Because each spouse owns one-half of all community property, the value of his or her interest is not taxable as part of the estate of the first to die. However, this amount is set off against the marital deduction allowed for separate property passing to a surviving spouse. In fact, the marital deduction was introduced into the federal estate tax laws to equalize the treatment of domiciliaries of common law and community property states. Although one-half of the community assets belong to the survivor, they usually are retained in the estate for purposes of administration and payment of community debts. California and Washington, though, have procedures for "confirming" community property to the survivor, regardless of how title had been held. This has the advantage, in most cases, of removing the survivor's share from the probate process, thereby reducing commissions and fees.

Other Considerations. On top of the complexities community ownership sometimes creates, often because it is not well understood outside the community property states, most of the jurisdictions that have this system also recognize some forms of common law co-ownership. In New Mexico, for example, property may be held in co-tenancy or jointly between a husband and wife, but if so, it is treated as separate property. On the other hand, in California, property that ostensibly is jointly owned or even titled in the name of the husband or wife alone, might be either community or separate, depending upon the intent of the spouses. None of the community property states recognizes tenancies-by-the-entirety, but joint tenancy combined with the homestead laws of the West serves essentially the same purposes.

FACTORS TO CONSIDER

Because so many variables, financial and otherwise, are involved, the best husband-wife property ownership arrangements usually depend upon the unique facts of each case. Moreover, as family situations change, what is appropriate at one time might be inappropriate at another: the estate conservation concerns of struggling young parents are far removed from those of elderly, well-to-do grandparents. Of course, all estate planning is to some extent ephemeral, so the best you can do is take your situation as it exists, factor in foreseeable major changes, obtain the most reliable information and advice available to you, and proceed from there.

The Tax Factor

Although effective estate planning goes well beyond saving taxes, to disregard their impact could adversely affect the ultimate goal of providing the most family benefit and protection with the assets you have. An understanding of the basic rules might help you avoid some costly mistakes.

Prior to 1977, conventional wisdom held that anyone with much more than a modest estate should view co-ownership skeptically. There was ample reason to do so, for joint ownership posed all sorts of gift, estate, and income tax risks. It still does, but to a lesser extent.

Presently, estate tax considerations are not quite as pressing a concern for most people, because under the 1976 Tax Reform Act, the estate tax marital deduction has been increased from one-half of a decedent's adjusted gross estate to $250,000 (or 50% of adjusted gross estates that exceed $500,000); gifts between spouses, up to a cumulative maximum of $100,000, are now tax free (formerly, one-half the value was not taxed, and everyone had a $30,000 lifetime exemption); and a unified estate and gift tax credit that equates to an exemption of about $147,000 in 1979 (and increases in annual increments to the equivalent of about $175,000 in 1981) has been introduced (see Appendix D).

With respect to income taxes, new laws have also changed the tax basis (the sum deductible from the sales price to determine taxable gain or loss) for inherited property. Previously, the basis had been "stepped-up" to the property's value on the date of death (or six months later). Now, it is the decedent's basis (usually his cost) for property acquired after 1979, or for determining gain, the value on 31 December 1979 for property held on that date (or the last day of 1976 if held then). If the property is other than marketable securities, its "fresh-start" value is arrived at by a complex formula that gives some recognition to prior appreciation. Essentially, though, in the past if a decedent had purchased stock in his name for $2,000 that was worth $10,000 at the time of his death, its later sale for $11,000 would have meant a taxable gain of $1,000; in the future, assuming the stock had been acquired after 1979, the taxable capital gain would be $9,000. Because of this change, there now is less income tax advantage in separate ownership of long-term investment assets.

Why Not Joint Ownership?

Although some of the tax incentives for not going overboard about co-ownership have disappeared, it would be a mistake to conclude that any married couple with assets below the $425,000 level (the $250,000 marital deduction plus, after 1980, the credit equivalent of $175,000) should hold all their property in some survivor-take-all manner. For one thing, such arrangements could prove unnecessarily costly to the ultimate beneficiaries (usually, their children). For example, if a husband died, having $100,000 of life insurance with his wife as named beneficiary, and owning $200,000 of other property jointly with her, there would be no federal estate tax liability. However, when his widow later dies, and assuming the $300,000 is still intact, her estate would be taxed $37,200. This entire sum could have been saved if he had left her a total of $150,000 (either outright or in trust) and had established a trust giving her a lifetime benefit of the other $150,000 with the remainder to go to their children on her death. Various other less costly arrangements also are possible. Whether any is appropriate might depend, of course, upon matters other than the prospective tax savings.

When Joint Ownership Is Indicated

For most people, even those who must be tax-conscious, joint ownership of a checking account and joint tenancy in the family home usually are sound steps. Aside from other considerations, the extent to which such co-ownership might contribute to family harmony and a wife's sense of security cannot be dismissed lightly.

With respect to other family assets, not everyone has to worry about tax savings, although with incomes and property values constantly increasing in response to the dollar's decline in purchasing power, more and more people will be affected. Nevertheless, toward the lower end of the size-of-estate spectrum (where most families are), different considerations obviously prevail. For example, assume a husband and wife with two young children have an annual family income of $14,000, a small "equity" in a $35,000 house, modest household furnishings, a $6,000 savings account, $25,000 insurance on the life of the husband, a three-year old car, and personal effects of nominal value. In their circumstances, the most pressing need if the husband were to die probably would be to have everything go to his widow in the simplest, fastest, and least expensive manner. Hence, joint ownership of all their titled assets (the house, savings account, and car) is indicated. The non-titled property is likely to be of limited value, so if they are domiciled in a state that permits summary proceedings for small estates, its transfer would be relatively simple and inexpensive. As a practical matter, though, most similarly situated families avoid any judicial supervision by simply keeping or distributing articles such as household furnishings and personal effects in whatever manner they believe the decedent would have desired. In fact, studies suggest that there are more than twice as many deaths as there are probate proceedings.

Joint Ownership is Not a Panacea

Even in those cases in which the maximum use of joint ownership might be beneficial, both the husband and the wife should have wills, particularly if there are children. Assuming both parents died when the children were still minors, whatever small wealth the family had accumulated should be used as advantageously as possible for the children's needs. If the assets went directly to them, an unwieldy and expensive property guardianship would be necessary. To avoid this, both parents' wills might provide for a contingent trust for the children, or if an unfunded life insurance trust existed, the estate assets could be poured over into it. A will also would enable the parents to nominate a personal guardian, which could help avoid the squabbles that otherwise might occur among relatives.

The principal purpose of this brief discussion has been to acquaint you with husband-wife co-ownership arrangements and to alert you to some of the complications that could develop from their indiscriminate use. No definitive solutions have been provided. By this point, though, you should realize that effective estate planning, whether it concerns accumulation or distribution, rarely results from happenstance, but instead is a function of informed deliberation abetted, as appropriate, by competent professional advice and assistance. A prerequisite to these is the ability to recognize potential pitfalls and problems. Too many people fail to plan their estates effectively. When death comes, it is too late.

chapter 11

Wills

Throughout history, all societies have recognized some heritable rights in lands and goods, and today every civilized nation permits, to a greater or lesser extent, property interests to pass from the dead to the living. Although the social planners in this country, in their egalitarian drive to redistribute incomes, have made many inroads on personal liberties and property rights of all types, everyone still retains considerable freedom to decide who will inherit most of his worldly possessions. If someone neglects to exercise this right, a scheme of inheritance prescribed by state law will take over. In either event, ownership will devolve upon others.

PROBATE AND NON-PROBATE ASSETS

In the next few pages, we shall examine briefly and generally the legislative and judicial answers to the question: who gets what? Before we start, though, a distinction must be made between what are known as *probate assets* and *non-probate assets*. Probate assets pass to other persons under the terms of the owner's will (if he had a valid will) or under the laws of succession of some state, and pursuant to an order of distribution entered by a court that has jurisdiction over such matters. On the other hand, non-probate assets pass independently. Examples of the latter are trust interests that become effective upon the death of the trustor; a survivor's interest in property he or she held in joint ownership with the decedent; and life insurance proceeds paid to a named beneficiary.

Although non-probate assets are not administered with the decedent's other property, they are part of his estate and, to the extent of his interest in them, they are subject to death taxes. Such property is not, however, subject to the owner's testamentary disposition—in other words, who receives it is determined separately from the testator's will, and any provisions he might have made in his will with respect to it are ineffective.

This distinction should be kept in mind because (as we have seen in the two preceding chapters) there are many arrangements that will take property out of the probate estate. To the extent that these have been used, the owner would not be able to control what happens to the property after his death. But even if he has deliberately tried to arrange his estate so as to avoid probate, he still needs a will. First, consider what happens when someone dies without one.

INTESTACY

Just as everyone, whether he wishes it or not, has a domicile, so everyone has a will. Assuming he has not made his own, some state legislature has made it for him, in which event he is known after death as an "intestate," and his condition is called "intestacy." Those who are entitled to an intestate's real property are, strictly speaking, heirs, and those who take his personal property are distributees. For simplicity, we shall refer to both classes as heirs.

Just who the heirs are and what they receive depends upon statutes known as laws of succession. In detail, these vary from state to state, but in principle there are marked similarities. For example, if an intestate is survived by a wife and children, his wife invariably will receive a portion of his property, generally one-third or one-half, and the balance will go to the children. In some states where remnants of the old common law distinction between real and personal property persist, a surviving wife's interest in her husband's real property may be no more than common law "dower," which is only a life interest in one-third. In these states, title to all the real estate, subject to the widow's limited interest, vests in the children.

If there is a widow but no surviving children, most states follow one of two general patterns: the widow either receives everything, or else a specified minimum plus half the remainder, with the balance going to the husband's relatives. Where there is no widow but children survive, the laws of succession uniformly provide for equal distribution among the children. If an intestate has neither widow nor children surviving, most states give the estate to the parents first, or if none, to brothers and sisters, then to nephews and nieces, and finally to cousins. Assuming no one within the specified degree of relationship can be located, the deceased's property will escheat to the state.

Widows of intestates who were domiciled in community property states (California, Washington, Idaho, Nevada, Arizona, New Mexico, Texas, and Louisiana) generally fare somewhat better than their common law sisters, because most or all of their husband's assets usually consist of community rather than separate property. As to the community estate, each spouse has an undivided half interest in the whole. Consequently, the widow always takes her half and, in all but two of the states, she will also receive all of her spouse's half, whether or not children also survived.

Although the laws of succession are designed to dispose of an intestate's estate in a manner that customarily would accord with his desires, had he made a will, intestacy can have some unfortunate results. None of the laws of succession gives any consideration, of course, to the needs or ages of the heirs. Hence, needless hardships sometimes occur. Assume, for example, that a man dies survived by a wife and young children. In common law states, his widow will receive a fraction of his property, say one-third, and the children the rest. Normally, the widow would be appointed guardian of the children's property, and as such she would administer it during their minorities. However, she would have to post a surety bond, obtain authorization from the court for unusual expenditures, and file annual accounts explaining how she had used her children's property, all of which could have been avoided had the decedent exercised his testamentary privilege. What is more, as the children reach majority, the balance of their shares must be distributed to them.

The consequences of intestacy might be even less desirable if the children have already reached majority, for in most cases the widow's financial needs are more than her part of the decedent's estate will provide, while the children may be self-sufficient. Regrettably, the benevolence of offspring cannot always be relied upon in such situations.

In many states, equally undesirable results may ensue if the decedent leaves a widow but no children. Here again, the financial needs of the person for whose welfare the decedent was primarily responsible may be needlessly sacrificed to enrich others. In some cases, property might even go to a distant relative whom the intestate scarcely knew and had little desire to benefit.

Aside from enabling a person to decide, within statutory limits, who shall succeed to his property, a will also permits him to select his executor and, if he wishes, avoid the costs of a surety bond; nominate a guardian for minor children if his wife does not survive him; save taxes in many situations; and create a testamentary trust. Thus, intestacy should be avoided unless the laws of succession provide for the same disposition as an individual would make by will, or unless the size or condition of an individual's estate is such that a will is unnecessary. (Summary administration statutes in many states permit the transfer to certain relatives of small estates, consisting entirely of personal property, without going through the usual process of administration.)

WILLS

There are various methods of avoiding the consequences of intestacy. Inter vivos gifts, living trusts, or joint tenancy, despite drawbacks in some situations, remove property from the operation of the laws of succession. But all of these can have limitations in individual cases and none is likely to dispose of an entire estate. The only comprehensive way an individual may decide who shall receive his property after his death is by the ancient device of a will.

The Vocabulary of Wills

Before considering what a will is or how it operates, a quick glance at some of the common language of wills may be helpful. To begin with, the word "will" formerly was used only in connection with real property, while "testament" referred to disposition of personal property. Hence, if the same document disposed of both real and personal property, it was known as a will and testament.

The distinction disappeared long ago, and "will" now encompasses the disposition of both classes of property, although the phrase "last will and testament," despite its redundancy, is sometimes still used.

The maker of a will is called a testator (or, if a female, purists prefer testatrix), and upon his death he is said to have died testate. Any gift of real property by will is a devise, and the recipient is a devisee. Strictly speaking, a gift of money by will is a legacy, while the gift of any personal property is a bequest; however, the terms are now used interchangeably, and donees of personal property are called legatees.

The person designated by the testator to administer his estate is known as the executor or, if a female, the executrix. In several states, however, the term, "personal representative," has been substituted for the person (or corporation) appointed to serve in this capacity. If a decedent did not have a will, the court would appoint someone known as the administrator (or administratrix) to perform the same functions.

To probate simply means to prove, and probating a will is the procedure of proving to the appropriate court that the document is the decedent's valid last will and that it meets the requirements of law. Probate court proceedings are *in rem* rather than *in personum*, which is to say that the court's judgment is binding on the whole world, not just the parties. With this elementary vocabulary in mind, we may next turn our attention to what makes a will valid.

What Is Necessary to Probate a Will

After a testator dies, one of the first responsibilities of his executor is to petition the appropriate court (usually known as a probate court or, in a few states, a surrogate's court) to admit the will to probate and to issue *letters testamentary* to the executor. Notice that this petition has been filed must be furnished, in a prescribed manner, to beneficiaries and also to all persons who would take any of the estate had the decedent died intestate, so that they will have an opportunity to contest the petition.

Thereafter, the executor must prove that the statutory requirements for a valid will have been met. These vary in detail from state to state, but there are fundamental similarities. In general, it must be established that the will signing ritual was performed and that the decedent had testimonial capacity. If not contested, testimony of one of the witnesses usually is sufficient proof of these matters, or if no witness is available, proof of the handwriting of the testator and one of the witnesses is an acceptable substitute. A few states permit an "affidavit of proof," signed before a notary by the testator and witnesses, to establish the matters necessary for admitting a will to probate; if there is no contest, this procedure dispenses with other proof.

No right exists to make testamentary disposition of property, except in accordance with the legislative mandates concerning the manner of executing or authenticating a will. Hence, strict compliance with these statutory modes is demanded, and any variance might result in intestate distribution of a decedent's property. There are five basic requirements to a legally effective will-signing ritual. On the surface, these may seem procedural, but there is a valid reason for each.

1. The testator must have "published" his will. Publication, in this sense, means he declared the document to be his will in the presence of the witnesses (most states require two witnesses, but some require three). This act tends to show he knew what he was signing.
2. The testator must have signed his will in the presence of all witnesses. "Presence of" means all the witnesses must have been together at the same time and all must have been observed the testator making his signature. (Some states, however, permit a testator, in the presence of all witnesses, to acknowledge a previously made signature.) This requirement is designed not only to minimize forgery, but to lessen the opportunities for force, duress, or fraud.
3. The testator must have signed at the end of the will. This prevents later additions, perhaps by someone other than the testator.
4. The testator must have expressly asked the witnesses to witness his signature and to sign the will themselves.
5. The witnesses must have actually signed in the testator's presence and, in most states, in the presence of each other.

Aside from proof of the required utterances and acts at the time the will was signed, there must be proof of other more basic requirements. The testator must have been at least 18 years old in all states except Georgia (14) and Alabama (21 to dispose of non-personal property), and he must have had testimonial capacity. Testimonial capacity means, generally, sufficient mental capacity to understand what he was doing (that he was "of sound and disposing mind and memory"). Additionally, of course, the will must have been voluntary, that is, the testator must have made it unfettered by any physical or mental force, duress or coercion. If there is no contest, testimonial capacity normally may be shown sufficiently by the attestation clause which precedes the witnesses' signatures.

As indicated, the courts are strict and sometimes seemingly harsh in requiring compliance with statutory procedures in making and executing a will. This judicial severity is not captious, but rather it is essential to protect all parties who may have an interest in a decedent's estate. Consequently, if for no other reason than to assure probate, a testator should have his will drawn and executed under the supervision of a lawyer. While so-called "standard form" wills are available at most stationery stores, the law of wills is intricate and a will, by its nature, is a highly personalized document. Anything short of competent draftsmanship and execution might defeat a testator's desires, which Lord Neaves aptly illustrated in his tribute to "The Jolly Testator Who Makes His Own Will":

> Ye Lawyers who live upon litigants' fees,
> And who need a good many to live at your ease;
> Grave or gay, wise or witty, what e'er your degree,
> Plain stuff, or State's Counsel, take counsel of me:
> When a festive occasion your spirit unbends,
> You should never forget the profession's best friends;
> So we'll send round the wine, and a light bumper fill
> To the jolly testator who makes his own will.

The Anatomy of a Will

Too many people neglect to make wills, which is regrettable mainly because of the unnecessary costs or hardships intestacy often imposes upon family survivors; additionally, a will is needed to effectively coordinate the various non-probate assets passing to others. Apart from the common tendency to procrastinate when something is not thought to be pressing, and the reluctance of most people to plan for death, there appears to be a mystique of sorts about wills. A good part of this is probably the fault of the legal profession itself, which often seems to revel in obscurity and which has a tendency to use words and phrases unfamiliar to others. (In many situations, however, such usage is essential for precision, simply because a particular word or phrase might be legal shorthand for a concept that could not otherwise be expressed concisely and effectively.) Also, many lawyers fail to explain clearly to clients (a great number of whom are reluctant to ask) what certain provisions mean and what effect they have.

In the belief that greater familiarity can breed greater understanding, we'll hastily dissect the relatively simple will of a hypothetical testator. He's a moderately successful, married man in his late 30s, with two teenage children; his financial situation does not yet warrant sophisticated tax-saving arrangements, yet he has progressed beyond the everything-to-my-wife stage, and he has established a life insurance trust. First, scan his will, Figure 11.1, then see if the explanations and comments that follow help foster a little better understanding of just what it is designed to accomplish and why.

FIGURE 11.1. *Will of Thomas T. Testator.*

WILL OF THOMAS T. TESTATOR

I, Thomas T. Testator, a resident of Santa Barbara, California, declare this to be my Will, and revoke all former Wills and Codicils.

FIRST: I direct that all estate, inheritance and other death taxes payable by reason of my death on any property included in my estate for tax purposes shall be paid as an expense of administration without contribution from any person and without apportionment.

SECOND: I am married and my wife's name is Barbara T. Testator. Any references to my wife are to her. We have two now living children, Mark, born December 5, 1963, and Joan, born March 31, 1965. Any references to my children are to them as well as to any children subsequently born to or legally adopted by me.

THIRD: All property in which I have any interest, other than property held in the names of myself and my wife as joint tenants, is community property. It is my intention to dispose of all property that I am entitled to dispose of by Will, other than my disposable interest, if any, in any property held in joint tenancy.

FOURTH: I give the following property or sums of money to the following persons:

(a) To my wife, if she survives me, my automobiles, boats, silver, books, pictures, paintings, works of art, household furniture and furnishings, clothing, jewelry, personal effects and other tangible personal property, together with any insurance policies and claims under such policies on such property. In the event my wife does not survive me, I give such property to my children who survive me, in shares of substantially equal value, to be divided among them as they, and such other person as my Executor may select to represent any child of mine believed by my Executor to be incapable of acting in his own best interest, shall agree. In case my children and such other person do not agree within six months after my death as to the division among them, my Executor shall make the decision. If any child of mine has not attained the age of eighteen, my Executor may deliver his or her share of such property to his or her guardian or to the person with whom he or she resides for the benefit of the child, and the receipt of the guardian or such person shall discharge the Executor. Notwithstanding the foregoing, should my Executor, in its sole judgment, determine that it would not be in the best interest of my children to receive possession of any item of such property, such as an automobile or firearms, my Executor may sell such item and add the proceeds to the residue of my estate.

(b) To my sister, Jane McGiffin, of Newport Beach, California, two hundred (200) shares of the capital stock of Intel Corporation, now owned by me. If she dies before I do, this legacy shall go to her son, Robert F. McGiffin, Jr., of San Diego, California.

(c) To my sister, Lois Testator, of Santa Barbara, California, a new Lincoln Continental or comparable automobile, to be selected and equipped as my Executrix or Executor, in her or its sole discretion, shall determine.

(d) To my friend, Amy Talbott, of Santa Barbara, California, ten thousand dollars ($10,000), to be paid as far as possible out of sums on deposit to my credit at the time of my decease in the Commercial and Farmers National Bank of Santa Barbara, California.

(e) To The Regents of the University of California, the sum of five thousand dollars ($5,000), to use for the purchase of books for the Boalt Hall Law Library at the Berkeley campus.

FIFTH: If any legatee above mentioned in Article FOURTH shall die before I do, the gift to that person, except as otherwise provided, shall fail.

SIXTH: I give the residue of my estate, including all failed and lapsed gifts, to my wife, Barbara T. Testator, if she survives me by thirty (30) days. If my wife does not so survive me, I give such property to the Security First National Bank, a national banking association, as Trustee under its Declaration of Trust No. T-518, dated January 16, 1976, wherein I am Trustor, to be added to and become a part of the corpus of said trust, and to be held, administered and distributed according to the terms and provisions thereof and any amendments thereto in effect at my death; however, if the Declaration of Trust is revoked or otherwise terminated before my death, I give the residue of my estate to my issue by representation who survive me by thirty (30) days.

SEVENTH: No interest shall be paid on any legacy given under this Will or any Codicil to it.

EIGHTH: If any provision of this Will is unenforceable, the remaining provisions shall, nevertheless, be carried into effect.

NINTH: If my wife, Barbara T. Testator, does not survive me, I nominate my sister and her husband, Jane and Robert McGiffin, of Newport Beach, California, or the survivor, as guardians or guardian of the persons and estates of my children during their minorities. If neither my sister nor her husband survives me, or if they fail to qualify or cease to act as guardians, then I nominate my sister, Lois Testator, of Santa Barbara, California, as such guardian.

TENTH: I appoint my wife, Barbara T. Testator, as Executrix of this Will. If my wife does not survive me or for any reason fails to qualify or ceases to act as Executrix, I appoint the Security First National Bank, a national banking association, as Executor. I authorize my Executrix or substitute Executor to sell or lease property of my estate subject to such order of court as may be required by law.

ELEVENTH: I direct that no Executor, Executrix or guardian, or any successor, shall be required to give any bond in any jurisdiction.

The foregoing instrument is subscribed by me on the 5th day of July 1979, at Santa Barbara, California.

THOMAS T. TESTATOR

The foregoing instrument, consisting of one page, was subscribed on the date which it bears, by the Testator, Thomas T. Testator, and at the time of subscribing was declared by him to be his last Will. The subscription and declaration were made in our presence, we being present at the same time; and we, at his request and in his presence, and in the presence of each other, have affixed our signatures hereto as witnesses.

_____ residing at _____
_____ residing at _____
_____ residing at _____

Preamble. The preamble to most wills consists of certain basic information, such as the testator's name and domicile, together with a statement identifying the document as his will and revoking all former wills and codicils. This, incidentally, is one of the few ways an effective revocation can be made.

The Superfluous Debt Clause. The initial paragraph of most wills directs the executor to pay all the decedent's just debts. As he is required to do this anyway, modern draftsmen usually omit this direction as surplus. Such a clause might be advisable, though, if a creditor is also a legatee, because it tends to negate any inference that the bequest is to satisfy the debt; in other circumstances, a direction to pay debts could require the residue to be used to discharge encumbrances (such as a mortgage note on specifically devised property), unless the devise or bequest provides otherwise. In most wills, this clause is superfluous, but usually harmless.

Payment of Death Taxes. In our example, the testator has directed that all estate and inheritance taxes be paid from the residue of his estate (what remains after the other gifts have been satisfied). This might be an appropriate provision if the probate estate is large enough, but its inclusion might be questionable if the non-probate assets constitute most of the estate. Whether or not the taxes should be apportioned among the beneficiaries depends, obviously, upon the circumstances of each case and the testator's desires.

Identifying Heirs. The next paragraph may identify the testator's wife, children, and other legal heirs. Mention should always be made of each child and the issue of deceased children, and provision either should be made for them or an intent not to provide for them should be shown. Otherwise, they will take as pretermitted heirs, which we shall consider later. Also, the nebulous word "heirs" should always be avoided. If a testator means the whole range of his descendants, he should use the word issue rather than children. Further guessing at his desires might be prevented if he makes known whether or not adopted children and adopted descendants are included.

Disposal of Tangible Personal Property. After the preliminaries, a bequest of personal and household effects may come. Specifically disposing of such property not only promotes family harmony, but also avoids the problem of converting it into cash if the residue goes into trust. In this connection, a careful draftsman will use the description "tangible personal property" rather than "personal effects" to prevent a dispute about whether such things as a boat, airplane, or car are personal effects. A very cautious draftsman might even go further by adding "except money," for some cases have held that cash has its own inherent value.

If any of the decedent's tangible personal property, such as a ring, a watch, or an heirloom, is bequeathed to a minor, the testator might avoid an unnecessary guardianship appointment if he gives his executor power to deliver the gift directly to the minor or to the person with whom he lives. Similarly, if the decedent wishes his tangible personal property to be divided among several people, he may circumvent considerable bickering among the legatees if he confers broad discretion on his executor to allocate the goods.

A few states permit tangible personal property to pass according to a separate memorandum left by a decedent, if he has directed such disposition in his will. Take advantage of this opportunity if you live in one of them.

Specific, General, and Demonstrative Devises and Bequests. After the tangible personal property has been bequeathed, the next provision usually disposes of the testator's real property and intangible personal property. A devise or legacy may be in one of three forms: specific, general, or demonstrative. At one end of the testimonial spectrum is the specific gift of property, while at the other end is the general devise or legacy; the demonstrative gift lies in between. A specific legacy specifies a particular thing that belongs to the testator at the time he makes his will, such as "my 100 shares of Ford Motor Company common stock." At the other extreme, a general legacy, such as "$5,000" or "100 shares of Ford Motor Company common stock," does not designate specific property. If the legacy is general and the property is other than money, the executor is required to purchase it if it is not contained in the decedent's estate. A demonstrative legacy, as the term suggests, indicates the source from which the property is to come, such as "100 of my 500 shares of Perkin-Elmer common stock" or "$1,000 to be paid so far as possible out of sums deposited to my credit at the Exchange National Bank of Colorado Springs at the time of my decease."

The distinctions in the form of legacies and devises may seem academic to the testator when he makes his will, but, as we shall see, the differences could be significant if, at the time of his death, the amount or nature of his estate has changed substantially.

The Residue Clause. After the specific, general, and demonstrative devises and legacies, a will should dispose of the balance of the estate. Draftsmen wedded to ancient terminology prefer the phrase "rest, residue, and remainder," rather than merely "residue," to describe these assets, but either term refers to the same property. The testator might give this residue to a certain person or class of persons, or he may place it in trust or have it "pour over" into an already established trust.

The Guardian for Minor Children Problem. Anyone with minor children should nominate a personal guardian for them, in case both parents were to be killed in an automobile collision or some other accident, or otherwise die while their children were still young. Frequently, a provision of this sort is overlooked, or the parents simply assume that some relative will care for their children if the need were to arise. Such a lack of foresight could be harmful to the children's welfare in those occasional cases in which a tug-of-war develops between well-meaning relatives, all of whom believe they are acting in the children's best interests. A sensible approach is for the testator and his wife to decide who is best qualified for this responsibility, then confer with the prospective guardian as to his or her willingness to serve.

In deciding who is best qualified, the children's welfare should be paramount, of course. Consideration should be given to such factors as the ages of the children; the ages, financial circumstances and size of the prospective guardian's family; religious and cultural environment; and the effect of a future divorce or the death of the guardian's spouse.

Whether the personal guardian should also be guardian of the children's estates depends upon several factors. Assuming that provisions have been made to place the estate in trust for the benefit of the children were neither parent to survive (which almost always is the soundest solution), appointment of the same person as both personal guardian and guardian of the children's estates, so that he might hold small amounts of property which the children acquire, is a convenient answer. However, if the trust device is not used, the parents must decide whether the person they believe is best suited to raise their children also has sufficient financial acumen to manage what might be a sizeable estate. This is seldom the case.

Once a husband executes a will in which he nominates a personal guardian for his children, his wife should make a will in which she names the same person or persons. Otherwise, the spouse's best conceived plans could be defeated, were both to die at about the same time or if the wife survives but then dies intestate while the children are still minors. In this connection, in almost every conceivable situation a wife needs a will as much as a husband does, if for no other reason than the uncertainty as to the order of deaths.

Appointment of the Executor and Trustee. Next, the executor and, if a testamentary trust is established, the trustee, should be appointed. Actually, these ostensible appointments are merely nominations, for the court makes the appointments, but it usually appoints the testator's selections, assuming they are qualified. Many states have restrictive rules which prevent appointment of nondomiciliaries as executors or trustees. If a domiciliary of such a state nominates a foreign corporate fiduciary or person to act as executor, the result is that the local court will appoint an administrator-with-the-will-annexed, and also require a bond. After naming the executor and trustee, a will normally recites what powers they are to have. If the estate is small and a family executor, such as a surviving spouse, is nominated, some saving will result if the testator directs that the executor be permitted to serve without bond.

Depending to a large extent upon the nature of the estate, many other clauses might be appropriate, of course, such as an exercise of a power of appointment, a provision for periodic payment to certain beneficiaries during administration, or a severable provision.

Conclusion. Then appears the date and the testator's signature. Following this, an attestation clause, the form of which is usually prescribed by statute, is customary. This clause normally is not a legal requirement, but it may be useful in reinforcing the presumption of due execution. Finally, the witnesses' signatures and addresses appear.

Codicils. After a testator has executed a will, he may wish to change it for any number of reasons. This is his privilege, provided he complies with all statutory requirements. For obvious reasons, he is not permitted to make modifications by the simple expedient of deleting, adding to, or changing provisions in the will itself. Instead, he may lawfully change his will only by either revoking it and making a new one or executing a codicil. A codicil is simply an amendment to a will, but all the formalities of execution required for the will itself must be observed. Consequently, unless the will is complicated and the amendment minor, or unless time is short, making a new will is usually preferable.

STATUTORY AND OTHER LIMITATIONS UPON TESTAMENTARY FREEDOM

Although a will may meet all statutory requirements to be admitted to probate, even the best laid testamentary plans may go awry. Hence, we shall consider next a few of the more common reasons why an estate may sometimes be disposed of in a way the decedent did not direct. Specifically, we shall limit our study to the problems of the widow's share, pretermitted heirs, lapse, ademption, and abatement.

Can a Wife Be Disinherited?

Most common law states have legislative substitutes for the archaic right of dower (a life interest in one-third of a husband's lands). These statutes provide that, regardless of the husband's will, the widow is entitled to a certain fractional share of his estate. Consequently, a husband may not deprive her of this interest by will, and if he attempts to do so, the usual result is that the widow may elect whether to take what is given her under the will or what she would be entitled to under the laws of intestate succession. Comparable results occur in community property states if a husband attempts to exercise testamentary control over his wife's undivided half of the community assets. Since this half is not his, the surviving widow may take it either as heir of her husband or by operation of law.

What Happens to an Unmentioned Child?

Although every state except Louisiana permits a testator to disinherit a child, to do so he must clearly express his intention. Merely ignoring the child in the will does not accomplish the desired purpose, for then the child will succeed to his parents' estate as a *pretermitted heir* (an heir whom the testator fails to mention). Odd as it may seem, sometimes a child is overlooked because of forgetfulness or because of carelessness in drafting a will. More often, though, a testator simply neglects to provide for afterborn children or for grandchildren whose parent (the testator's child) predeceases the testator. Under these circumstances, the pretermitted heir is entitled to his intestate interest. In most states, this revokes the will to the extent of the neglected heir's interest, although in some jurisdictions total revocation results.

What Happens if a Beneficiary Dies First?

A beneficiary's death before that of the testator, or an inability or unwillingness to take a legacy or devise, is another circumstance which might cause a testator's estate to be disposed of in some manner other than by the terms of his will. In this situation, the gift is said to *lapse* and, unless there is a provision in the will covering such a situation or unless an anti-lapse statute applies, the lapsed property becomes part of the residuary estate. Although anti-lapse statues exist in most states, they might not save all gifts because they normally apply only to persons who have a particular relationship to the testator and who are survived by certain relatives (usually only lineal descendants). In any event, a testator should always consider what he wishes to happen if a particular beneficiary predeceases him, and then express his intent. For example, were a married child to predecease the testator, the testator might desire (particularly if the estate is small) that the legacy go to the deceased child's spouse. To accomplish this, an express provision is necessary. Similarly, if the testator desires to preclude the results under an anti-lapse statute, a gift should be made contingent upon survival.

What if Specific Property Has Been Disposed of?

A principal characteristic of a specific devise or legacy is that it may be *adeemed* by extinction, that is, fail completely if the specific property is not part of the testator's estate at the time of his death. At common law, this result was based upon the presumption that when a specific gift was destroyed or disposed of by a testator, he did not intend the gift to be made, for otherwise he could have changed his will so as to give something else to the specific legatee. Today, most courts do not regard intent as material; instead, they base ademption upon the Statute of Wills, preferring to follow the strict prerequisites to passing property by will, rather than to search for a nebulous intent. In a few states, such as California, ademption results only if it appears that the testator intended to deprive the legatee or devisee of the gift. In most states, however, if a testator sells property he has specifically bequeathed or devised, neither the proceeds from the sale nor similar property purchased with the proceeds passes to the beneficiary, for the specific property is not in his estate. For example, if a testator bequeathed "my 100 shares of General Motors common stock to my friend, Gaylord Manor," but later sold this stock, the gift would be adeemed, even though the testator did not intend this result. However, insubstantial changes will not deprive the legatee of his gift. Thus, if in the example General Motors split its stock two-for-one and the 200 shares were part of the testator's estate, Gaylord would be entitled to all 200 shares. To avoid ademption, either a general gift or an alternate gift should be considered.

The Results of Giving Away More Than You Have

Sometimes a testator's estate may have changed materially between the time he made his will and his death or, for other reasons, it may not be adequate to fulfill all the devises and legacies. When this occurs, some or all of the gifts must be reduced by the probate court. *Abatement* is the legal term for this reduction process, and the principal question presented in such situations is what gifts must first give way. Assuming the testator has not specified any priorities, generally the residue first abates. If this is exhausted and a deficiency still exists, the general legacies are next to go. Finally, specific legacies may be reduced. The hybrid demonstrative legacy may be considered in the same category as either a general or a specific gift, depending upon whether or not the designated source of the legacy is part of the estate. If the assets are insufficient to satisfy all the specific legacies and the demonstrative legacies that rank with the specific, a prorated abatement among these gifts results. *Because the persons most important to the testator are usually provided for in the residue, it is they who have the risk of abatement.* Consequently, a testator should consider the possibility of substantial losses in his estate and provide safeguards (e.g., condition specific or general bequests to others upon a minimum estate value, or provide for a pro rata or other reduction of such gifts).

THE EXECUTOR'S RESPONSIBILITIES

Having taken a cursory look at a typical will and a few of the problems that may arise in connection with it, we shall conclude our study of wills by briefly considering what an executor (personal representative) does.

As previously noted, the executor is the person (either an individual or corporation) who administers the estate between the time of death and the time of distribution to the beneficiaries. In effect, he is a trustee for the decedent's heirs and creditors and, because of this fiduciary relationship, he must strictly observe all judicial requirements.

Initial Duties

Although an executor's appointment must be confirmed by letters testamentary issued by a competent court, his responsibility commences when the testator dies, for he must protect the estate property in the interval between death and his confirmation by taking whatever steps are reasonably necessary to prevent loss, such as arranging for livestock to be fed or personal property to be stored. Also, he arranges for the survivors' immediate living expenses, if necessary, and notifies interested parties and agencies, such as the post office and banks, of the death.

Filing for Probate

One of the executor's primary duties is to offer the decedent's will for probate (which is done, of course, by an attorney of his or the testator's selection). Those who must be notified of the proceedings are determined and notified, and if a contest ensues, the executor must defend the will (attempt to establish that it was duly executed and that the testator had testamentary capacity).

Inventory of Assets

Another basic duty is to ascertain what assets belonged to the decedent at the time of his death and to have these appraised for administration and tax purposes. The executor's job is considerably simplified if the deceased has left a data sheet of some sort, in which he has listed his various assets and liabilities, the location of important papers, and the names of persons whom it might be essential or desirable to contact. In fact, everyone should compile such information, which should be updated as often as necessary, and leave it in a place where it can be readily located, not only to help his executor but, more important, to minimize the danger that certain assets (e.g., personal loans receivable, savings or checking accounts, brokerage accounts, life insurance policies) might never be discovered. While this risk exists even if there is a surviving spouse, it is much more likely in those cases in which a husband and wife die close to each other. Such a data sheet might be as comprehensive as the individual desires, but as long as it contains the essential information, it serves the purpose. The form set forth in Appendix H illustrates the type of information which should be easily accessible to survivors or the executor. It may be detached and used as is or modified to suit a particular situation.

For the benefit of all interested persons, an inventory of assets must be filed with the probate court, and the deceased's property must be actually or constructively taken into the executor's possession, for he is responsible for its safety and preservation. In this connection, ordinary prudence usually suggests that an executor obtain adequate insurance against all insurable risks.

Paying Claims

The executor is required to publish notice to creditors advising them to file claims within the prescribed statutory period, which is six months in many states. When presented, he must determine which claims are legally enforceable and which are doubtful, then pay those that are just and reject the others. He may compromise claims, if authorized by the court, or if litigation results he must defend against it. Also, the executor must obtain tax waivers to transfer certain property, prepare and file all forms required for reporting estate assets to the state and federal taxing authorities, and pay all estate, inheritance, and income taxes.

Other Duties

Aside from the usual steps that must be taken to settle an estate and distribute the assets, there are many other acts which an executor may be called upon to perform during administration. Some of these are necessary because of the nature of the estate, while others are discretionary. If certain of the testator's property is located outside the state, for example, the executor must arrange to obtain it by "ancillary administration," which involves retaining a lawyer in the other state and going through usually long and sometimes costly proceedings there.

Although estate administration, strictly speaking, involves only the collection, preservation, and distribution of the estate, and not property management in the ordinary sense, management sometimes becomes an incidental function. An executor might have occasion, for example, to invest excess funds; to continue a business if authorized by the will or by court order; to sell real or personal property, including estate securities; to encumber property or borrowed money; to lease property; or to complete contracts. Usually, these managerial functions must be authorized by the court. However, an executor risks being surcharged if he fails to take certain common-sense actions. For example, an executor should not hold cash in a substantial amount in relation to the size of the estate, without making it income-producing in some way. Hence, if there were $50,000 cash in an estate, an executor who leaves this sum in a checking account during the period of administration, say two years, might be liable to the beneficiaries for the interest which might have been earned, perhaps $5,000. In such a situation, many courts would hold that the funds should have been placed in Treasury bills or in a commercial bank savings account. Investments in corporate debt securities probably would be improper, though, without specific judicial approval, as would the purchase of common stocks. Similarly, it is not likely that many courts would regard either credit unions or savings and loan associations as prudent receptacles of estate funds, so any resulting loss might be charged to the executor who placed money in them.

Distribution

The ultimate act of the estate proceedings is final distribution. After the statutory period for creditors to present claims has expired, the executor files a final account and a petition for distribution with the probate court. If the court finds that all the appropriate steps have been taken, it will issue an order (actually prepared by the estate's lawyer) determining who is entitled to share in the balance of the estate and the proportions of each, and direct distribution of the property. The executor then delivers the property to the persons designated, including the trustee if a trust is established, obtains receipts for it and, after filing an affidavit for final discharge, is released by the court.

Compensation

An executor is entitled to compensation for his services, of course, as is the attorney for the estate. Minimum commissions and fees often are set by the laws of the state and usually are based on a percentage of the estate's value. If the estate is complicated, however, and special services are required, additional remuneration may be authorized by the probate court. As a rule of thumb, at least 5% to 7% of the value of an estate will go for the executor's commissions and attorney's fees. In a simple estate, where the assets are limited and involved problems are not likely to be encountered, some saving may result if the principal beneficiary under the will, such as the surviving spouse, is nominated as executor and waives the commission. If the estate is very large or complicated, though, the testator usually is wise to appoint someone skilled in business and in performing an executor's functions. Corporate executors, such as the trust departments of most large banks, are well suited for this purpose, and the proportionately small added cost may be saved many times over by their skill and experience. If an individual's situation suggests the use of a corporate executor, he might also consider appointing his spouse as a co-executor, which will give her a voice in decisions that may be of paramount importance to her.

appendices

A. What's Your Interest?

Despite the seeming straightforwardness of a statement such as, "Your annual percentage yield will be 7.75%," trying to determine the actual dollar amount of interest earned on various types of savings deposits can be a baffling experience. The difficulty stems, in large part, from the failure of financial institutions to use a standard approach, with the result that yields might be calculated in any of a hundred or so different ways.

Savers, as well as the banks and thrift institutions that serve them, would benefit from the lucid approach and comprehensive tables developed by Dr. Richard L. D. Morse, Professor of Family Economics at Kansas State University. Anyone with more than very modest savings should consider mailing two dollars to Morse Publications, 2429 Lookout Drive, Manhattan, KS 66502 for a copy of *Check Your Interest*, which will provide the reader with (1) a basic understanding of savings accounts; (2) an ability to calculate simply and accurately the yields available from different prospective uses of savings, so that he or she can choose the most advantageous; and (3) an awareness of whether he or she is actually being paid the earnings that are due. In addition, the book sets forth a number of questions that a prudent saver should ask before opening a savings account.

What's Your Interest? 235

To give you an idea of one application of Dr. Morse's approach, the following work form is used to determine earnings by what he refers to as the "terminal date method."

TABLE A.1. *Work Forms.*

TERMINAL DATE METHOD

Date of activity	Days to end	Cents per $100. (See tables.) ×	$ Amount of activity	Divide by 10,000 (to convert to $ and ¢)	Earnings (+ or −)
		(balance at beginning of term)			
_____	_____	_____	$_____		+$_____
		(deposits made during the term)			
_____	_____	_____	$_____		+ _____
_____	_____	_____	_____		+ _____
_____	_____	_____	_____		+ _____
		(withdrawals made during the term)			
_____	_____	_____	$_____		− _____
_____	_____	_____	_____		− _____
_____	_____	_____	_____		− _____

Total earnings for the term—from the *beginning balance* plus from *deposits* less *withdrawals* made during the term................. $_____

Table A.2. is an extract from one of several *Morse Daily Rate Tables*. The novel technique of using cents per $100 avoids the confusion of decimals and provides the user with a better sense of the sums being calculated. The extract shows the cents earned by $100 in the number of days indicated, if the principal is compounded daily at a 5.25% annual rate on a 365-day basis. Although the tables provide factors for up to 366 days, if an account is posted at least quarterly, all that is required are factors for the first 92 days or 91¼ days for quarters that are one-fourth of a year. Also, unless an account exceeds $100,000, there is no need to use more than the first four digits after the decimal.

TABLE A.2. Cents Earned by $100 in Indicated Number of Days.

Days	Cents	Days	Cents	Days	Cents
1	1.438 3561643	26	37.464 5759328	51	73.620 5658867
2	2.876 9192156	27	38.908 3208375	52	75.069 5113106
3	4.315 6891834	28	40.352 2734042	53	76.518 6651444
4	5.754 6660976	29	41.796 4336627	54	77.968 0274182
5	7.193 8499879	30	43.240 8016429	55	79.417 5981618
6	8.633 2408842	31	44.685 3773747	56	80.867 3774054
7	10.072 8388161	32	46.130 1608878	57	82.317 3651789
8	11.512 6438134	33	47.575 1522124	58	83.767 5615122
9	12.952 6559060	34	49.020 3513781	59	85.217 9664354
10	14.392 8751237	35	50.465 7584149	60	86.668 5799786
11	15.833 3014961	36	51.911 3733528	61	88.119 4021716
12	17.273 9350532	37	53.357 1962216	62	89.570 4330445
13	18.714 7758247	38	54.803 2270511	63	91.021 6726273
14	20.155 8238404	39	56.249 4658715	64	92.473 1209501
15	21.597 0791301	40	57.695 9127125	65	93.924 7780428
16	23.038 5417237	41	59.142 5676040	66	95.376 6439356
17	24.480 2116509	42	60.589 4305761	67	96.828 7186583
18	25.922 0889416	43	62.036 5016585	68	98.281 0022411
19	27.364 1736256	44	63.483 7808814	69	99.733 4947141
20	28.806 4657328	45	64.931 2682745	70	101.186 1961071
21	30.248 9652929	46	66.378 9638679	71	102.639 1064504
22	31.691 6723359	47	67.826 8676915	72	104.092 2257739
23	33.134 5868915	48	69.274 9797752	73	105.545 5541078
24	34.577 7089896	49	70.723 3001490	74	106.999 0914820
25	36.021 0386601	50	72.171 8288428	75	108.452 8379267

Days	Cents
76	109.906 7934719
77	111.360 9581476
78	112.815 3319841
79	114.269 9150113
80	115.724 7072593
81	117.179 7087583
82	118.634 9195383
83	120.090 3396295
84	121.545 9690619
85	123.001 8078657
86	124.457 8560709
87	125.914 1137078
88	127.370 5808063
89	128.827 2573967
90	130.284 1435091
91	131.741 2391735
92	133.198 5444203
91¼ (one quarter of a year)	132.105 5458357

Courtesy of Morse Publications (2429 Lookout Dr., Manhattan, KS).

B. Federal Income Tax Withholding Rates (1979)

For a MONTHLY payroll period, multiply the total number of exemptions claimed by $83.33, then subtract the product from the amount of taxable wages for that month. The result is the "amount of wages" in the following tables:

Single Person

If the amount of wages is	The amount of tax to be withheld is
Not over $118	0

Over	But not over		Of excess over
$ 118	$ 275	15%	$ 118
$ 275	$ 567	$ 23.55 + 18%	$ 275
$ 567	$ 850	$ 76.11 + 21%	$ 567
$ 850	$1,183	$135.54 + 26%	$ 850
$1,183	$1,433	$222.12 + 30%	$1,183
$1,433	$1,875	$297.12 + 34%	$1,433
$1,875		$447.40 + 39%	$1,875

Married Person

If the amount of wages is	The amount of tax to be withheld is
Not over $200	0

Over	But not over		Of excess over
$ 200	$ 550	15%	$ 200
$ 550	$ 908	$ 52.50 + 18%	$ 550
$ 908	$1,250	$116.94 + 21%	$ 908
$1,250	$1,600	$188.76 + 24%	$1,250
$1,600	$1,967	$272.76 + 28%	$1,600
$1,967	$2,408	$375.64 + 32%	$1,967
$2,408		$516.64 + 37%	$2,408

C. Federal Individual Income Taxes (1979 Tax Year)

Taxable Income[a]	Tax	Single Tax as % of taxable income	Marginal tax rate[b]	Tax	Married (joint return) Tax as % of taxable income	Marginal tax rate[b]
$5,000	$422	8.4%	18%	$224	4.5%	14%
$7,500	$884	11.8%	19%	$614	8.2%	16%
$10,000	$1,387	13.9%	21%	$1,062	10.6%	18%
$12,500	$1,963	15.7%	24%	$1,530	12.2%	21%
$15,000	$2,605	17.4%	30%	$2,055	13.7%	21%
$20,000	$4,177	20.9%	34%	$3,225	16.1%	24%
$25,000	$5,952	23.8%	39%	$4,633	18.5%	32%
$30,000	$7,962	26.5%	44%	$6,238	20.8%	37%
$40,000	$12,657	31.6%	49%	$10,226	25.6%	43%
$50,000	$18,067	36.1%	55%[c]	$14,778	29.6%	49%
$100,000	$50,053	50.1%	68%[c]	$41,998	42.0%	59%[c]

[a] "Taxable income" means "adjusted gross income" reduced by (1) the deduction for personal exemptions plus (2) the amount by which deductions, if itemized, exceed the "zero bracket amount" (ZBA). "Adjusted gross income" is the total of all wages, salaries, other income, and taxable interest and dividends, minus certain adjustments (mainly for directly related business expenses). For 1979, the "zero bracket amount" (which replaced the "standard deduction" used before 1977) is $2,300 for a single person and $3,400 for a married couple filing a joint return. A personal exemption of $1,000 is allowed for each taxpayer and dependent. The table above takes into account the zero bracket amount, so unless your itemized deductions exceed your ZBA, the only sum that you should subtract from your adjusted gross income is the deduction for personal exemptions.

[b] The marginal tax rate is the percentage at which the next $1 of taxable income would be taxed; this is commonly referred to as the taxpayer's "bracket."

[c] "Personal service income," which is "earned" income such as wages, salaries, and commissions, is taxed at a maximum rate of 50%; "unearned" income, such as dividends, interest, rents, and capital gains, is taxed up to a maximum of 70%.

D. Federal Estate and Gift Tax Rates

Rate Schedule

Amount of Taxable Gift or Estate	Tax
Not over $10,000	18%
$10,000–$20,000	$1,800 plus 20% of amount above $10,000
$20,000–$40,000	$3,800 plus 22% of amount above $20,000
$40,000–$60,000	$8,200 plus 24% of amount above $40,000
$60,000–$80,000	$13,000 plus 26% of amount above $60,000
$80,000–$100,000	$18,200 plus 28% of amount above $80,000
$100,000–$150,000	$23,800 plus 30% of amount above $100,000
$150,000–$250,000	$38,800 plus 32% of amount above $150,000
$250,000–$500,000	$70,800 plus 34% of amount above $250,000
$500,000–$750,000	$155,800 plus 37% of amount above $500,000
$750,000–$1,000,000	$248,300 plus 39% of amount above $750,000

(Progressively higher rates, up to 70% for gifts/estates above $5 million, apply.)

GIFT/ESTATE TAX CREDIT

A credit in the following amounts is applied against gift and estate taxes, permitting transfers to be made tax-free in the amounts indicated. Any part of the credit that is used as a setoff against gift taxes is subtracted from the amount available as a setoff against estate taxes.

	Tax Credit	Equivalent Exemption
1977	$30,000	$120,666
1978	34,000	134,000
1979	38,000	147,333
1980	42,500	161,563
1981 or later	47,500	175,625

TAXATION OF GIFTS

1. Gifts up to $3,000 per donee per year ($6,000 for husband-wife gifts to a third person) are exempt.
2. There is no gift tax on the first $100,000 of lifetime gifts between a husband and wife; between $100,000 and $200,000, such transfers are fully taxable; above $200,000, 50% of the value of the gift is taxed.
3. All gifts made within three years of death (in excess of the $3,000 annual exclusion), plus the gift taxes paid on such gifts, are included in the donor's estate.
4. The amount of the gift tax is determined by applying the rate schedule to all taxable transfers the donor made during his life, then deducting the gift tax paid in previous taxable periods.

TAXATION OF ESTATES

1. $250,000 or 50% of the adjusted gross estate passing to the surviving spouse, whichever is larger, is allowed as a marital deduction. This amount is reduced when community property is involved.
2. One-half the value of "qualified joint interest" property held by a decedent and his or her spouse is excluded from the taxable estate. To qualify, the joint interest (joint tenancy or tenancy-by-the-entirety) must have been created by either or both of the spouses. If personal property is involved, the interest must have completed a gift for purposes of gift taxes; if real property, the donor must have treated the creation of the interest as a taxable event.
3. A decedent's gross estate includes the proceeds of any insurance on his life, payable to his estate or to others, unless he had given up all incidents of ownership in the policy.

E. Compound Interest Table

How Much $1 Would Amount to If Compounded Annually at Different Rates of Interest for the Number of Years Shown

Number of Years	4%	5%	6%	8%	10%
1	1.0400	1.0500	1.0600	1.0800	1.1000
2	1.0816	1.1025	1.1236	1.1664	1.2100
3	1.1249	1.1576	1.1910	1.2597	1.3310
4	1.1699	1.2155	1.2625	1.3605	1.4641
5	1.2167	1.2763	1.3382	1.4693	1.6105
6	1.2653	1.3401	1.4185	1.5869	1.7716
7	1.3159	1.4071	1.5036	1.7138	1.9487
8	1.3686	1.4775	1.5938	1.8509	2.1436
9	1.4233	1.5513	1.6895	1.9990	2.3579
10	1.4802	1.6289	1.7908	2.1589	2.5937
11	1.5395	1.7103	1.8983	2.3316	2.8531
12	1.6010	1.7959	2.0122	2.5182	3.1384
13	1.6651	1.8856	2.1329	2.7196	3.4523
14	1.7317	1.9799	2.2609	2.9372	3.7975
15	1.8009	2.0789	2.3966	3.1722	4.1772
16	1.8730	2.1829	2.5404	3.4259	4.5950
17	1.9479	2.2920	2.6928	3.7000	5.0545
18	2.0258	2.4066	2.8543	3.9960	5.5599
19	2.1068	2.5270	3.0256	4.3157	6.1159
20	2.1911	2.5633	3.2071	4.6610	6.7275
21	2.2788	2.7860	3.3996	5.0338	7.4002
22	2.3699	2.9253	3.6035	5.4365	8.1403
23	2.4647	3.0715	3.8197	5.8715	8.9543
24	2.5633	3.2251	4.0489	6.3412	9.8497
25	2.6658	3.3864	4.2919	6.8485	10.8347
26	2.7725	3.5557	4.5494	7.3964	11.9182
27	2.8834	3.7335	4.8223	7.9881	13.1100
28	2.9987	3.9201	5.1117	8.6271	14.4210
29	3.1187	4.1161	5.4184	9.3173	15.8631
30	3.2434	4.3219	5.7435	10.0627	17.4494
...	...	...	...	...	...
40	4.8010	7.0400	10.2857	21.7245	45.2593
...	...	...	...	...	...
50	7.1067	11.4674	18.4202	46.9016	117.3909
...	...	...	...	...	...
60	10.5196	18.6792	32.9877	101.2571	304.4816
...	...	...	...	...	...
70	15.5716	30.4264	59.0759	218.6064	789.7470

F. Periodic Investment Table

Approximate Sum That Must Be Saved Each Year, at Different Rates of Compound Interest, to Equal $100 after a Stated Number of Years

Number of Years	5%	6%	8%	Number of Years	5%	6%	8%
1	$95.24	94.34	92.59	21	$2.67	2.36	1.84
2	46.45	45.80	44.52	22	2.47	2.17	1.67
3	30.21	29.63	28.52	23	2.30	2.01	1.52
4	22.10	21.57	20.55	24	2.14	1.86	1.39
5	17.24	16.74	15.78	25	2.00	1.72	1.27
6	14.00	13.53	12.62	26	1.86	1.60	1.16
7	11.70	11.24	10.38	27	1.74	1.48	1.06
8	9.97	9.53	8.71	28	1.63	1.38	.97
9	8.64	8.21	7.42	29	1.53	1.28	.89
10	7.57	7.16	6.39	30	1.43	1.19	.82
11	6.70	6.30	5.56	31	1.35	1.11	.75
12	5.98	5.59	4.88	32	1.27	1.04	.69
13	5.38	5.00	4.31	33	1.19	.97	.63
14	4.86	4.49	3.82	34	1.12	.91	.58
15	4.41	4.05	3.41	35	1.05	.85	.54
16	4.03	3.68	3.05	36	.99	.79	.50
17	3.69	3.34	2.74	37	.94	.74	.46
18	3.39	3.05	2.47	38	.88	.69	.42
19	3.12	2.79	2.23	39	.84	.65	.39
20	2.88	2.57	2.02	40	.79	.61	.36

To determine how much a particular number of dollars saved each year, at a stated, compounded interest, would amount to after a given number of years, multiply the annual investment by 100, then divide by the sum required to accumulate $100 in the same period. For example, if $600 is invested each year for 20 years at 6% compounded, at the end of the twentieth year there would be:

$$\frac{600(100)}{2.57} = \$23{,}346$$

G. Consumer Prices

1820–1978
(1967=100)

Year	Index (Adjusted)	Annual Change[a]	Year	Index (Adjusted)	Annual Change[a]	Year	Index (Adjusted)	Annual Change[a]
1978	202.9	9.0%	1945	53.9	2.3 %	1912	30.1	6.0%
1977	186.1	6.8	1944	52.7	1.7	1911	28.4	0
1976	174.3	4.8	1943	51.8	6.1			
			1942	48.8	10.9	1910	28.4	5.2
1975	166.3	7.0	1941	44.0	4.8	1909	27.0	0
1974	155.4	12.2				1908	27.0	(3.9)
1973	138.5	8.8	1940	42.0	1.0	1907	28.1	5.2
1972	127.3	4.9	1939	41.6	(1.4)	1906	26.7	3.5
1971	121.3	4.3	1938	42.2	(1.9)			
			1937	43.0	3.6	1905	25.8	0
1970	116.3	5.9	1936	41.5	1.0	1904	25.8	(1.1)
1969	109.8	5.4				1903	26.1	4.8
1968	104.2	4.2	1935	41.1	2.5	1902	24.9	2.5
1967	100.0	2.9	1934	40.1	3.6	1901	24.3	2.5
1966	97.2	2.9	1933	38.7	(5.4)			
			1932	40.9	(9.7)	1900	23.7	3.9
1965	94.5	1.7	1931	45.3	(9.4)	1899	22.8	2.7
1964	92.9	1.3				1898	22.2	0
1963	91.7	1.1	1930	50.0	2.5	1897	22.2	1.4
1962	90.7	1.3	1929	51.3	0	1896	21.9	1.4
1961	89.6	1.0	1928	51.3	(1.3)			
			1927	52.0	(1.9)	1895	21.6	0
1960	88.7	1.6	1926	53.0	1.0	1894	21.6	(2.7)
1959	87.3	0.8				1893	22.2	(2.6)
1958	86.6	2.7	1925	52.5	2.5	1892	22.8	1.3
1957	84.3	3.6	1924	51.2	0.2	1891	22.5	6.1
1956	81.4	1.5	1923	51.1	1.8			
			1922	50.2	(6.2)	1890	23.1	0
1955	80.2	(0.4)	1921	53.5	(10.8)	1889	23.1	0
1954	80.5	0.5				1888	23.1	2.7
1953	80.1	0.8	1920	60.0	15.8	1887	22.5	0
1952	79.5	2.2	1919	51.8	15.1	1886	22.5	1.4
1951	77.8	7.9	1918	45.0	17.2			
			1917	38.4	17.8	1885	22.2	(2.6)
1950	72.1	1.0	1916	32.6	7.2	1884	22.8	(5.0)
1949	71.4	(1.0)				1883	24.0	(5.9)
1948	72.1	7.8	1915	30.4	1.0	1882	25.5	3.7
1947	66.9	14.4	1914	30.1	1.7	1881	24.6	3.8
1946	58.5	8.5	1913	29.6	(1.7)			

Index (Adjusted)		Annual Change[a]	Index (Adjusted)		Annual Change[a]	Index (Adjusted)		Annual Change[a]
1880	23.7	1.3	1860	18.1	(3.2)	1840	17.8	(15.2)
1879	23.4	(1.3)	1859	18.7	(8.3)	1839	21.0	0
1878	23.7	0	1858	20.4	(1.4)	1838	21.0	(1.4)
1877	23.7	(1.3)	1857	20.7	3.0	1837	21.3	6.0
1876	24.0	(5.9)	1856	20.1	1.0	1836	20.1	12.9
1875	25.5	(2.3)	1855	19.9	4.7	1835	17.8	17.9
1874	26.1	0	1854	19.0	0	1834	15.1	(12.2)
1873	26.1	(2.2)	1853	19.0	6.7	1833	17.2	1.8
1872	26.7	1.1	1852	17.8	0	1832	16.9	1.8
1871	26.4	(2.2)	1851	17.8	11.3	1831	16.6	3.8
1870	27.0	(3.9)	1850	16.0	6.0	1830	16.0	(7.0)
1869	28.1	(3.1)	1849	15.1	(5.6)	1829	17.2	1.8
1868	29.0	(4.1)	1848	16.0	(7.0)	1828	16.9	0
1867	30.2	(1.0)	1847	17.2	0	1827	16.9	3.7
1866	30.5	1.0	1846	17.2	7.5	1826	16.3	(5.2)
1865	30.2	7.5	1845	16.0	3.9	1825	17.2	1.8
1864	28.1	21.6	1844	15.4	2.0	1824	16.9	(6.6)
1863	23.1	18.1	1843	15.1	(7.4)	1823	18.1	(4.7)
1862	20.4	9.1	1842	16.3	(8.4)	1822	19.0	3.3
1861	18.7	3.3	1841	17.8	0	1821	18.4	4.7
						1820	19.3	

[a] The figures in parentheses indicate *declines* in prices.

Sources: Federal Reserve Bank of New York Index (1820–1913);
Hoover Consumer Price Index (1851–1880);
Bureau of Labor Statistics' Consumer Price Index (1911–1978).

H. Information For My Executor

Name	Date of Birth	Place of Birth

Religion	Social Security Nr.	Permanent Address

Name of Spouse	Date of Birth	Place of Birth

Date of Marriage	Place of Marriage	Location of Marriage Certificate

Names and Addresses of Spouse's Parents, Brothers and Sisters

Previous Marriages (name of former spouse; dates; dates and places of marriage and divorce; names and addresses of any children)

Previous Marriages of Spouse (furnish same data)

Name(s) of Child(ren)	Date(s) of Birth	Place(s) of Birth	Location of Birth Certificates

Mother's full name	Mother's Address, if Living

Father's full name	Father's Address, if Living

Names and Addresses of My Brothers and Sisters

I entered military service at	Date	Service Nr.	Grade	Separated (date, place)

Employer

Address	Name of immediate supervisor

Life Insurance

Company	Amount	Policy Nr.	Location of Policy	Beneficiary

245

Bank, Savings and Loan, Credit Union Accounts
Name   Address   Checking/Savings   If Joint, Name of Co-owner

I (do) (do not) have a safety deposit box. (Name and address of bank; attach schedule of contents)

Securities
I have accounts with the following brokerage firms:
Name   Address   Acct. Nr.   Securities (are)(are not) held in
                                                     Street Name

Stocks (attach list, if necessary)
Name of Company   Nr. Shares   Cert. Nr.   Location of Certificate

Bonds (attach list, if necessary)
Issuer   Denomination   Serial Nr.   Maturity   Location

Real Estate
Description   Location of Deed   If mortgaged, name & address of mortgagee

Property is insured with   Type of Insurance   Location of Policies

Personal Property
   (Attach inventory of valuable items. Where appropriate, indicate location of title or other papers; types of insurance and location of policies; liens)

Description and Location of Property in Storage, if Applicable

Debts I Owe
Name of Creditor   Amount   Purpose   How Payable

Money Owed to Me
Name of Debtor   Address   Amount   Purpose   Location of Note

Income Taxes

Returns have been filed and taxes paid through _____. Duplicate copies of returns are located at _____

Names and Addresses of Advisors

Attorney

Stockbroker

Insurance agent

Other

Will

A copy of my last will (is) (is not) attached. The original was executed at _____ on _____.
It is located at _____

Burial Instructions

I wish to buried at _____, (with) (without) military honors.

Other information

_____
(signature)

Index

Abatement, 229
Ademption, 228, 229
Administration of estate (*see* Wills)
Adjustable life insurance, 88
Adjusted gross income, defined, (*footnote*) 239
Allen's law, 11
American Stock Exchange, 138
Amount necessary for survivors (*see* Estate programming)
Annuities:
    straight, 85
    tax-deferred, 87
    variable, 86, 87
Association of Closed-End Investment Companies, 145
Association life insurance, 81
Automobile insurance, 24, 27–38
    assigned risk plans, 36
    collision:
        amount needed, 30
        deductibles, 30
        protection provided, 31
    comprehensive:
        deductibles, 31
        protection provided, 30
    costs, how determined, 35, 36
    deductibles, 30, 31
    development, 24
    extended non-owned automobile coverage, 32
    financial responsibility laws, 28, 29
    liability coverage:
        amount needed, 28
        for bodily injuries, 28, 29
        costs, 29
        for property damage, 28, 29
    medical payments
        costs, 31
        protection provided, 31
    no-fault systems, 32–35
        death benefits, 34, 35
        development, 32–34
        loss of income, 34
        medical expenses, 34
        pain and suffering, 34
        personal services, 34
        protection provided, 33, 35
    persons insured, 28
    rental reimbursement, 32
    theft of personal property from car, 32
    types, generally, 27, 28
    uninsured motorists coverage, 31, 32
    what to do if you have a collision, 37, 38
Avoiding probate (*see* Probate)

Babson's *Reports*, 153
Balance sheet, personal:
    purpose, 8, 9
    table, 8
Barron's, 134, 145
Belth, Joseph M., 106–108

Best's *Flitcraft Compend*, 106, 108, 169
Best's *Life Insurance Reports*, 103, 169
Best's *Review*, 174
Bonds (*see* Corporate bonds; Government securities; Municipal bonds)
Borrowing money, 16–19
    costs, 17–19 (*see also* Credit: costs)
    installment loans, 17
    secured loans, 17
    sources:
        commercial banks, 17
        credit unions, 18
        industrial banks, 19
        life insurance loans, 18
        mail-order loans, 19
        small loan companies, 19
    unsecured loans, 17
Bowles, *Where the Life Insurance Industry Is Headed*, 174
Brokerage firms (*see* Common stock)
Budget, 5–7
    defined, 5
    maintaining, 6
    purpose, 5, 6
    using, 6, 7
Business Week, 132

Call options (*see* Options)
Capital stock (*see* Common stock)
Cash-equivalent funds (*see* Mutual funds)
Cash surrender value (*see* Life insurance: nonforfeiture provisions)
Certificates of deposit, 116, 118, 125, 126
Changing Times, 7
Chicago Board Options Exchange (CBOE), 129, 132, 138
Clasing, Henry K., Jr., 132
Clayton, C. & Co., 140
Cleveland, Grover, 3
Clifford trusts, 189
Closed-end funds, 144, 145, 150, 153
    advantages, 145
    description, 145
    information, 145
    types, 145
Codicils; 226, 227
Collectibles, as investments, 153, 154
Columbine Securities, 140
Commissioners Standard Ordinary (CSO) 1958 Mortality Table, 74, 75
Commodities, as investments, 153, 154
Common stock:
    advisory services, 134
    American Stock Exchange, 138
    books, suggested reading, 134
    brokerage firms:
        account, opening an, 140
        commissions, 140
        discount firms, 140, 141
        selecting a, 139
    buying and selling, 138–142, 181
    commencing an investment program, 139–153, 180, 181
    dollar-cost averaging, 143, 144, (*figure*) 144
    Dow-Jones Industrial (DJI) Average, 1945–1978, (*figure*) 176
    "growth" stocks:
        defined, 135
        determining growth rates, 136, 137
        examples, 136–138
        price-earnings ratios, 135
        rates of growth, (*table*) 136
        representative, (*table*) 137
    inflation, relationship, 174–178
    investment counseling firms, 151–153
    investment guidelines, 179–181
    management investment companies (*see* Mutual funds; Closed-end funds)
    margin accounts:
        costs, 141
        example, 142
        requirements, 141, 142
    New York Stock Exchange, 138, 139
    over-the-counter market, 138, 139
    periodic investment of small sums, 142–151
        advantages, 142–144
        example, 143, 144, (*figure*) 144
    price-earnings (PE) ratios, 135
    prices, determining, (*figure*) 133, 134, 139
    rates of return, 175–178
        1926–1975, (*table*) 176
        projected, 1975–2000, (*table*) 176
        "real" compared to "nominal," 175–178
    selecting, 134–138
    short selling, 142
    transactions, reports of, (*table*) 133, 134
    where traded, 138, 139
Community property, 208–210
    common-law concepts in community states, 210
    "confirming" the survivor's interest, 210
    control, 209
    defined, 208, 209
    disposition on death, 209
    states, 208, 209, 216
    taxation, 209, 210
Condominium owners' insurance, 41
Consolidated Quotation System, 139
Consumer prices, 54, 170–174, 248, 249
    (*see also* Inflation) 1820–1978,

Consumer prices (*continued*)
    (*figure*) 171, (*table*) 248, 249
    since World War II, (*figure*) 172
Consumerism, 7
Consumer Reports, 7
Consumers Union Report on Life Insurance, 106
Convertible debentures, 124, 125
Convertible preferred stock, 128, 129
Corporate bonds:
    advantages and disadvantages, 123, 124, 125
    bearer bonds, 123
    bond funds, 124, (*table*) 127
    convertible debentures, 124, 125
    registered bonds, 123
    when *not* to buy, 124
    yields, 123, (*table*) 127
Cost of life insurance (*see* Life insurance: costs)
Coupon life insurance policies, 88, 89
Credit, 10–21 (*see also* Borrowing money)
    costs, 12–21
        constant-ratio formula, 20
        disclosure, when required, 19, 20
        installment sales, 21
        methods of computing, 20, 21
        skip-period formula, 21
    excessive, what is, 12
    expanded use, 10, 11
    securities margin accounts, 141, 142
    Truth-in-Lending Act, 19, 20
    types, 12–15
        credit cards, 14, 15
        extended-payment plans, 13
        installment purchases, 13, 14
        regular charge accounts, 12, 13
        revolving charge accounts, 13
    use of, when justifiable, 11, 12
Credit cards, 14, 15
    comprehensive cards, 14, 15
    costs, 14, 15
    liability for use if lost or stolen, 15
    special purpose cards, 14
Credit life insurance, 15, 16
    costs, 16
    growth, 16
    protection provided, 16

Danforth Associates, 153
Death taxes (*see* Estate taxes; Inheritance taxes)
Debt, when justifiable, 11, 12
Denenberg, *Insurance in the Age of the Consumer*, 174
Dependency and Indemnity Compensation (DIC), 56

Deposit-term life insurance, 81, 82
Descent and distribution (*see* Intestacy)
Disinheritance:
    children, 227, 228
    wife, 227
Disintermediation, defined, 116, 117
Dividends on life insurance policies, 92
Dollar-cost averaging, 143, 144, (*figure*) 144
Double indemnity, 94
Dow-Jones Industrial (DJI) Average, 1945–1978, (*figure*) 176
Drew, Daniel, 131

"Educational" life insurance policies, 83, 166, 167
Ehrbar, *The Long Term Case for Common Stocks,* 174, 177, *Some Kinds of Mutual Funds Make Sense,* 148
Emergency fund, need, 180
Employee Retirement Income Security Act of 1974, 86, 87
Endowment (*see* Life insurance)
Engel, Louis, *How to Buy Stocks,* 134
Equity capital (*see* Common stock; Investments)
ERISA, 86, 87
Estate programming, 58–72
    administration of estate, costs, 68, 69
    college costs, providing for, 68, 83
    constructing a chart, 59–72
        deferred annuity, determining amount, 62–67
        figure, 61
        immediate annuity, determining amount, 62–67
        monthly income required for survivors, 59
        present value, 62, (*table*) 64, 65, 66
        present value of annuity, 62, (*table*) 63, 65, 66
        social security benefits, 60–62
    death taxes, estimating, 68, 69
    debts, providing for payment, 67, 68
    expenses incident to death, 59
    size of estate required, (*exercise*) 70–72, (*figures*) 70–72, 162
Estate taxes:
    community property, 209, 210
    credits, 189, 192, 211, 212, 241, 242
    estate liquidity, need for, 163
    gifts prior to death, 200, 201, 242
    government savings bonds, 207
    joint checking and savings accounts, 207
    jointly owned property, 202, 207, 211, 212, 242, 243
        "consideration-furnished" test, 207
        exclusion, qualifying for, 207

Estate taxes (*continued*)
  life insurance proceeds, 158, 159, 243
  marital deduction, 191, 207, 210, 211, 242
  rates, 241
  Tax Reform Act of 1976, 159, 207, 211, 212
  saving, how to, 188–192, (*table*) 191, 199–201, 207, 210–212
  trusts:
    generation-skipping, 188
    irrevocable, 188, 189
    revocable, 187, 188
    savings by using, 187–192, (*table*) 191
    testamentary, 190–192
    Totten trusts, 202
  unified credit, 211, 241, 242
Executor (*see* Wills: executor)

Family-income life insurance, 84
Family-plan life insurance, 84
Federal Deposit Insurance Corporation (FDIC), 115
Federal Insurance Contributions Act (*see* Social security)
Federal Reserve Board:
  function, 115, 117, 141, 142
  monetary policy, affect on inflation, 171–174
Federal Savings and Loan Insurance Corporation (FSLIC), 116
Federal Trade Commission, 20
FICA (*see* Social Security)
Fidelity Management and Research, 141
Financial responsibility laws, 28, 29
Financial success, key to, 9
Fire and casualty insurance (*see also* Automobile insurance; Homeowners insurance; Personal property insurance)
  amounts needed, 43
  creditors' rights, 26
  development, 23
  legal considerations, 24–26
  protection provided, 22–24
  types available, 24
Fisher and Lori, studies, 177
Fixed-dollar uses of money, (*figure*) 113 (*see also* Corporate bonds; Government securities; Inflation; Life insurance; Municipal bonds; Savings)
Forced savings (*see* Life insurance: premiums)
Fortune, 148, 174

Gaines, *The Question Marks of Property,* 164
Gastineau, Gary L., *The Stock Options Manual,* 132
Gifts, use in reducing estate taxes, 195, 200, 201
Gift taxes (*see also* Tax Reform Act of 1976):
  annual exclusion, 188, 200, 242
  credits, 241, 242
  husband-wife gifts, amount excluded, 205, 211, 242
  rates, 241
  returns, timely filing, 207
  trusts:
    irrevocable, 188, 189
    revocable, income from, 188
  unified credit, 211, 241, 242
Gold, as an investment, 175
Government securities:
  Federal Land Bank bonds, 119
  Federal National Mortgage Association ("Fannie Mae"), 119
  Government National Mortgage Association ("Ginnie Mae"), 119
  savings bonds, 112–115, 119, (*table*) 127, 164–170, 180, 207
    advantages and disadvantages, 113–115, 180
    education fund, use as, 114
    estate taxation, 207
    interest, deferral of income taxes, 114
    missing bonds, reissuance, 114
    series E, exchanging for series H, 114, 115, 166
    series EE, 112–115
    series HH, 112–115
    term insurance plus savings bonds, 164–170
    yields, 113, 114, (*table*) 127
  Treasury bills, 18, 117–119
  Treasury bonds, 119
  Treasury notes, 119
  yields, (*table*) 127
Graham, Donn, and Cottle, *Securities Analysis,* 134
Group life insurance, 80, 81
Guardian:
  of estate, 225, 226
  nomination, 225, 226
  of person, 225, 226
  trust, advantages of, 190

Health maintenance organizations (HMO's), 42, 43
Heirs, defined, 215
Homeowners insurance, 40, 41

Homeowners insurance (*continued*)
  condominium owners' policies, 41
  lessors' policies, 41
  protection provided, 41
  renters' policies, 41
Hospitalization insurance (*see* Medical and hospitalization insurance)
Husband-wife property arrangements (*see* Community property; Joint ownership; Tenancy-by-the-entirety; Tenancy-in-common)

Ibbotsen and Sinquefield, studies, 177
Income:
  adusted gross, (*footnote*) 239
  from personal services, (*footnote*) 240
  taxable, (*footnote*) 239
  "unearned," (*footnote*) 240
Income taxes:
  adjusted gross income, defined, (*footnote*) 239
  "brackets," (*footnote*) 240
  "dividends" on life insurance policies, 92
  government savings bonds, deferral of income taxes, 114, 115
  government savings bonds registered in child's name, 115
  individual, rates, 239
  inherited property, tax basis, 211
  interest on loans to pay insurance premiums, 85
  interest on proceeds left with insurance company, 101
  life insurance proceeds, 160
  municipal bonds, interest, 119, 120
  rates, 239
  taxable income, defined, (*footnote*) 239
  Totten trusts, 202
  trusts:
    irrevocable, income from, 188, 189
    revocable, income from, 188
  withholding rates, monthly (1979), 237, 238
  zero bracket amount (ZBA), defined, (*footnote*) 239
Indemnification, defined, 25, 26, 28
Individual retirement accounts (IRA's), 86, 87
Inflation, 170–178
  causes, 172–174
  common stocks, relationship, 174–178
  consumer price index (*see* Consumer prices)
  fixed-dollar assets and inflation, 174–178
  life insurance settlement options, effect on selection, 101

protecting purchasing power, 174–178
  uses of savings, effect, 22, 170–178, 193
Inheritance taxes (*see also* Estate taxes):
  on jointly-owned property, 207
  life insurance proceeds, 158, 159
  provision to pay from estate, 223, (*figure*) 221
Insurable interest:
  defined, 25
  dollar amount, 25, 26
Insurance, 22–43, 73–110
  amounts needed, guide, 27, 43
  fire and casualty (*see* Automobile insurance; Fire and casualty insurance; Homeowners insurance; Personal property insurance)
  hospitalization (*see* Medical and hospitalization insurance)
  legal considerations, 24–26
    disaffirmance by minor, 25
    indemnification, explained, 25, 26, 28
    insurable interest requirement, 25
    legality of purpose, 25
  liability (*see* Personal liability insurance; "Umbrella" coverage; Automobile insurance)
  life (*see* Life insurance)
  medical (*see* Medical and hospitalization insurance)
Interest:
  add-on, (*example*) 17
  calculating amount, 234–236, (*tables*) 235, 236
  discounted, (*example*) 17
  table of compound, 244, 245
Inter vivos trusts (*see* Trusts)
Intestacy, 215–217
  in common-law states, 215, 216
  in community-property states, 216
  defined, 215
  disadvantages, 216, 217
Intestate succession (*see* Intestacy)
Investment Company Act, variable life insurance exemption, 88
Investments, 111–154
  advisory services, 134
  bonds (*see* Corporate bonds; Government securities; Municipal bonds)
  books, suggested reading, 134
  brokerage firms (*see* Common stock)
  closed-end funds, 144, 145, 151, 153
  commissions, 140, 141
  common stock (*see* Common stock)
  convertible debentures, 124, 125
  convertible preferred stock, 128, 129
  counseling firms, 151–153

Investments (continued)
    costs, 152
        services provided, 152
    defined, 112
    flexibility, maintaining, 181
    individual needs, tailoring to, 111, 112
    information, obtaining, 133, 134
    lending, distinguished, 112
    life insurance as an, 118
    by life insurance companies, 91
    management, by trustee, 187, 188
    management investment companies (see Closed-end funds; Mutual funds)
    margin accounts (see Common stock)
    money-market funds (see Mutual funds)
    mutual funds (see Mutual funds)
    non-traditional, 153, 154
    options (see Options)
    periodic investments, (table) 246
    periodic investments of small sums (see Common stock)
    preferred stock, 128, 129, 135
    real estate as an, 153, 154, 175
    savings accounts (see Savings)
    savings, possible uses, (table) 113
    selecting securities, 134–138
    time deposits, 116–119, (table) 127
    trustee's powers, 196–199
    where securities are traded, 138, 139
IRA, 86, 87

Jensen, *The Performance of Mutual Funds in the Period 1945–1964*, 148
Johnson's *Investment Company Charts*, 150
Joint ownership:
    "joint" checking and savings accounts, 202
    survivorship, right of, 206
    tax factors:
        disadvantages, 212
        estate taxes, 202, 207, 211, 212
        gift taxes, 207, 211
        income taxes, 211
        inheritance taxes, 202, 207
        "qualifying" jointly-owned property for exclusion, 207
    when use indicated, 212, 213
    will, prevents disposition of property by, 206
Joint tenancy (see Joint ownership)
Journal of Business, 177
Journal of Finance, 148

Kaiser-Permanente Plan, 42
Keogh plans, 86, 87

Lapse, defined, 228
Letterman Transaction Services, 140
Life insurance, 15, 16, 18, 24–26, 44, 73–110, 118, 155–170, 178–181, 190, 192–195, 209, 215
    amount:
        affordable, 160, 161
        needed, 111, (figures) 162 (see also Estate programming)
        paid to beneficiary, 77
    association term, 81
        death-cost index, (table) 109
    cash surrender value (see nonforfeiture provisions)
    cash value policies:
        advantages, 163, 164
        amount of actual insurance provided, 77, 156, 157
        inflation, effect of, 174
        loans, 18
        replacing with term insurance, 178, 179
        savings component, 118, 156–158, 166
    commissions, 157, 158
        on variable life policies, 88
    Commissioners Standard Ordinary (CSO) 1958 Mortality Table, 74
    companies:
        expenses, 158
        mutual companies, 89, 102, 103
        selecting, 102, 103
        stock companies, 89, 102, 103
    contractual clauses:
        aviation, 94
        double indemnity, 94
        entire-contract clause, 93
        misstatement of age, 93
        suicide, 93, 94
        waiver of premium, 95
        war or civil disturbance, 94
    costs:
        comparative, 156–158, (table) 160, 161
        death-cost index, 107–110, (table) 109
        interest-adjusted method, 105–107, (table) 107
        term compared to cash value policies, 160, 161
        "traditional" net cost analysis, 103–105
    credit policies (see Credit life insurance)
    creditors' rights, 26
    disaffirmance by minor, 25
    dividends:
        nature, 91, 92, 158

Life insurance (*continued*)
    options with respect to, 92
    tax treatment, 92
  endowment, 80, 83, 165–167
    "college education" policies, 166, 167
    costs, 165–167
    graphs, (*figure*) 90, (*figure*) 166
  extended term (*see* nonforfeiture provisions)
  financial protection provided, 156, 157
  incidents of ownership:
    tax consequences, 159
    transfer, 158, 159
  insurable interest, defined, 26
  investment, as an, 118
  investments by companies, 91
  lifelong coverage, need for, 161, 162
  limited-payment life:
    death-cost index, (*table*) 109
    graph, (*figure*) 90
    nature, 82
    premium components, 82, 156, 157
  loans, 18, 97, (*table*) 98
  mortality risk, 75–76, (*table*) 74
  need for life insurance, if no dependents, 180
  nonforfeiture provisions:
    cash surrender value, 95, 96, 158
    extended term, 96, 97
    paid-up whole life, 97
    values, (*table*) 98
  nonparticipating policies, 89, 91, 92, 158
    comparative costs, 91, 92, 158
  paid-up life (*see* nonforfeiture provisions)
  participating policies, 89–92
    dividends, 92, 158
  permanent policies (*see* cash value policies)
  premiums, 74–77, 156, 157
    amounts of different types of insurance same premium might buy, (*table*) 160
    difference in costs, term and cash value policies, 77–80, 156–158
    forced savings, 77, 156, 157
    level-premium method, 76
    loading charges, 76
    mortality-risk cost, 74–76
    for non-participating policies, 91, 92, 158
    for participating policies, 91, 92, 158
  purpose, 73
  savings, as a method, 118, 157, 158, 166
  services available from agents, 163, 164
  settlement options, 98–101
    which is best, 100, 101
    life income, 99, 100
    limited installments, 99
    lump sum, 98, 99
    proceeds left with company, 100
    trusts, compared, 193, 194
  taxation, 92, 160, 243 (*see also* Estate taxes; Income taxes; Inheritance taxes)
  term policies:
    costs, 156, 161, (*example*) 167, (*figures*) 166, 168
    death-cost index, (*table*) 109
    graph, (*figure*) 90
    investment of savings in premiums, 164–170
  trusts, life insurance, 186, 192–195
  "twisting," 178, 179
  types of policies:
    adjustable life, 88
    association life, 81
    coupon policies, 88, 89
    deciding which to buy, 179–181
    deposit-term, 81, 82
    "educational" policies, 83, 166, 167
    endowment, 80, 83, 85, 86, (*figure*) 90, 165–167, (*figure*) 166
    family income, 84, (*figure*) 90
    family plan, 84
    group life, 80, 81
    illustrated, (*figure*) 90
    limited-payment life, 82, (*figure*) 90
    minimum-deposit life, 84, 85
    modified life, 82, 83, (*figure*) 90
    ordinary life (*see* whole life)
    retirement-income policies, 85, 86, (*figure*) 90, 165–167
    Servicemen's Group Life Insurance (SGLI), 81
    straight life (*see* whole life)
    term, 78, 79, (*figure*) 90
    variable annuities, 86, 87
    variable life, 87, 88
    Veterans' Group Life Insurance (VGLI), 81
    whole life, 79, 80, (*figure*) 90
  whole life, 74–77, 79, 80, 90, 109, 156, 157, 167–170
    costs, 167–170
    death-cost index, (*table*) 109
    graph, (*figure*) 90, (*figure*) 168
    premium components, 74–77, 156, 157
Limited-payment life insurance (*see* Life insurance)
Living trust (*see* Trusts)
Lloyds of London, 23
Load funds (*see* Mutual funds)

Index 255

Loading charge (*see* Life insurance: premiums)
Loans (*see* Borrowing money)
Loeb, Gerald M., *The Battle for Stock Market Profits*, 134

McCabe, W. T. & Co., 140
Malkiel, *A Random Walk Down Wall Street*, 150
Management investment companies (*see* Mutual funds; Closed-end funds)
Margin accounts (*see* Common stock)
Marital deduction (*see* Estate taxes)
Massey, "For the Long Haul," 177
Medical and hospitalization insurance (*see also* Health maintenance organizations)
    amount needed, 42
    costs, 42, 43
    protection provided, 24, 42, 43
Minimum-deposit life insurance, 84, 85
Modified life insurance, 82, 83
Money-market certificates (MMC's), 117, 118
Money-market funds (*see* Mutual funds)
Moody's, 134
Morris Plan, 19
Morse "Daily Rate Tables," (*tables*) 235, 236
Mortality risk:
    cost (*see* Life insurance: premiums)
    table, 74
Municipal bond funds:
    compared with unit trusts, 121, 122
    list, 122, 123
    nature and purpose, 121, 122
Municipal bonds, 119–123, (*table*) 127
    interest, exempt from federal income taxes, 120
    interest, taxable equivalent, (*table*) 121
    types, 119, 120
    unit trusts, 120–122
    yields, (*table*) 127
Mutual funds:
    accumulation plans:
        front-end load, 150, 151
        voluntary plans, 150
    advantages and disadvantages, 145, 146, 180, 181
    cash-equivalent funds, 125–127
    information about, 150
    load funds, 146–151
        commissions, 146
        compared with no-load funds, 148–150
    money-market funds, 125–127
        initial investment required, 125
        list, 126
        nature and purpose, 125, 126
        yields, 125, 126, (*table*) 127
    muni-funds (*see* Municipal bond funds)
    no-load funds, 146–151
        compared with load funds, 148–150
        list, 149
        rating service, 149
    performance records, 147, 148
    table, 147
    types, 146, 147
    withdrawal plans, 151

National Association of Insurance Commissioners, 16, 74, 105
National Association of Securities Dealers (NASD), 139
National Underwriting Company, 106
Neaves, Lord, 220
Net worth, determining personal, (*table*) 8
New York Insurance Department, 105, 106
New York Stock Exchange, 138
No-fault insurance (*see* Automobile insurance)
No-load mutual fund directory, 149
No-load funds (*see* Mutual funds)
NoLoad*X, 149
Non-participating life insurance policies, 89–92
Non-probate assets, 214, 215
Non-probate transfers (*see* Gifts; Joint ownership; Payable-on-death accounts; Totten trusts; Trusts; *Uniform Gifts to Minors Act*)
Nuveen, John & Co., 121

Old age, survivors, and disability insurance (OASDI) (*see* Social security)
Open-end funds (*see* Mutual funds)
Options, 129–132
    buying options, 131, 132, 135
    calls, 129–132
    prerequisites for trading, suggested, 132
    puts, 129–132
    table, 131
    where traded, 129
    writing options, 130, 131
Over-the-counter markets, 138, 139
Participating life insurance, comparison, 89–92 (*see also* Life insurance)
Passbook accounts, 115, 116
Payable-on-death accounts, 202
Personal catastrophe liability insurance (*see* "Umbrella" coverage)
Personal injury protection (*see* Automobile insurance: liability)
Personal liability insurance, 24, 40–42

Index

Personal property insurance, 38–41, 43
  "all-risk" coverage, 39
  amount needed, 43
  floaters, 39
  homeowners insurance, included in, 41
  inventory, importance, 39, 40
  protection provided, 38
  "scheduled" and "unscheduled" property, 39
  value, proving, 39, 40
Personal representative (*see* Wills: executor)
Porter, Sylvia, *Money*, 7
Powers of appointment, 191, 192
Precious metals, as investments, 153, 154, 175
Preferred stock, 128, 129, 135
Pretermitted heirs, 227, 228
Probate:
  avoiding, 185–202
    by gifts, 200, 201
    joint accounts, 213
    joint ownership, 205, 206, 212, 213
    life insurance trusts, 193–195
    payable-on-death accounts, 202
    Totten trusts, 202
    trusts, *inter vivos,* 187, 188
  definition, 218
  requirements, 218–220
Probate assets, 214, 215
Property co-ownership (*see* Community property; Joint ownership; Tenancy-by-the-entirety; Tenancy-in-common)
Purchasing power (*see* Inflation)
Puts and calls (*see* Options)

Rates of growth, compound, (*table*) 136
Real estate:
  home ownership, 180
  inflation, as protection against, 175
  as an investment, 153, 154
Remaindermen (*see* Trusts)
Renters' insurance, 41
Retirement-income life insurance, 85, 86, 165–167
Resources, allocation, 155–181 (*see also* Investments; Inflation; Life Insurance; Savings)
Rose & Co., 140, 141

Saving, 3–9
  defined, 4
  minimum suggested goal, 7
  purpose, 3, 4
  ways to, 4–7, 9
Savings:
  savings accounts:
    commercial banks, 115
    credit unions, 116
    joint accounts, 202
    passbook accounts, 115, 116
    payable-on-death accounts, 202
    savings and loan associations, 115, 116
    Totten trusts, 202
  cash reserve, suggested amount, 111, 143
  interest:
    calculating, 234–236, (*tables*) 235, 236
    periodic investments, (*table*) 246, 247
    table of compound, 244, 245
  life insurance cash values, 118, 157, 158
  money-market certificates (MMC's), 117, 118
  money-market funds (*see* Mutual funds)
  possible uses, (*figure*) 113
  purpose, 3, 4, 155
  savings bonds (*see* Government securities)
  time deposits, 116–118, (*table*) 127
  yields on representative uses, (*table*) 127
Securities (*see* Investments)
Securities and Exchange Commission (SEC), 88, 139
Self-insured, when to be, 27, 30–32, 38, 43
Series EE bonds (*see* Government securities)
Servicemen's Group Life Insurance (SGLI), 81
Sherwood, Hugh C., *How to Invest in Bonds*, 134
Sinclair, Upton, 10
Size of estate needed (*see* Estate programming)
Small loan companies, 19
Smith, Adam, *The Money Game*, 173
Social Security, 44–57
  AIME, 50–52, 60
  amount of benefit:
    for the disabled, 49, 50, 53
    how to estimate, 50–55
    as multiple of primary insurance amount (PIA), (*table*) 53
    reduction or elimination, 49, 54, 55
    replacement rates, (*table*) 54
    for the retired, 48, 53
    for surviving dependents, 48, 49, 53, 61
  average indexed monthly earnings, 50–52, 60
    how computed, 51
    indexing, 51, 52
  beneficiaries:

Social security (*continued*)
    the disabled, 49, 50, 53
    the retired, 44, 45, 48, 53
    surviving dependent children, 48, 49, 53
    surviving spouse, 48, 49, 53
  cost-of-living increases, 54
  development, 45–47
  eligibility:
    "currently" insured, 48, 49
    "fully" insured, 48, 49
  importance in estate planning, 44–47
  Medicare, 42
  nature of the system, 46
  other income, effect on benefits, 54, 55
  primary insurance amount (PIA), 52–54, 60
    benefits as multiple of, (*table*) 53
    formula, 53
    significance, 53, 54
  remarriage, 49
  taxes:
    combined employee-employer costs, (*figure*) 47
    on employees, (*table*) 51
  how to verify your credits, 52
Source Securities, 140
Springer, *The Mutual Fund Trap,* 148
Standard and Poor's:
  Outlook, 134
  Stock Reports, 136
Stock brokers (*see* Common stock: brokerage firms)
Stocks (*see* Common stock)
Succession, laws of (*see* Intestacy)
Survivors' Benefit Plan (SBP), 56

Taxable income, defined, (*footnote*) 239
Taxation of life insurance proceeds (*see* Estate taxes; Income taxes; Inheritance taxes)
Tax Reform Act of 1976:
  estate tax changes, 159
  gift tax changes, 159, 189
  joint ownership, 207, 211
  marital deduction increased, 211
Tenancy-by-the-entirety, 208
Tenancy-in-common, 202, 205
Terminal date method for calculating interest, (*table*) 235
Term life insurance (*see* Life insurance)
Time deposits, 116–118, (*table*) 127
Totten trusts, 202
Transportation insurance, 24
Treasury securities (*see* Government securities)

Trust departments, investment management services, 152, 153
Trustee (*see also* Trusts):
  appointment by will, 226
  corporate, 196
  fees, 186, 187, 196
  investments by, 196–198
  powers, 196–199
  selection, 196
  spouse as co-trustee, 196
Trusts, 185–199 (*see also* Trustee)
  administrative provisions, 195–199
  advantages, generally, 186, 187
  as alternative to transferring life insurance, 159
  beneficiaries, types, 186
  Clifford trusts, 189
  common trust funds, 196
  distributive arrangements, 195–199
  estate tax savings through trusts, (*table*) 191
  family trusts, 191, 192
  generation-skipping, 188
  gift taxes (*see* Gift taxes)
  guardian's needs, providing for, 198, 199
  history, 186
  income beneficiaries, defined, 186
  income taxes (*see* Income taxes)
  inter vivos (living) trusts:
    irrevocable, 188, 189
    revocable, 187, 188
  life insurance trusts, 192–195
    contingent, 194, 195
    settlement options, compared, 193, 194
    testamentary trust, compared, 193
  living trusts (*see inter vivos* trusts)
  for minors, advantages, 194, 195
  miscellaneous provisions, 199
  nature, 185–187
  powers, 196–199
    invasion of principal, 197, 198
    investments, 196–198
  remaindermen, defined, 186
  spendthrift clause, 199
  ten-year trusts, 189
  testamentary:
    advantages, 189–192
    contingent, 190
  2503 (c) trusts for minors, 195
Truth-in-Lending Act, 19, 20
"Twisting" (*see* Life insurance)

UGMA (*see* Uniform Gifts to Minors Act)
"Umbrella" coverage:
  costs, 41, 42
  protection provided, 41, 42

Unfunded life insurance trusts, 192–195
Uniform Gifts to Minors Act:
   example, 210
   provisions, 201
   2503 (c) trusts compared, 195
United Business Service, 134
Unit trusts (*see* Municipal bonds)

Van Caspel, Virginia, *The New Money Dynamics*, 134
Variable life insurance (VLI), 87, 88
Veterans' Group Life Insurance (VGLI), 81

Waiver-of-premium clause, 95
War clause, 94
The Wall Street Journal, 134, 145
Whole life insurance (*see* Life insurance)
Wiesenberger's *Investment Companies*, 150
Wills, 214–233 (*see also* Intestacy)
   abatement, 229
   ademption, 228, 229
   administrator (*see* executor)
   advantages, 216, 217
   age of testator, minimum, 219
   ancillary administration, 232
   attestation, 226
   if beneficiary dies first, 228
   child, failure to mention, 227, 228
   codicils, 226, 227
   disinheritance of wife, 227
   distribution of estate, 232, 233
   if estate insufficient to satisfy all gifts, 229
   executor, 217, 218, 230–233
      appointment, 226
      compensation, 233
      distribution of estate, 232, 233
      duties, 230–232
      information to leave, (*sample*) 250–253
   gifts, types, 224
   jointly-owned property, 206
   lapse, 228
   letters testamentary, 218
   limitations on testamentary freedom, 227–229
   personal property:
      disposal of before death, 228, 229
      gifts by memorandum, 224
   personal representative (*see* executor)
   "poor-man's will," 205–207
   pour-overs, 190
   pretermitted heir, 227, 228
   probate, requirements, 218–220, 230
   property subject to, 214, 215
   provisions:
      death taxes, payment, 223
      debts, payment, 223
      demonstrative gifts, 224
      general gifts, 224
      guardian for minor children, 225, 226
      heirs, identifying, 223
      personal property, disposal, 223, 224
      preamble, 223
      residue clause, 225
      specific gifts, 224
   requirements for validity, 219
   sample will, (*figure*) 221, 222
   standard forms, use, 220
   testimonial capacity, defined, 219, 220
   vocabulary, 217–220
   wife, attempt to disinherit, 227
   wife's need for a will, 225, 226
Withholding, federal income taxes (1979), 237, 238

Zero bracket amount (ZBA), defined, (*footnote*) 239